# THE ETHICS OF RESEARCHING WAR

MANCHESTER
1824

Manchester University Press

# New Approaches to Conflict Analysis

Series editor: Peter Lawler,
Senior Lecturer in International Relations,
Department of Government, University of Manchester

Until recently, the study of conflict and conflict resolution remained comparatively immune to broad developments in social and political theory. When
the changing nature and locus of large-scale conflict in the post-Cold War
era is also taken into account, the case for a reconsideration of the funda-
mentals of conflict analysis and conflict resolution becomes all the more stark.

*New Approaches to Conflict Analysis* promotes the development of new theoretical insights and their application to concrete cases of large-scale conflict,
broadly defined. The series intends not to ignore established approaches to
conflict analysis and conflict resolution, but to contribute to the reconstruction of the field through a dialogue between orthodoxy and its contemporary
critics. Equally, the series reflects the contemporary porosity of intellectual
borderlines rather than simply perpetuating rigid boundaries around the
study of conflict and peace. *New Approaches to Conflict Analysis* seeks to uphold
the normative commitment of the field's founders yet also recognises that the
moral impulse to research is properly part of its subject matter. To these ends,
the series is comprised of the highest quality work of scholars drawn from
throughout the international academic community, and from a wide range
of disciplines within the social sciences.

# The Ethics of Researching War

## Looking for Bosnia

ELIZABETH DAUPHINÉE

Manchester University Press

Published by Manchester University Press
Altrincham Street, Manchester M1 7JA, UK
www.manchesteruniversitypress.co.uk

*British Library Cataloguing-in-Publication Data is available*

ISBN 978 0 7190 7609 1 *hardback*
ISBN 978 0 7190 7615 2 *paperback*

First published by Manchester University Press in hardback 2007

This edition first published 2018

Printed by Lightning Source

# CONTENTS

# Contents

# ACKNOWLEDGEMENTS

This project was made possible through the generous financial support of the Social Sciences and Humanities Research Council of Canada and the Canadian Consortium on Human Security. The Centre for International and Security Studies at York University in Toronto provided much appreciated intellectual and fieldwork support. I am also particularly indebted to my new colleagues in Politics at the University of Manchester, who have warmly welcomed me and helped to make leaving yet another country an easier process. Those who supported me personally throughout this project are spread across Canada, the United States, the United Kingdom, Bosnia and Hercegovina, and Serbia and Montenegro. They are too many to name, but they know who they are, that I am grateful to them, and that I love them.

Vladimiru Blagojeviću, još uvijek . . .

# 1

# *An accusation in the course of fieldwork*

Before one is guilty, one is already uniquely and irreplaceably in a position of shame in regard to those about whom one is to write.[1]

I am building my career on the loss of a man named Stojan Sokolović (and on the loss of many millions of others, who may or may not resemble him). And one night, he told me: 'You write about violence – you say that fear is a violence – that the things that cause fear and insecurity are violences. But you do not know how that fear sits like a bear on my heart. You talk about fear, as though you understood what it tasted like – what it smelled like – that electrified, trembling scent of mortar dust and artillery shells. You talk about guilt, but you look in from a place that does not allow you to see it well. Violence must be quantifiable in your world. It must count bodies, burned houses, livestock, and graves – lost libraries, churches and synagogues, mosques. It must count the flood of refugees driven across the border from their own fields into those of others – into fields that do not want to shelter them. You have no scale with which to weigh the contents of heart or soul. And so, you can identify victims – static, immobile entities – but you have not asked yourself about the violence the committer of violence has done to himself, and you have not bothered to theorize that. You have not watched as he sleeps to see if he cries out, or if he weeps, and you have no gauge with which to look behind his eyes. Your scales are a failed chimera.

No one wants to talk to those who hid behind the artillery wearing sneakers because their army did not have proper boots for them. No one wants to ask them if they will ever be alright again, trapped as they are in this life and hemmed in on all sides by the measure of their own responsibility. You do not see it, because you have never been consumed by fear, though you think you have observed it. If you had heard our wailing – killer and killed alike – you would say something other than what you are

1

saying at your seminars and conferences. I don't know what it would be, but I know that it would not be the same.

We were bankrupt of love, but if all of you there who condemned us here had cared so much about what had happened to the thin fabric of our lives, you would not have come to observe us like tourists on safari. You would not have come to talk to taxi drivers as you drove through the hail of our artillery fire only to go home again and boast about how you survived that, and how exhilarating it was. You would not have snapped so many photographs, looking always for the frame that would 'shock the conscience of mankind'[2] – some obscenity – but you would have sold your hefty Nikons on the borders that only you could cross and given us the money to pay the UNPROFOR soldiers who charged five thousand German marks to take our children across the lines.[3] You would have held our heads, because we could not stop trembling, even when we were killing, even when we came to be defined by the killing we had done. You would have come to help us bury the dead and to sing prayers over their souls, because we did not have enough clergy from any faith to do it. If you had really cared so much, you would not have written about what primitive beasts we were, or how deranged our leaders were (many of us knew that already), but you would have wept for us. Your rendering of us was a violence of similar measure to the violence we committed. Because even the winners in Bosnia lost, and the bottom line is that you got tenure-track positions and scholarly awards and publications and we are the ones who paid for them. They were paid for with the dust from the gypsum in the collapsed heaps of our homes and with our exile and our lives.

You determined guilt and innocence with ink lines on the pages of books and journals in your subfield of an academic subfield, but none of it helped anything to be more bearable. You delineated between categories of ethnicity and language, you passed your pronouncements and decrees – you divining judges and juries – but you did not teach us anything. You had nothing to teach from your mountain of learning, even from the beginning – from the first stroke of your pen – from the first tap of your manicured fingertips across the keyboard of your laptop with its mobile Pentium processor on your Lufthansa flight out of Zagreb. You pretended to understand what we had done – you organized conferences over it – you developed theories about it – but you never really cared what had happened to us, because it was not you. We were not *you*. And so, what you wrote about us – what you wrote about who we were – was its own measure of destruction.'[4]

'What do you know about Bosnia? Why did you come, and what did you think you would find?' Stojan Sokolović was not angry, and I believe even now that he loved me not despite, but *because of* my treachery. He spoke to me thus out of love.

## An accusation in the course of fieldwork

I was bankrupt of love, and walking one day with my hefty Nikon in the ancestral mountains of eastern Bosnia, in the *opština*[5] of Rogatica, when I saw something that froze the flow of blood in my heart and filled me with terrible regret. The handful of houses on the road closest to the edge of the village were gutted and burned, their terracotta roof tiles smashed and blackened and strewn across the yellow grass. Even now, I think of those burned houses, but I did not forge into the spaces between their twisted walls at the time I encountered them. There were landmines in the living rooms. One did not need to see the municipal registry to know that the occupants of those houses fled (or died) because they felt that Yeshua was not the Christ, but only a prophet of God. What bothered me particularly about it was that, in one of these places, a stove was rusted in the tall grass behind the charred, skeletal structure of the house. It was rusted, and I regret it. I know what a burden it is to prepare a proper meal – and how satisfying it is to share one with people you love. Who among us does not? There, that rusting metal thing, which was a stove. There was a woman who once knew intimately all of the details of that stove – a woman who knew when it was too hot, or not hot enough – a woman who knew exactly when to take the *tepsija* out, because she knew the character of that stove, when it would yield, and when it would not.[6]

There it stood, a strange tumour in the tall grass with sheep walking absently past. I looked at those houses for a long time, passing back and forth a few times with my camera at the ready. After some time, I noticed that there was an old man staring at me from the other side of the narrow road. He wore a vest made of sheepskin, and I saw as he approached me that he had cracks in the skin of his hands like pavement. I was ashamed to not greet him, but I was anxious at the thought of doing so (because I was not a master of the language of that place, and because I had been warned by the US Secretary of State's travel advisory website that foreignness is a dangerous cloak to wear). He greeted me and smiled.

'Come down out of the midday sun', he said, and stretched his hand out. He disregarded my obvious foreignness, he overlooked it, ignored it (perhaps he forgave it), and we walked back toward the centre of the village together. I had followed a narrow dirt road on foot from the place where I started to the place where I happened upon him, but he led me in a different direction back over the mountain along a barely perceptible path. You would have to be a tracker to see that path, I thought to myself. Was it even a path at all? (And are there landmines in these hills?)

'I don't see where we're going', I confessed to him.
'I know the way during the new moon as well as I know it at daylight', he responded promptly.

He had seen me looking at the burned houses, but gave no indication as to whether he thought anything about this one way or the other. I did not bring it up, because there were also potential landmines in the filling of those silences.[7] After a time, he asked me to whom I belonged. 'Čija si ti? – Whose are you?' I told him that I did not know. In truth, I was no one's – at least not in a way that would mean anything to him.[8]

Outside the narrow wooden gate to his house he implored me to come in out of the sun for a cup of coffee. It was bitter and thick, and he served it from his scarred hands in cracked porcelain cups. Had he lit the match that started the fires? Had he set the landmines in the living rooms? When the coffee was gone, he kissed my cheeks three times, in the Serbian fashion, and I ducked through the doorway and continued walking down the road. This man, the potential lighter of matches, the potential layer of landmines, expressed his capacity for love in the serving of coffee from cracked teacups. And it was truly love, because there was no gain to be had from serving a foreigner in the midst of those mountains – a foreigner who did not even know from whom she had come.

## On expertise

What expert am I? This is what Stojan Sokolović demanded of me and to which I had (and have) no good answer. Perhaps I did not understand the question. I believed at the time of his asking that I occupied a more or less secure place in a discipline that provided a sense of coherence even in its divisions (and perhaps precisely *because* of its divisions). I believed that its debates and paradigms were part of the metaphysical trajectory of its very existence, and that this could be well-ordered, mapped out, and under-stood, if subjectively in content and context, then objectively in what we have all tacitly agreed upon (or have been forced to agree upon) as its basic ordering frameworks. The questions that I was prepared to answer were finite questions that were inherently formed and nurtured within the context of the discipline. 'Where do you stand? What position do you take? To what side do you belong? What tradition, perspective or community do your labours faithfully represent? These are questions that we ask one another from the first moment of our entry into the field [and into the spaces between the fields]. These are the questions, we are given to know from the start, to which we must have our already prepared replies.'[9]

What expert am I? This was not an enquiry that could be answered within the parameters of that framework, because it did not ask me to iden-tify the disciplinary ground on which I stood or the window from which I spoke. It did not require me to expound on the history or genesis of my 'expertise' – my travels and research, my interviews and contacts in the

4

southeast of Europe, my theoretical fears or commitments (or my fears of theoretical commitment itself). It charged me with faithlessness *writ large*, with an unforgivable violence, to which I could simply make no adequate response. It asked me not with which experts I had spoken, or what they had said. It asked me not what scraps of truth were contained on the tiny little audiocassettes that comprised my burgeoning library of interview archives. It asked, instead, if I had noticed the slant of the setting sun on the terracotta tiles on the houses by the coast. It asked me if I had stuck my fingers absently in the honeycomb brickwork of the buildings along the Vrbas River or run the flat palm of my hand along the stuccoed gypsum plaster of the borrowed house in which I slept. It asked me if I had endured the rain at an inopportune moment, or if I had even noticed the rain at all – if I had divined anything in it. It asked me what the future held as read through the dried coffee grounds on the bottom of my coffee cup. It asked me if there was even a possibility of truth – whether anyone could actually apprehend, process, signify, and render it in speech or text or microform. The questions that presupposed the form (if not the content) of acceptable answerability were obliterated in that single sentence – *what expert are you?* – asked rhetorically, perhaps, because there was no possibility of making an answer along the lines for which my training had prepared me to make an answer and at some level, Stojan Sokolović knew that. The validity of those questions, in a single flash of well-placed enquiry, was obliterated.

How can I speak of war or death or peace operations or democratization or privatization or post-conflict environments or the political economy of insecurity in the maze of uncertainty to which Stojan Sokolović led me? How can I do that, when I have already had to accept the non-existence of an Archimedean point that drags us along a preordained teleology of being (or Being) and progress toward the grotesque flower of objective, universal truth? As soon as I speak, I must impart the universal or else no one can understand me, complained Søren Kierkegaard. I can only speak of my impressions, perceptions, and sensations, which are momentary, fluctuating, contingent, ethereal dust in the recesses of my memory – now vanished in that imperceptible ether of the air in my lungs and the marrow in my bones. I can only speak of the impressions left in darkness and in falling rain at night in fields fundamentally marked by insecurity. For example, in July 1999 I was driving from the revised south of Serbia back into Bosnia, where the armoured vehicles of the North Atlantic Treaty Organization (NATO) are too large for the narrow mountain roads.[10] The weather turned bad and there was nowhere to sleep because the guest-houses were all filled up with Kosovo refugees, and the landlords were bitter because those refugees had to be kept and fed free of charge. ('What shall

I do?' demanded the owner of the hostel who had no room to rent. 'Shall I turn them away?' He shrugged and waved us onward through a sheet of rain. 'Find another place!')

All along the road, there were terrible scars in the earth. At the border at Karakaj, between those two republics which not long ago were undefended and inseparable, the soldiers stared interestedly at my strange blue passport. They seemed very young in the rain – in the dark – as they begged me for patience. One of them had sneakers on his feet. He asked from where I had come. I told him in my grammarless way that I had paused last in Belgrade, where I had a discussion with an old colleague and friend over two brown bottles of beer in Republic Square. One of the soldiers asked if the buildings along Kneza Miloša had really been so badly destroyed by the bombs. I told him they had, and that it was the same in Niš, Čačak, Kragujevac, and Pančevo. I told him that, although Belgrade was a showcase of targeted warfare at its technological pinnacle (or at least somewhere in that general vicinity), the same could not be said for other cities and villages, in which cluster bombs had been dropped on marketplaces (Niš) and cruise missiles on homes huddled together for protection against nights marked by war (Aleksinac).[11] Two of the soldiers took my passport inside and it began to rain harder. The soldier with the sneakers on his feet told me that he had heard the bombers coming every night as they passed over Karakaj for Serbia. I fished out two local cigarettes from a crumpled package and offered one to him through the window of the car. He cradled it carefully in his hand while he rummaged through his numerous pockets in search of a match.

All around us, the fields stretched out into an unseen distance, marked in the imagination with bales of hay and distant, clustered collections of houses. Everything was already finished, and nothing could be done then to take it back. The road was more poorly lit than usual because the switching stations and refineries had all been bombed, and there remained a state of energy emergency as a result of that war, which it was said in Belgrade from the beginning had smelled thickly of death and defeat. It was more terrible to drive in the darkness, if only because the image produced by one's imagination is sometimes more difficult to grasp than the reality of things – and this is the case even when one has already seen what was done. And so, when the sun was yet low in the sky and the earth was scorched in places by deep black craters that had collected blackish groundwater in their centres, the sight was somehow bearable. It was bearable because you could talk about it. You could murmur at it, and then hear the terrible tale of the night that it (whatever it had been) was struck by the missiles that were satellite-guided and fired from the safety of a thousand miles away. You could hear them coming, it was said. They made terrible whistling noises in the seconds before the very earth trembled and the concussions rippled through the surrounding houses, imploding all the glass windows for a kilometre and wrenching the nearest buildings from their very foundations. My security studies mind rattled on about air-to-surface, wing-mounted, laser guided missiles, defended against poorly by the anti-aircraft artillery, which was useless anyway, because those bombers hid up beyond the clouds at a full 15,000 feet. It was because of this that they made so many mistakes in their target identification, and the reason why the gunners could not find them up there.

It was better to see it in the day, because your research-oriented mind could order and catalogue the damage. The rational parts of you could engage in intellectual assessment – could grasp the blast radius and the corresponding damage done to structures 20 metres, 40 metres, 100 metres from the point of impact. It was a neat trick, how the intellect was able to master the heart in daylight. But at night, along that road, passing unseen gnarled transformer towers, charred roof tiles, smashed windows, structures bent at crazy angles, bridges broken in half, the intellect could not function. At night, there was no rational order, because without seeing, you cannot order, but you can imagine. And imagining is sometimes worse than seeing, because seeing allows you to find the parameters of something – allows you to delineate things – whereas imagining has no parameters, and because it goes on and on long after the seeing is finished.[12] It keeps me awake at night. I waited in the rain at the Karakaj crossing, and I thought these things – things which I was sure that my discipline would never provide a place for me to say, and to which I still cannot do justice, because darkness is something Other in a world apprehended and mediated by vision. We huddle against it.

The soldier with the sneakers on his feet smoked my cigarette thoughtfully under the cover of his waterproof overcoat. He gathered himself beneath that coat, squinting his eyes against the rain as he waited for his colleagues to return with my passport. I thought that it was unfair for me to think about him – to wonder why he didn't have proper boots or to contemplate the question of why he had so many pockets in his coat or to wonder what he thought when he had heard the NATO warplanes crossing on their way to Serbia. I thought it was unfair for me to wish that I had the time and the money to ask him for a drink when that desire was only so that I could represent him better in some narrative or other, as I am representing him now. I thought it was unfair to want to write about him, to want to capture him like some strange animal in his authentic surroundings, a hastily constructed border post in a seemingly random spot. I felt that I was on a safari of some sort, scouting Serbs like lions. I felt that then, and I feel it still – the narrow line between fieldwork and tourism, between scholarship and voyeurism. When it was finished, the soldier that I wanted to interview tossed the cigarette out into the side of the road and said that he would go inside to see why in Christ's name it was taking so long. He came back promptly with my passport and regretfully announced that his colleagues had forgotten about me. He wished me a safe and pleasant journey and I gave him another cigarette before I drove on. The stamp in my Canadian passport was thick-lined and wet. It read **KAPAKAJ**, and the ink had bled into the fibres on the opposite page as well. The rain had let up a bit, and I was pleased about that, because those roads going up through the mountains were dangerous enough without that they should also be wet.

I remember now how that soldier's eyes had been so strangely blue that they were almost colourless, with silver flecks in the irises that expanded and contracted with the tenor of his voice. I could not write that when I got back home, because there was nothing academic in that, and it did not further the potential for knowledge; it did not lay the ground-work for an acceptable research agenda, and my faculty (which stands vigil over me from places now farther, now closer, and to which I am still answer-able) would not have liked it at all. Now, it seems imperative to gather the guts to remember it better, to gather the guts to indicate clearly that these impressions are the groundwork of the ethics of interaction, the politics of friendship, the imperative to responsibility for even what I do not under-stand and cannot grasp. The need to do well by the Other, even as I lay certain that I do not know how to do well by the Other, and that all my pleasant intentions are fictions and dangers. To leave this imperative behind, to theorize it out, to discipline it into a perverse uniformity, to squander the presence, the imminence of that imperative, would be uncon-scionable. 'I squander what is given me. I, a squanderer with a thousand hands.' Thus spoke Zarathustra.

I have always tried to anticipate what may befall me. Is this not what seals my place of privilege and what allows for the wealth and luxury of anticipation? Is this not what marks the difference between a good scholar and a poor one? Is this not the very question of one's judgment? I have always tried to pre-empt injurious things, and to be aware of where they may lie in wait for me. But I have not examined myself as the inju-rious one – as the perpetrator of violence. I do not know how I can defend myself against future charges. I am crushed by the weight of the texts that have come before this one, the weight of the texts that demand to know how this text dares to count itself among them, even as it seeks with some semblance of dignity to discipline those texts so that it might say some-thing sane; that is, so that it may find a place to sleep peacefully on the birch shelves in my landmine-free living room that are so painfully

illuminated by the afternoon sun. Stojan Sokolović fundamentally compromised the foundational moment of my faith (or my faithlessness) in the
discipline in which I have been trained and from which I claim to speak.
It is for this reason that the slant of the sun, the grounds in my espresso,
or the contracting, expanding, hostage-taking silver flecks in the colourless eyes of the soldier at the Karakaj crossing are here, in this place, a
cause for concern that I have indeed fallen over the edge of academic acceptability. I am just trying to respond to Stojan Sokolović – to speak of what
he asked and to admit, here, in this space, that I am bankrupt of any
currency with which to answer the charge.

Academic writing is only one kind of writing.[13] And in this case, it does
not allow me to attempt to answer the charge. I cannot enter a plea of 'not
guilty', because Stojan Sokolović will never sit on the jury that is empowered to decide my fate. Stojan Sokolović is not my peer in the empire of
knowledge, and no court comprised of my itinerant colleagues would
convict me for having wronged him. I was only following the rubrics of
acceptable scholarship. There would be irrefutable evidence: my degrees
and diplomas and qualifying examinations, my fellowships and research
funding, my publications and conference presentations, my fieldwork, my
groaning birch bookshelves, the well-paved road that led from my doctorate
to a permanent academic position in less than ten weeks, and which no
longer has any exit ramps. Who can be convicted for having followed the
letter of the law?

But the charge of my faithlessness yet remains, spoken in the rain
against a smudge of smoke from the tyres that burned along the banks of
the Vrbas River in homage to St Peter in the beginning of July. Faithlessness
is not a charge that I have experience answering to. I would have walked
away from it, would that it had not slipped through the tight weave of my
consciousness and prevented me from sleeping well at night.[14] I wanted to
walk away, then, to tell myself that it was nothing, nothing – just a mirage,
brought on by the burning tyres, or a hallucination brought on by sleeplessness, or the taste of the rain. But I could not escape it. It made demands
of me that could not be dismissed. It demanded of me an admission that I
cannot claim to have a formula, to craft a sentence, which will ever have
been enough – which will ever have said enough – captured enough –
transmitted enough. I can only do what I can do, which is all that I can
do and which is probably all that can be reasonably asked of one being.
So my task could be to say that impressions are knowledge, that the taste
left in the mouth from a half-remembered conversation is knowledge, that
my grief and the grief that others have allowed me to see is knowledge,
that love and the ability to love is knowledge.[15] I could make such a case,
because I could draw on resources that have made it before.[16]

But perhaps the better task is to simply abrogate the centrality of knowledge itself (as though I, a student ineffably guided by the viole(n)t shadows of the Enlightenment, could do such a thing); to say instead that knowledge is a pompous, baseless thing, crafted itself on foundations of faith (or of faithlessness); to say instead that knowledge, and the world of onto-logic that motivates the tapping of my fingers across the keyboard, is better left to those who want to make a business of knowing. Impressions are *not* knowledge. The taste left in the mouth from a half-remembered conversation is *not* knowledge. My grief and the grief that others have allowed me to see is *not* knowledge. But this should not prevent me from writing it. It may be because these things are not counted as knowledge that we are in desperate need of them, that we may need to consciously carry them, along with the burden of love (which is not so dissimilar) into our philosophical and political oblivion.

It was Stojan Sokolović himself (prosecutor from another world) who provided me with the mitigating circumstances that may allow me to answer the charge if I might see my way clear to ignore the law from now on. I may yet escape with my soul (and maybe my academic credentials) because he did not say that what I was doing was *wrong*. He said that 'had I been standing elsewhere' I would have seen something else, which is also not the same thing as saying that what I would have seen from my erstwhile elsewhere position would have been the truth, or complete, either. For even he, who was presumably standing somewhere near that Other place did not make any claim to know what I *should* have said. What he asked was simply that I stand responsible for not only my words, but also for the position I occupy that allows me to say what I say, and write what I write, in the first place. What he asked for was an ethical rereading, a rewriting, of what I had seen and heard, read and written.[17] He asked me to suspend the law. He asked me to embody something Other – he asked me to consent to Otherness itself. He did not ask for authenticity, or for me to go and do and be where, what, and who I am not and cannot be.

Moreover, because I am still concerned with my own defence, or at least with the possibility of making restitution, could I have said something that was purely non-violent? I cannot decide. John Caputo argues definitively that: 'There is no pure non-violence, only degrees and economies of violence, some of which are more fruitful than others.'[18] In any event, undecidability stops somewhere – at the foot of my bed, perhaps, or at the bottom of my coffee cup, or at the Karakaj crossing, or in the single, particular words of a (wo)man who bears a proper name – and responsibility begins. The Infinite stops at the moment of disaster(s), where undecidability ends and one must come down, either for this or that or for something (or someone) else.[19] And so I am not left speechless, which is fortuitous because I have problems keeping my mouth shut. I am not left with a fundamental inability to say anything at all. It does not mean that I should not speak, lest I commit unawares (as I already have) violence against those Others who would wish me to say something else – something perhaps less violent (or perhaps more so). Stojan Sokolović does not relegate me into fearful silence, for even silence is a potential form of violence. Silence is a decision. Silence, for example, can signal complicity – the silence of the body politic that allows the internment and death camps to crop up in train yards, farms, and factories.

> In derelict sidings the poppies entwine
> with cattle trucks lying in wait for the next time.[20]

Silence is also the herald of violence, or its co-conspirator. I could not have written something non-violent, because representation itself is always a form of violence and there is no writing without representation because writing *is* representation, even when we are aware and mindful of what we are up to. Perhaps I could have written something less violent, perhaps I could have accepted greater responsibility for the inherent violence that comes to pass in all speech and in all speech acts that stake claims about this or that thing, event, or person, to the detriment of Other possibilities, which would themselves be violent, but perhaps less so (or perhaps not). And this is the point, made in the shadow of the sun, as a fugitive from the law. We are trapped in violence, discursive and material, and discursive that leads to material, and material that emanates from and leads back to discursive. Accepting that there is no pure non-violence simply requires (as though it were indeed simple) that the writer of violence (that is, myself) keep a vigil of sorts over the ever-present possibility of violence, always trying to minimize its impact – to choose what is less violent – to be aware, as it were, that there are ever only 'degrees and economies of violence, some of which are more fruitful than others.'[21]

## Phonologies

The awareness that there is no pure non-violence is the vocative call – that which summons me – to be responsible for my decisions, for the words I choose and the stances I take. It demands that I stand responsible for and before the unwavering gaze, the inescapable charge, of Stojan Sokolović. But here is an interesting problem, raised (not of my will, to be sure) in the use of the vocative case. Emmanuel Levinas conceives of the vocative as a salutation – a greeting – because I must greet the Other who faces me – to speak *to*, but not *for* – which is in part why the nominative is insufficient (which is, in fact, why the nominative can be seen as its own sort of violence). But the vocative does not only greet, nor does it simply call. The vocative also commands. Can I call:

*Stojane!*[22]

Without that I also *require* him to turn back to face me, even if and when he wants to have done with me? That which greets in the vocative case can also command:

*Stojane!*

And he replies:

*evo me!*[23]

Stojan Sokolović is other – *drugi* – who requests a politics of friends – *drugovi*. My Other friend – *moj drugi drug*. My Other friends – *moji drugi drugovi*. And what if I call out in the vocative case using a different character set? What if I call out:

*Стојане!*[24]

If I call out:

*Стојане Соколовићу!*

What if I call for a politics of friends – *другови?* And if I speak of my other friend – *мој други друг?* My other

friends – *моји други другови?* If I call out:

*Стојане!*

Will he reply as he did above?

*ево ме!*

Changing the letters does not change the meaning of the words, but it might change their politics, might it not? Yes, indeed. And is it an accident that, in Stojan Sokolović's tongue, the word for 'friend' (*drug/друг*) is so similar to the word for 'other' (*drugi/други*)? I am not a linguist of Slavic tongues (though I like their phonologies), but this is an interesting question.

We academics – we products of those violent shadows receding into centuries that themselves precede and define us; we defend and console ourselves with the thin blade of rationality that wards off our enemies, arguing in conferences that ours is the proper research question, the best methodology, the only way to know. The academy creates knowledge (I know this because I am one of its keepers – a keeper of knowledge), it covets knowledge (and thereby covets what it creates, which must be the symptom of some illness or other); and all this creating and coveting serves to discern the parameters of the possible. Even in these post-post-post places we occupy, even in this strange, empowering oblivion, we are still caught in the straitjacket of our theism.[25] Can we journey beyond the parameters of the politically possible? Will we even retain a claim on the ability to speak to the discipline – to speak *from* it? My ability to speak is partial and situated, and my words, my speech, my acts – the deeds done or left undone by my small hand – can never claim what cannot be said of them. And it is the case that we Enlightenment sojourners and mourners have identified what is not knowledge (though I confess, I have a hard time seeing my way out of that). And though knowledge as a category, and what counts as knowledge, may be in flux and the boundaries may move around from time to time, the walls as such seem ever to remain.

My pride in the calibre of my intellect has led me to believe that it is better to be the one who holds the stick in the seminar than the one who gets hit with it – that it is better to be right than to be wrong, to humiliate than to be humiliated – that it is better to have a defensible truth, even if I know in my heart that my truth is nothing more than something that happened to cross my mind as I wandered around in the ancestral mountains of eastern Bosnia, even if I know that my truth is nothing more than the itinerant fragments I managed to capture on my tiny little audiocassettes.[26] I cannot separate myself now, from the layers of landmines, from the ones who hid behind the artillery. The divisions are blurring. As Raul Hilberg reminds us, it is when we succeed at our scholarly task that we are in the most danger of having usurped that which we wrote about. It is precisely our success that indicts us.[27]

Now, I look elsewhere for ethics.

## Responsibility

Stojan Sokolović has attenuated me to the fact that I am responsible, to everyone, all the time, and for everything. (I borrowed this from Levinas, who borrowed it from Dostoevsky.) This is the moment when the possibility of possibility comes crashing in: when I laugh and weep and mourn all at the same time, and with the same breath of air in my lungs. But this responsibility is also a thing that I fear and despise because it is inexplicable, beyond all description or rendering of it. It is the boundless possibility that I have theorized myself out of, that I have trained myself to ignore, in the same way that, because I was born beside the sea, I never really heard it crashing against the shore unless there was an unusual quality to it – unless a hurricane had come, for example. I have recently noticed that I can stand in the middle of something for what feels like a thousand years and still fail to definitively identify its most salient points, and still fail to apprehend what it 'really is' or come to terms with the idea that it might not be anything at all.

What expert am I, because I saw the stove in the grass behind the house that had landmines in its gutted living room? What expert am I for falling ill beneath the charge of Stojan Sokolović, who disappeared into the folds between borders that only moments ago were undefended, interre-publican borders, rent in ways that defied the intention of their crafters? Stojan Sokolović knew that there was no way to ever go home again not because there were landmines in his living room, but because he proceeded now from what had ceased to exist.[28] I loved him because he changed me, because he enabled me to write what I am writing now (which is my attempt to beg that particular court for mercy, but which is also an attempt to say something both to him and to my knowledge-producing colleagues in a language that allows me to), no matter how strange or unsuccessful it may ultimately be. He loved me because of my treachery, as he loved even the ones with proper names who hid behind the artillery in sneakers because their army did not have proper boots for them. He loved them even though they had killed others, who also bore proper names, *whom he had loved equally well*. Now, how shall I ask him to order that love? How shall I deny that one can love the ones who did the killing despite one's love for the ones who were killed? Stojan Sokolović did not order his love on the basis of guilt and innocence. He loved because he loved.

This is an indiscriminate, wasteful love that recognizes the most radical of all ideas – that the world unfolds every day – that in every day, and in every moment, and in every second, the beginning of the unfolding of the world takes place, without coherence, without systematization. This is a love that is not bankrupt of justice (as so many systems of justice are bank-rupt of love). It is a love that contemplates the possibility of forgiveness.[29] And it is only the truly unforgiveable that can be forgiven. It is a love that admits that I and the one who sits across the table facing me over a cup of espresso on the coast beside the sea are indiscernible, ethereal, gossamer-thin, inapprehensible, subject to change, subject *of* change. I didn't believe this until I realized that I could make no acceptable answer to Stojan Sokolović, that my faculties and my training had simply failed me. I didn't see it until I was smacked with the awareness that there is love inside hatred and happiness in horror. I didn't see it until I began to believe that fevers are the hallmark of health, that luck and fortune are encased in sorrow, that disgrace and ineptitude and failure are ingrained in all know-ledge systems, that love is not singular or unitary but multiple and fractal, that incoherence is not lunacy, that my inability to explain and under-stand is not the mark of my ignorance, but is the very basic form of my existence.

## An accusation in the course of fieldwork

If I had been willing to see back when I was writing the things that Stojan Sokolović called me to account for that I did not (could not) occupy a coherent place in the observatory of innocence, I could not have written what I wrote. I would have seen the possibility of love, the violence of love that takes you hostage, that demands coexistence with, and often betrays, the intellectual, the rational, the scientific, the knowable. Life is bound in love. And it is precisely the love in life that offers the heaviest burdens. I am not burdened by my love of the innocent. (Who is burdened by love of innocence?) The burden lay in the love of the guilty, in the love *for* the guilty (which does not, however, entail ignoring the call for justice). And this binds me in measure beyond measurement, because of my love, because of my lack of it, and because grief, like violence, is not a thing that can be washed from the skin like salt.

NOTES

1  James Hatley, *Suffering Witness: The Quandary of Responsibility After the Irreparable* (Albany, NY: State University of New York Press, 2000), p. 131.
2  See Michael Walzer, *Just and Unjust Wars* (New York: Basic Books, 2000).
3  A 1999 *Toronto Star* article noted that 'Canadian peacekeepers were suspected of being paid cash to smuggle refugees across no-man's land in war-torn Bosnia in 1994, confidential military documents show ... No charges were ever laid because no witnesses could be found.' Allan Thompson, 'Canadian Troops Smuggled Bosnian Refugees, Memos Say', *Toronto Star*, 28 November 1999.
4  I have not dutifully transcribed what Stojan Sokolović said to me that night while the thunder rolled off the eastern horizon and the soldiers gathered together beneath the balcony to find shelter from the summer rain. I have produced here my *impression* of his statement – the feeling it left me with that I had failed incontrovertibly. Perhaps some scholars would charge my 'methodology' as suspect, but I charge anyone who has ever interviewed another human being to dare say that she herself has not served as the sole interpreter of the significance of words captured on tiny little audiocassettes and manipulated them to fit carefully, seamlessly, into the text she has crafted around the interview – or the text which has itself crafted the interview and the interview's content. We craft these statements to serve our own purposes – we tease them out in ways that serve us – to underwrite and legitimize our own intellectual projects and projections. I do not pretend to have spoken for Stojan Sokolović – instead, I have rendered the substance of what I heard in his words, what it meant for my scholarship, and for my ability to be responsible. I have rendered the transcription that I heard in the charge – and so the translation is mine (as all translation invariably is and will ever be) and should not be attributed to those I interviewed. Finally, while Stojan Sokolović is an existing pseudonymic individual with whom I have had extensive interview contact, for the purposes of this text, where he appears, he should not always be taken by the reader as one person, but rather representative of a number of interviews I conducted in which the informant expressed essentially the same sorts of challenges to my project. Given the propensity of International Relations to project individuality and personification onto units of analysis, such as states, it would not seem that I am guilty of any greater misrepresentation.

15

5   An *opština* is roughly equivalent to a county or municipality.

6   A *tepsija* is an all-purpose baking pan.

7   Derrida argues that 'friendship does not keep silence, it is preserved by silence.' in George Collins (trans.) *Politics of Friendship* (London: Verso, 1997), p. 53.

8   The question 'čija si ti?' translates literally into English as 'whose are you?' or 'to whom do you belong?' In the cultural context, however, the speaker is querying my ancestry – referring to my father, grandfather, my clan or kinship ties, my *slava* or family's saint day – all factors that would serve to identify me as *proceeding from* and therefore *tied to* a particular teleological lineage that is presumably bounded and traceable.

9   Richard Ashley, 'The Achievements of Post-Structuralism', in Steve Smith, Ken Booth, and Marysia Zalewski (eds), *International Theory: Positivism and Beyond* (New York: Cambridge University Press, 1996), p. 241, brackets mine.

10  Here is the need of the universal reference. This trip took place in July 1999. This point of temporal (date) and spatial (southern Serbia) departure will likely lay the groundwork for the reader to fill in more information than I can provide with everything that follows. The place is southern Serbia – a new Serbia without Kosovo in the post Operation Allied Force environment. The refugees are Serbs.

11  After cruise missiles were dropped on the small mining town of Aleksinac, CNN correspondent Brent Sadler reported seeing 'quite clearly that these were civilian homes . . . I saw body parts inside these buildings.' See 'More Explosions in Yugoslavia; Civilian Casualties Reported', 5 April 1999: http://cnn.com/WORLD/europe/9904/05/nato.attack.04/ (accessed on 5 April 1999).

12  Derrida asks, '[w]hat happens when one writes without seeing? A hand of the blind ventures forth alone or disconnected, in a poorly delimited space; it feels its way, it gropes, it caresses as much as it inscribes, trusting in the memory of signs and supplementing sight.' See Jacques Derrida, *Memoirs of the Blind: The Self-Portrait and Other Ruins*, Pascale-Anne Brault and Michael Naas, trans. (Chicago: University of Chicago Press, 1993), p. 3.

13  I am grateful to Sandra Whitworth for reminding me of this in an earlier articulation of this chapter.

14  See Emmanuel Levinas, *Of God Who Comes to Mind*, Bettina Bergo, trans. (Stanford, CA: Stanford University Press: 1998), p. 75.

15  It might also be said that my failure – the failure pointed to by Stojan Sokolović – can form the baseline for the development of a body of knowledge, properly understood. Iris Murdoch argues that: 'What is experienced as most real in our lives is connected with a value which points further on. Our consciousness of failure is a source of knowledge. We are constantly in process of recognising the falseness of our "goods", and the unimportance of what we deem important.' See *Metaphysics as a Guide to Morals* (London: Chatto & Windus, Ltd, 1992), p. 430.

16  For example, Patricia Hill Collins has argued in the context of black feminism(s) that black women's songwriting, poetry, and literature can be utilised as part of a corpus of black women's intellectual history in an effort to reclaim a black women's intellectual tradition. See *Black Feminist Thought: Knowledge, Consciousness, and the Politics of Empowerment*, 2nd edn (New York: Routledge, 2000).

17  Many feminists have been asking for a similar kind of responsibility for more than a decade. See particularly Donna Haraway, *Simians Cyborgs and Women* (New York: Routledge: 1991) particularly chapter nine, 'Situated Knowledges: The Science Question in Feminism and the Privilege of Partial Perspective.' Haraway argues that 'traditionally what can count as knowledge is policed by philosophers codifying cognitive canon law' (p. 183). For Haraway 'situated knowledges require that the object of knowledge

16

be pictured as an actor and agent, not a screen or a ground or a resource, never finally as slave to the master that closes off the dialectic in his unique agency and authorship of 'objective' knowledge.' (p. 198). Haraway's point is that the epistemological and ontological boundaries of what constitutes proper knowledge need to be expanded. The difference here is precisely one of querying 'knowledge' as a category and as a bounded phenomenon with particular, definitive characteristics. I would argue here that it is more useful to suggest that knowledge itself should not necessarily be expanded, but rather challenged by other forms of cognition. It is this possibility that I think might allow for movement beyond the epistemological and ontological paradigm of inside/outside and other modes of binary thinking. Anthony Burke makes a case for reading poetry 'outside security', arguing that 'a certain kind of poetry provides a way of thinking past the dominant ontological assumptions and emotional promises of prevailing political discourses of security ... it can help liberate subjectivity from a powerful modern technology of the soul that binds state and subject into an intimate, but ultimately destructive, relation.' (p. 307). What is most instructive here is the idea of thinking *past*, a suggestion that means significantly more than just expanding boundaries – a suggestion, perhaps, that provides a way of collapsing these ontological categories in on themselves, thereby doing away with the very concept of boundaries. This does not, however, solve the first order ontological problem that 'naming' entails. Levinas points to the problem of the 'said' in the 'saying' – the problem, as it were, of naming. This naming is its own ontological technology – a theoretical move that totalizes the named in the very moment in which the naming takes place. See 'Poetry Outside of Security', *Alternatives* 25, 2000, pp. 307–321; see also Emmanuel Levinas, *Otherwise Than Being Or Beyond Essence* (Pittsburgh: Duquesne University Press, 1998).

18  John D. Caputo, ed., *Deconstruction in a Nutshell: A Conversation with Jacques Derrida* (New York: Fordham University Press, 1997), p. 47.

19  John D. Caputo, *Against Ethics* (Indianapolis: University of Indiana Press, 1993), particularly Chapter 5, 'The Epoch of Judgment'.

20  Roger Waters/Pink Floyd, 'Your Possible Pasts', *The Final Cut* (Phantom Records, 1983).

21  Caputo, *Deconstruction in a Nutshell*.

22  The Serbian vocative case of the name Stojan.

23  The Levinasian *'me voici!'*

24  The Cyrillic transliteration of *Stojane!*

25  I use the term 'theism' here to refer to the Enlightenment trinity of rationality, science, and knowledge. These *replaced* the triadic theism of Christianity, but they did not disrupt the universal absolutes that theism entailed. Thus, the legacy of the Enlightenment remains an insular, unassailable species of theology, with science standing in for God. William Connelly notes that: 'Contemporary social theory contains within it a set of secular reassurances that compensate for those lost through the death of God ... (p. 16) [T]his phenomenology presupposes a relatively stable and serene context of self-identity, social practice, state and interstate relations, and temporal projection.' (p. 19). Human freedom, of course, is the chief compensation. See *Identity/Difference: Democratic Negotiations of Political Paradox* (Minneapolis: University of Minnesota Press, 1991).

26  Grace M. Jantzen writes that: 'once the model of a battle is taken as central to philosophical thinking, then the likelihood increases that instead of engaging in creative exploration of the issues, a student who is trying to learn to think philosophically will think not of what gives her insight or how that insight could be extended, but of how her position could be attacked and what she needs to do about it. When such students write essays or present seminars of their own, they will naturally try to make only a small and easily defended case (if indeed they are brave enough to try out their own

ideas at all), since in an adversarial paradigm the discussion that follows a paper is not one that tries to take up points to see how they could be developed further, but rather one which tries to demolish questionable bits. If arguments are set up so that they must be "won" or "lost", most people, at whatever academic level, will try to present cases which they feel confident that they can "win". Nobody enjoys being a loser. But this means that, in a more important sense, everybody loses, since fewer people will risk trying out adventurous ideas. Innovative thinking may well contain inadequacies. If students expect that these will be pounced upon, rather than that their creativity will be fostered (while being helped to avoid potential pitfalls and dead ends), they will quickly learn to curtail their innovative or exploratory inclinations and reproduce the attacks and defences of traditional philosophical battle.' *Becoming Divine: Towards a Feminist Philosophy of Religion* (Manchester, UK: Manchester University Press, 1998), p. 70.

27  Raul Hilberg, 'I Was Not There', in Berel Lang, ed., *Writing and the Holocaust* (New York: Holmes & Meier, 1988), p. 25.

28  In this formulation, what has ceased to exist is the Socialist Federal Republic of Yugoslavia (SFRY), but this does not make Stojan Sokolović a refugee. Stojan Sokolović was not a refugee; he was not properly stateless and he was not forcibly displaced. He was, perhaps, in a place stranger still: he possessed a passport issued by the post-war SFRY (it was a nice burgundy colour), even though there was, in fact, no recognized post-war SFRY to issue such a document. When the Federal Republic of Yugoslavia began issuing a new passport that reflected the membership of only Serbia and Montenegro in the reconstituted federation, the document was virtually useless for travel because the 'new' federation had not been recognized by the international community. Visas to visit other states were generally issued only if the bearer of the new blue passport also had permanent resident status in a second country. So, for example, the United States consulate in Toronto issued tourist visas to blue-passport-holding Yugoslav citizens only if they were also in possession of Canadian- or third-party issued landed immigrant documents. US visas were not embossed in the bearer's passport, but were provided on separate pieces of paper, because the United States did not recognize the federation that had issued the passport. US visas, however, continued to be embossed in the old red passports of the SFRY, an entity comprised of six constituent republics, even after the US had recognized three of those republics as independent states. So what had ceased to exist was the SFRY, but what followed, the Federal Republic of Yugoslavia comprised of Serbia and Montenegro, had yet to exist. This was the strange placelessness of a people who now occupied a space that had no legal facticity.

29  Caputo argues that: 'Forgiving lets the web of human relations hang loose. It cuts the event loose, gives the Other space, room to breathe, to try again.' See Caputo, *Against Ethics*, p. 112.

# 2

# *Responding to Others*

Every actual relationship in the world is exclusive; the other breaks into it to avenge its exclusion.[1]

Virginia Dominguez argues that: 'It is important that we all pay attention to the presence or absence of love and affection in our scholarship – at all stages of the production of our scholarship. If it is not there, it is important to ask ourselves why and what we should do about it. If it is there, we owe it to our readers to show it, to enable them to evaluate its role in the nature of our work.'[2] I began researching the wars of secession in Yugoslavia in fulfillment of a promise that two undergraduate Serbian political science students extracted from me in a café at York University in Toronto in 1997. Those students were centrally involved in organizing a movement in Toronto protesting against the electoral sleight of hand that had seen Slobodan Milošević retain power in Belgrade in October of 1996. I attended their rallies in Nathan Phillips Square in the dead of winter, which were held in solidarity with student protests in Yugoslavia and which were almost exclusively ignored by the media. I attended their house parties. I served them tea. They taught me to speak Serbian – *ekavica* – which I speak poorly. They introduced me to the man I later married, who speaks *ijekavica*.

Two years after beginning my research into identity and the politics of conflict in Bosnia and Kosovo the opportunity to visit the region presented itself. On 24 March 1999, NATO began a 78-day military air campaign against the Federal Republic of Yugoslavia, and more specifically, against Serbia as a constituent republic of that federation, with the stated intent of forcing Belgrade to pull its security forces out of Kosovo.[3] Over the course of the preceding decade, Serbian repression against the Albanian population in the province had deepened dramatically, manifesting in large-scale dismissals of Albanian professionals from their jobs, the closing of Albanian-language schools, and imprisonment of activists and demonstrators. By the spring of 1998, that repression had given rise to the independence-oriented Kosovo Liberation Army, and Serb security forces had resorted to the wholesale razing of compounds and villages to try to capture or kill those suspected of being involved. After the war which was not referred to as a war, and with an invitation from friends to accompany them on a trip to Bosnia and Serbia, I received a single-entry visa from the Yugoslav embassy – one of the few issued in Toronto following the NATO bombing.[4]

I arrived first in Bosnia, and I arrived as I think most academics do: to pursue the answers to those central questions that take up so much of the scholarly and policy terrain that has come to characterize Bosnia: How can democracy be implemented? How can civil society be strengthened? How can corruption be stemmed? Why are the nationalists (nearly) always elected? How can refugee return be ensured? How can multiculturalism be fostered? According to the vast majority of the literature of the 1990s on Bosnia, it was clear that the biggest problem with nationalist violence and intolerance was to be found in Republika Srpska. Comparatively few researchers have spent time in the Serb-allocated territory of Bosnia, however, and those who had were almost uniformly condemnatory of the aggressive, violent, exclusionary attitude of the Serbs. The peacekeepers were more uniformly cynical: 'If we weren't here, these people would still be killing each other', noted one Canadian Stabilization Force (SFOR) officer that I spoke with in Bosnia.[5]

I went to Bosnia for the first time to fulfil my promise. I arrived with a reasonable background in the academic literature, and in first hand relationships with Bosnians, Serbs, and Bosnian Serbs in Toronto who thought they had prepared me for my trip. I arrived with a few local contacts and a decent grasp of the language. I thought that, because of this background, I was more uniquely placed to experience and appreciate a more authentic 'truth' of Bosnia than most researchers ever see. That sentiment quickly faded, and after several years of passing back and forth, I began to see that the arrogance of that sentiment was not antithetical to the violence I was researching.

## Ethics

In *Ethics as First Philosophy*, Emmanuel Levinas argues that the ontological structure of knowledge always already involves a mechanics of appropriation. 'The immanence of the known to the act of knowing is already the embodiment of seizure.'[6] Knowledge manifests as a grasping – a groping – of perception, comprehension, repetition, a subsuming of the Other into a framework of intelligibility that orders alterity into a category or taxonomy for ease of analysis. As such, the primary characteristic of what

20

is known and of what *can* be known is its a priori status as *property* in a metaphysical world characterized by and built upon an ontological point of origin.[7] Here, the variable and the contingent are fashioned into the immobile – into the imperative need of the object and of the objectified in the realm of ontological certitude. The objects that emerge from this appropriation are displayed as the alibi and as the justification of the structure of knowledge that informs its own system. My academic and personal relationships and research background mediated and identified the salient points associated with identity and responsibility in Bosnia. These preceded my ever having stepped foot there and shaped the research agenda that I fashioned before I had even entertained the thought of my first fieldwork trip. Levinas proceeds from the question of whether thought understood as knowledge is not exhausted, and he wonders whether, 'beyond knowledge and its hold on being, a more urgent form does not emerge.'[8] For Levinas, that form, which is prior to and beyond knowledge and being, takes the shape of the desire for the Other, which is transcendence, and the extreme, inescapable exposure of the Other to the violence of my existence. Through a structure of desire in which what is desired can never be attained:

> The ego strives to comprehend, literally, to grasp the Other, but is unable. The Other expresses an infinitude which cannot be reduced to ontological categories. The ego is pulled out of itself toward the transcendent. This inability to comprehend the Other calls the ego and its self-sufficiency into question. Have I, merely by existing, already usurped the place of another? Am I somehow responsible for the death of the Other? The face calls the ego to respond before any unique knowledge about the Other. The approach of the human Other breaks the ego away from a concern for its own existence; with the appearance of the Other, *Dasein* is no longer a creature concerned with its own being.[9]

Here, the structure of ethics as that which emanates from and serves the Self/ego is demolished and I am found to be subordinated to the imperative posed by the unavoidable imminence of the face of the Other. In Levinas's transcendent formulation of responsibility, my very existence is an unavoidable violence despite my best attempts at innocence. It is this encounter in which the Other faces me – accuses me – that I become fundamentally responsible prior to any other claim or imperative. For Levinas, this entails a '[r]esponsibility for the Other, for the naked face of the first individual to come along. A responsibility that goes beyond what I may or may not have done to the Other or whatever acts I may or may not have committed, as if I were devoted to the other man before being devoted to myself.'[10] This ineluctable responsibility frames my fundamental orientation toward the Other, and this is a responsibility that I cannot pass off onto another person. No one can substitute for me. This means that: 'In the face of the other man I am inescapably responsible and consequently the unique and chosen one.'[11] In this formulation, fear for the Other becomes *my own* fear – the palpability of emotion as it moves through anxiety, joy, sadness – but it does not revert to fear for myself. Such a formulation reflects a crisis of being and selfhood, because it posits the cry of the Other as prior to my existence, for which I am already always responsible. The brother of the elder Zosima in Dostoevsky's *Brothers Karamazov* provides the groundwork for this sense of responsibility when he says that 'every one of us is answerable for everyone else and for everything. I don't know how to explain it to you, but I feel it so strongly that it hurts.'[12] Such a statement dispenses with the hard-and-fast distinction between guilt and innocence and levels ethics at the doorstep of a responsibility that binds one as a hostage to the other man: 'a responsibility for my neighbour, for the other man, for the stranger or sojourner, to which nothing in the rigorously ontological order binds me – nothing in the order of the thing, of the something, of the number or causality.'[13] Here, we find the 'infinite subjection of subjectivity.'[14]

For Levinas, like Dostoevsky, ethics is prior to being – prior to our ability to situate ourselves in a matrix of existence marked by the temporal fixity and metaphysical reliability of relationships and identities. For Levinas, ethics is stretched out and mapped congruently – simultaneously – onto the form of one's very existence and thereby onto any claim one could reasonably make from the ground of that existence. Here, the argument is that we are always already 'ethically situated' in relation to the face of the Other – the trace of the Other – which is the ultimate location of sensibility and sensuousness. Here, the Other regards me in the accusative (in Serbo-Croat: *sebe*) which does not correspond to a nominative or to an accusative of the self (*ja, mene*). The Levinasian relation to the Other, then, is not ontological or even phenomenological, but ecstatic: 'Ethics is not a moment of being, it is otherwise and better than being; the very possibility of the beyond.'[15] The command of the Other is experienced as a convulsive trauma – an incalculable shock – an ecstasy which falls outside of the net of reason and rationality:

> I cannot slip away from the face of the neighbor without avoidance, or without fault, or without complexes; here I am pledged to the other without any possibility of abdication. I cannot slip away from the face of the other in its nakedness without recourse ... My responsibility in spite of myself – which is the manner by which the other is incumbent upon me, or how he disturbs me, that is, the way in which he is close to me – is a hearing or an understanding of this cry. It is awakening. The proximity of the neighbor is my responsibility for him: to approach is to be the guardian of one's brother; to be the guardian of one's brother is to be his hostage. This is immediacy. Responsibility does

not come from fraternity, it is fraternity that gives responsibility for the other its name, prior to my freedom.[16]

Here, one becomes aware of a call that is nevertheless always present – to ignore the call is not to dispel or destroy its salience, even though the call is addressed to an 'I' who cannot be substituted by another. The awareness of the vocative call is described by Levinas as an awakening: 'The referring to another is awakening [éveil], awakening to proximity, which is responsibility for the neighbor to the point of substitution for him.'[17] Here, the trauma of responsibility is absolute, without the possibility of recourse, a totality of obligation in which my responsibility for Others is such that I keep nothing for myself.[18] Accordingly, then, one cannot substitute for the Other, or take the place of the Other, because the Other is not simply another position, but is rather a fundamental challenge to the blamelessness of my own life even in the space before it is my own. It is thus that I am responsible for events and Others that precede the temporality in which I dwell, as well as for events and Others that unfold in spaces that I do not occupy. This being apart from me, however does not mean that: 'The Other is . . . experienced as an empty pure place and means for the world to exhibit another perspective, but as a contestation of my appropriation of the world, as a disturbance in the play of the world, a break in its cohesion.'[19]

Michael Shapiro points out that the fundamental ethical position is an acceptance of the absolute exteriority of the Other, an understanding that the Other is not simply another 'I' in a different position, or speaking a different language, or harbouring different commitments, familial, social, political, ethical.[20] For Shapiro, attention to the Other means that 'we are responsible to alterity as absolute alterity, as a difference that cannot be subsumed into the same, into a totalizing conceptual system that comprehends self and other.'[21] The Other faces me, contesting me absolutely in the facing. This facing throws up a roadblock around which there is no detour. The facing thus prevents me from moving through time and space, through politics and ethics outside of responsibility. It challenges the way I am in the world, the sense of consanguinity that is said to exist between us as human beings; it undermines my claims before I have made them, it prevents me from assimilating, from appropriating and incorporating the statements of Stojan Sokolović. Yet, that facing, while contesting any possibility of affinity between us, nevertheless simultaneously binds me without recourse – without the possibility of abdicating my responsibility.

For Levinas, '[t]here is a paradox in responsibility, in that I am obliged without this obligation having begun in me, as though an order slipped into my consciousness like a thief, smuggled itself in, like an effect of one of Plato's wandering causes. But this is impossible in a consciousness, and clearly indicates that we are no longer in the element of consciousness.'[22] Outside of consciousness, the Other seizes me, which I experience as a moment of ecstasy, the sensibility of a caress, a grip of madness that falls outside the realm of rationality, function, or ontological analyses.[23] Responsibility takes place in ecstasy, else it could not happen at all. The madness identified by Kierkegaard is not only the madness associated with decision-making itself – as an act – but is also the madness associated with a particular choice, a particular decision which embraces the least of all the rational options from the viewpoint of self-interestedness. The ecstatic encounter, this brushing up against another world with a face and a skin that is more than a surface, but which is, at its core, a contestation, an accusation, a challenge. This is an order placed upon me that is simultaneously and fundamentally outside of my ability to thematize it. It is outside the realm of knowledge and of ontology. One experiences the command of the Other as an impact which cannot be absorbed. As Alphonso Lingis writes in the introduction to *Otherwise Than Being*: 'Not being able to take up the order put to me and appropriate it, and make it into my own principle, is just in what the sense of being contested consists.'[24]

## Politics

Levinas's formulation of the relationship with the Other – the face-to-face relationship – appears to be inevitably disrupted when it is stretched into a political world that is populated by other Others – by multiple Others who stake different and competitive claims. In this world, the Other is also faced by another Other. In other words, the Other is contested by a Third. While Levinas understands the ethical relation to involve the facing of the Other, he understands the political relation to always include at least three persons, which in turn gives rise to the question, which is a dilemma, of how to pursue justice. When the third person enters into and disrupts the ethical relationship, the ethical crosses over into the political. Here begins the Levinasian formulation and structure of justice; the need of deliberation, of arbitration, of the liberal state and its attendant institutions – of the courts, the legislature, constitutions, tribunals and truth commissions. For Levinas: 'The third party introduces a contradiction in the saying whose signification before the other until then went in one direction. It is of itself the limit of responsibility and the birth of the question: What do I have to do with justice? . . . Justice is necessary, that is, comparison, coexistence, contemporaneousness, assembling, order, thematization, the visibility of faces, and thus intentionality . . . Proximity takes on a new meaning in the space of contiguity.'[25]

In this formulation, the political aspects of proximity first appear as a challenge to the face-to-face relationship and responsibility to the Other, which has heretofore been an infinite responsibility. The question of determining who requires response, of who requires justice, of who is the neighbour to whom I am pledged unequivocally, disrupts my relationship with the Other through both an extending and a limiting of my responsibility. With the entry of the Third, my responsibility is extended insofar as I become responsible beyond the Other to other Others. But my responsibility is also limited in that my infinite responsibility to and for the Other is tempered by my responsibility to the Third, whom the Other may injure, kill, or persecute.

Insofar as the entry of the Third ushers in the realm of the political, the move from the Other to the Third marks the moment of violence. For Levinas, this is the move from ethics to an ontological system, which is marked fundamentally by violence. The ontological structure of law and justice cannot regard the face of the Other. Indeed, the transcendental responsibility-unto-death to and for the Other is destroyed by the entry of the Third because my attention to the Other is thus divided, diverted, distracted. As William Paul Simmons notes, 'It is not possible to respond infinitely to all Others. The original demand for an infinite responsibility remains, but it cannot be fulfilled. Ethics must be universalized, but in attempting to do so, the ego has already reneged on its responsibility for the Other. Thus, Levinas' peculiar formulation; justice is un-ethical and violent.'[26]

Yet, for Jacques Derrida, the violence associated with the *ineluctable, necessary, and just* entry of the Third suggests that there is also an ethical violence in the relationship of the face-to-face that the Third tempers or mitigates. For Derrida, the Third protects against the violence of the possibility of unicity – of absolute affinity – between the Self and the Other. The Third mitigates against the possibility of rapture or ecstasy, against the possibility of the fusion of the Other with the Self. Indeed, the Third requires us to adjudicate what is nevertheless an 'impossibility of discerning here between good and evil, love and hate, giving and taking, the desire to live and the death drive, the hospitable welcome and the egoistic or narcissistic closing up within oneself ... The third would thus protect against the vertigo of ethical violence itself.'[27]

The entry of the Third also requires an analysis of what it means to be in proximity, of how to adjudicate, to determine who requires response – *which* neighbour? For Levinas, ethical proximity is understood as 'contact with the other. To be in contact is neither to invest the other and annul his alterity, nor to suppress myself in the other. In contact itself the touching and the touched separate, as though the touched moved off, was always already other, did not have anything in common with me.'[28] Derrida rightly argues that one is always only able to respond to an Other because one failed to respond to an-other Other. For Levinas, this dilemma seems to be resolved spatially, with the question of 'who is closest to me?' solidifying in the image of 'the neighbour' as the answer. Yet, David Campbell notes that, in his discussion of proximity, Levinas also simultaneously denies the spatial dimensions evoked by the concept of proximity. It seems also that the notion of proximity may include cultural, linguistic, or customary ties – 'the priority of time over space'.[29] In this sense, the neighbour becomes the Other who can be identified within the logic of the borders of the state. It is thus the case that the ethicality commanded without regard to distance *within* societies is limited by the politics of the borders *between* societies. In other words, ethics is suspended at the border crossing. On the other side of the border, observes Patricia Molloy, we find the potential 'transformation of alterity into enmity.'[30]

It is this formulation, according to Campbell, that lays the groundwork for Levinas's infamous excision of the Palestinians from the realm of those to whom the Israeli 'I' is responsible.[31] Asked about the question of responsibility in the aftermath of the 1982 massacres of Palestinian refugees during the Israeli invasion of Lebanon, Levinas replied: 'If your neighbour attacks another neighbour or treats him unjustly, what can you do? Then alterity takes on another character, in alterity we can find an enemy, or at least we are faced with the problem of knowing who is right and who is wrong, who is just and who is unjust. There are people who are wrong.'[32]

Levinas does not deny that the absolute ethical relation founders on the shoals of the political. There is always the danger that, once the neighbour is identified as a victim, the victim may produce other victims in the name of self defence. Is this not the precise cornerstone on which accounts of ethical violence, 'just war', for example, rest? In his consideration of Levinas's limiting of the ethical in the transition to the political, John Caputo addresses the problem by divesting ethics of the a priori interiority that insulates responsibility from the realm of things that 'happen' – the world of events, of politics, of poverty, homelessness, and murder, for example. That Levinasian ethics – the absolute responsibility to the Other – is tempered by Levinasian politics; that some Others may become enemies is not particularly problematic for Caputo. Thus, with regard to the absolute infinity of the Other posed by Levinas, Caputo argues that: 'You have to be sensible. There are limits. For example, if the Other is shooting at you, then we say, that is not the Other. So we draw a circle around "ethics", marking off a domain of purity, and we point out that everything has its limits, including the ethics of infinity, which turns out to be relatively finite. In addition to being held hostage by the Other, one also keeps an army, just as a deterrent against hostage taking.'[33]

Here, we find a relatively immobile identification of victimhood: the neighbour called to the defence of the Other neighbour as the Third attacks him. This is an understanding of victimhood par excellence, an abject victimhood of genocide, of murder and expulsion; an assailment of one's very right to be. This is the formula of the Shoah. In these events we find a paradigm of abject victimhood associated with the mechanized annihilation of the Jews of Europe. Levinas stands watch over the Shoah, he keeps vigil over the events that produced the murdered in their nameless numbers. In the case of the Shoah, even after the intent of the National Socialists toward the Jews became clear, the Jews were still annihilated. The ethical relation to the Other foundered on the exigencies and difficulties of the political and six million were murdered. For Caputo, then, the interview with Levinas which saw him evade the question of Israeli responsibility to the Palestinian 'is a revelation . . . of the impossibility of ethics, the impossibility of drawing a line around ethics, of preserving an inner sanctum, a holy of holies, called ethics, and of the need for the deconstruction of ethics.'[34]

Also concerned with the apparent elision of responsibility in the transition from ethics to politics in Levinas, David Campbell relies on the deconstructive turn of Derrida as the 'supplement' to Levinas.[35] Campbell argues that deconstruction loosens the ontological categories that solidify in the Levinasian move from the Other to the Third, exposing the contingency and the non-necessity of things. Most importantly, deconstruction allows for political engagement while simultaneously exposing the contingent, variable, and mobile character of the political, its categories, and its claims to authority. For Campbell, the value of deconstruction lies in its continuous movement to expose particular iterations of politics as non-natural, non-necessary, and non-immutable. For example, the development of authoritative forms that in turn produce the normative conditions of international political life are not the inevitable consequence of the uncontested 'laws' governing the relationship between states. These relationships can be recognized as having developed within particular ordering principles that can be understood as having been established simply because others were not. No claim, then, can be understood as being based on something more than the very claim for which justification is continually being sought. In this way, laws and customs are without inherent ground or authority, without a priority, and without a fixed and identifiable once-and-for-all character. Derrida expands: 'The operation that amounts to founding, inaugurating, justifying law, [and] making law, would consist of a *coup de force*, of a performative and therefore interpretive violence that in itself is neither just nor unjust and that no justice and no previous law . . . could guarantee or contradict or invalidate.'[36]

For example, then, as identity is invoked and reinvoked, inscribed and reinscribed as truth or fact, it relies and *can* rely only on past conceptions and perceptions of itself. This is crucial to an understanding of the marginalization or denial of other iterations of identity. Thus, as Campbell argues in the case of Bosnia, the hardening of identity as an exclusionary, nationally based phenomenon can actually be read not as an immutable manifestation of primordial hatreds, but rather as a performative undertaking which mobilizes the resources of history in order to pursue a national politics in and of the present. In this formulation, there is nothing natural or necessary about the war in Bosnia or in the fracturing of intercommunal relationships along national/ethnic lines. The Serb is not an a priori subject with fixed characteristics who enters into relationships of violence as a necessity of history and of the history of politics. Rather, the point that Campbell makes in his use of Derrida's *coup de force* – the 'founding' act – is that the Serb as such is constituted in and by the violence that is inscribed by his body on the bodies of others. As Campbell argues: 'Conceiving of violence as a form of political inscription and transcription, rather than the product of a "psychogenetic" cause, as a performance rather than a purely instrumental practice, highlights its constitutive role in identity politics ... Far from being a natural outgrowth of historical animosities and earlier conflicts, we can think of these issues of ethnicity and nationalism as *questions of history violently deployed in the present for contemporary political goals.*'[37]

The basic ethicality associated with deconstruction lies in the fact that its very character is to avoid totalizing, exclusionary goals. For Levinas, the move from the ethical to the political is a totalizing one wherein the universal must be expressed. To recognize deconstruction's deferment to contingency is to recognize that deconstruction itself constitutes a basic ethical position. In the recognition that the ethical lies in the refusal to arrive at a totalizing outcome or iteration, the focus of attention falls on the idea of the undecidable. For Derrida, undecidability is precisely that crisis of confidence which renders decision-making simultaneously impossible and imperative. At the core of the decision lies a moment of madness because one can never calculate all of the effects of a particular choice. Furthermore, decision-making erupts out of the space of the fundamentally unknown and unknowable. The decision passes through a realm of indeterminacy, of Kierkegaardian fear and trembling, because it must include the contemplation of what cannot be identified or made certain. As Campbell notes: 'Were everything to be within the purview of the decidable, and devoid of the undecidable, then – as Derrida constantly reminds us – there would be no ethics, politics, or responsibility, only a program, technology, and its irresponsible application.'[38]

It is this ethos that Campbell identifies as being imperative to an understanding of the war in Bosnia. For Campbell, Levinasian thought is, in the main, 'appealing for rethinking the question of responsibility, especially with respect to situations like the Bosnian war, because it maintains that there is no circumstance under which we could declare that it was not our concern.'[39] Arguing that the triadic nexus of identity/citizenship/territory serves as the settled normative orientation of international (read: western) society, Campbell demonstrates that international response to the war in Bosnia was not only insufficient, but also complicit in the reproduction of the very nationalist imaginaries that made the war possible in the first place. In this regard, the limitations on conceptions and formulations of legitimate politics act to silence all challenges and dissent and to excise other, non-national iterations of identity. The point of Campbell's argument is to show that exclusionary, violent nationalism was not exclusive or necessary to understanding identity in Bosnia, that the conflict was thus not an inevitable outcome of 'primordial' ethnic hatreds but rather an iteration of a politics of exclusion that sought to justify itself in the framework of a naturalized history marked by various *coups de force*.

Furthermore, Campbell illustrates that it was possible to locate other voices in and around the conflict from all ethnicities which were antithetical to the claims of nationalists. Arguing that there is no single way to view the war in Bosnia, and thus no singular way to respond, Campbell points out that: 'Different problematizations produce different "Bosnias", and those different "Bosnias" are rendered as different problems to be addressed by different political options.'[40] For Campbell, the performativity, and thus the mobility, of identity and its unhinging from a naturalized trajectory of history means that there is never a possibility of one, transhistorical, trans-situational iteration of 'Serb', 'Croat', or 'Bosnian', regardless of claims to the contrary. For Campbell, history is deployed as a resource in the present, even while: 'The present always passes us by to become the past. Once it does, our relationship to the past, even the ever so immediate past (let alone that from which we are either spatially or temporally distanced) is necessarily mediated. More often than not, that mediation takes the form of a narrative, whereby contested events are connected in such a way as to give some meaning.'[41] Situating a rationale of inevitability in an unproblematic teleological narrative that is reified as 'history' works performatively to secure these political resources as natural, immutable, and inevitable.

As Campbell points out, 'the greatest acts of violence in history have been made possible by the apparent naturalness of their practices, by the appearance that those carrying them out are doing no more than following commands necessitated by the order of things, and how that order has often been understood in terms of the survival of a (supposedly pregiven) state, a people, or a culture. Then it is possible to appreciate that only if we examine, through strategies of deconstructive thought (among others), the *coup de force* that encloses this logic in a timeless quality can we resist such violence.'[42] In this regard, the absolution of the self on the basis that one's behaviour and position are required by the nature of things is a logical conclusion. It is thus that, even in the admission of responsibility for particular events, the question of responsibility remains, strangely, a non-sequitur, posing a fundamental disconnect between the ways in which individuals and groups see themselves as responsible for the course of events. By way of example, consider Hannah Arendt's report on the following exchange:

> Q. Did you kill people in the camp? A. Yes.
> Q. Did you poison them with gas? A. Yes.
> Q. Did you bury them alive? A. It sometimes happened.
> Q. Were the victims picked from all over Europe? A. I suppose so.
> Q. Did you personally help kill people? A. Absolutely not. I was only a paymaster in the camp.
> Q. What did you think of what was going on? A. It was bad at first but we got used to it.
> Q. Do you know the Russians will hang you? A. (Bursting into tears) Why should they? *What have I done?*[43]

Here we find an elision of responsibility – a sidestepping of responsibility in the refusal to regard the Self as complicitous, murderous, guilty; in the refusal to regard the Self as culpable in events through either direct or indirect participation.

## Disasters

In Dostoevsky's *The Brothers Karamozov*, Ivan argues bitterly that there can be no justification for the disaster that befalls the innocent. He argues that one cannot forgive in another's place for a crime that was not committed against him, and that the torture and murder of even one human being can never justify a greater good, even if it means that such a thing might never happen again. It is not possible to atone for shed tears, argues Ivan, or for torture against human or animal, and no future political, religious, or ethical order can justify that violence, whatever its cause or reason. In the context of this exchange with his brother, Alyosha, Ivan argues that the ultimate position of innocence is that occupied by the child. The child, declares Ivan, is wholly innocent, free of the cognition and knowledge of evil, trusting and helpless in the extreme – she occupies the radical place of blamelessness. It is for this reason that a child can be identified as an inescapably innocent victim. There is nothing the child could have done in his innocence to 'deserve' the disaster that is perpetrated against him. Ivan provides the example of an eight-year-old boy who, playing in a court-yard, inadvertently strikes and injures the General's favourite dog with an errant stone. When he is found out, the General locks the boy up and then, in the morning, the boy is set loose in the woods whereupon the General's hunting dogs tear him to pieces, limb from limb, and before the eyes of his own mother.[44]

For John Caputo, the imperative to obligation takes place outside of any properly ethical ontological order. We are not obligated because the order of philosophical metaphysics compels us to the Other, nor are we obligated because there is a universal, theological, or normative principle that enjoins us to one another. For Caputo, obligation boils down to one primary recognition and that is that *flesh suffers*. Every day, everywhere, people are faced with suffering that manifests in the flesh of the body. Obligation emanates from this simple fact of hunger, disease, poverty, and violence. He argues that divesting ethics of its metaphysical origins unbinds obligation, cuts it loose, allows it to embrace contingency, to embrace vulnerability, weakness, in other words, flesh. Cutting ethics loose allows us to recognize disaster – it unbinds us – frees us to respond. That, for Caputo, is the power of powerlessness – the obligation that the victim places inescapably on those who are obliged grows in direct proportion to the depth of the suffering that engenders the call for help. Here, Caputo observes that, 'a disaster is an economic notion. It refers to an unrecoverable loss. Disasters are events of surpassing or irretrievable loss. By irretrievable loss I mean a wasting of life, something that cannot be repaired, recompensed, redeemed. A disaster is a loss that cannot be incorporated into a "result", that cannot be led back into a gain. You cannot grow another body; you cannot regain wasted years.'[45] When the certitude of what constitutes disaster is established, the Other is identified as the widow, the orphan, the beggar, the leper, the child born with HIV/AIDS, the murdered. For Caputo, the names of the murdered are themselves the substance and the impera-tive of the call for justice. For Caputo, as for Ivan Karamazov: 'It is precisely in the name of the Other, of justice, of respect, in the names of the chil-dren, that resistance is called for.'[46]

For Caputo, then, *the origin of the vocative cry must be determined before response is considered*. One must identify the orphan, the widow, the stranger as such in order to respond to the orphan, the widow, and the stranger as orphans, widows, and strangers. The relationship of victims to perpetra-tors must be established a priori so that we can be sure the one to whom we are responding is the authentically Other and an authentic victim of an authentic victimizer. For Caputo: 'Vicious military leaders, exploitatious

31

capitalists, oppressive, dishonest government officials, rapists (homicidal or not) are not victims but victimizers, and so the restraint of their victimization practices does not constitute their "exclusion" but simply a just law or a just order.'[47] And, significantly: 'People who produce victims are not the "Other" to whom we owe everything. The other, as Levinas says, is always "the widow, the orphan, the stranger", that is, emblematically, the victim – not the victimizers.'[48]

Victims, as such, are assumed here to be quite easy to identify, and indeed, Caputo distinguishes unproblematically between those who victimize, and those who are victimized. These designations are ahistorical, non-contextual, and stripped bare of their complexity and their contingency. William Connelly identifies Caputo's formulation of victimhood as a metaphysical minimalism which 'impels him to treat devastated groups and helpless individuals as paradigm objects of obligation. Sick, homeless, helpless individuals. Peoples laid low by floods, conquest, famine, holocaust.'[49] Yet, while the direness of these and similar situations is undeniable, Connolly argues, 'they may not pose the most difficult cases in ethics.'[50] Indeed, 'the most difficult cases arise when people suffer from injuries imposed by institutionalized identities, principles, and cultural understandings, when those who suffer are not entirely helpless but are defined as threatening, contagious, or dangerous to the self-assurance of these identities, and when the sufferers honor *sources* of ethics inconsonant or disturbing to these constituencies.'[51] In short: 'To simplify obligation in an era of political pessimism, Caputo has quietly emptied ethics of its political dimension.'[52]

Indeed, one is rarely ever only a transhistorical and trans-situational voiceless victim or a cold-blooded perpetrator. The problem of assignation is that it reifies both individual and collective experience and it undermines the mobility – the multiplicity – which is inherent in human political relationships across time and space. It is not always clear who occupies the place of victim and who the perpetrator. People often occupy different positionalities depending on time, space, and circumstance. Indeed, they may occupy different positionalities even simultaneously. Thus, for example, the same Serbs who were posited as the aggressors in the Croatian Krajina were themselves 'ethnically cleansed' from that same region in a two-day offensive in the summer of 1995. Individual men and women, as well as collectivities of them, never just 'are'. There are no transhistorical ways of being and knowing. Rather, as Campbell points out, we are continually constituted in and through performance, through the mobilization of resources in a particular moment, and in particular relationalities. In this sense, the relationality between victims and perpetrators is not self-evident across time and space. The relationality between victimhood and responsibility for victimhood is not always clear in the complexities of the interstices, in the intersectionality that lies inevitably within the taxonomy – the ontology – of place and of naming. This is not to deny the abject position of the murdered as murdered, nor to deny the responsibility of the murderer by attenuating the reader to extenuating circumstances or to the fact that the murderer may also be a victim of another sort in another situation. The point is to suggest that the complexity of these relationships exposes the ethical water as fundamentally murky, and that there is a difficulty in assigning an ethical position to the belligerent violence of the resistance leader who nevertheless remains marginalized, disenfranchised, and victimized. How do we differentiate between different calls from different Others?

## Others

For James Hatley, the absolute command of the command transcends reason precisely because it does not give one time to distinguish between calls or to weigh their relative merits. As Hatley notes: 'in the face-to-face encounter, no time is given for me to ask whether the command of the other face is justified.'[53] If I attempt to distinguish between the innocent and the guilty, the command *in which I have already found myself* is radically undermined. 'Suddenly, some of the others command me more than the rest of the others.'[54] The absoluteness of the command is destroyed in the rational categorization associated with the question of which commands matter over against other commands. This is the controversy that Levinas engendered as a result of his commentary about the massacres of Palestinians in the Sabra and Chatila camps. As Hatley notes: 'Precisely because I have been so radically commanded to responsibility before the other, I must search out every way I am capable of responding to the other's violence as much as to the other's victimization.'[55] And yet, 'to be called as Levinas is called, one must write the text again for oneself. No one can write it for anyone else, since the very urgency of the relationship precedes its thematization.'[56] My encounter with the Other is singular and unique insofar as I am uniquely commanded by that Other and insofar as no one can stand in my place. If I am beholden to the first individual I happen upon, or who happens upon me, then I cannot pass that person by because I find out later that he is a killer. My responsibility is not contingent upon what I later determine about him. As Hatley puts it:

> The face *transcends* whatever the other might turn out *to be*. In coming before the face of the other, one does not simply confront a being whose projects differ from one's own and so would resist one's intentions with counterintentions, a balancing of identity against counteridentity. One finds that before

any intention might even have been expressed, before one might even have had the time to determine the identity of he or she who bears this face, one was already claimed by a responsibility to listen to the face, to the other. The face of the other addressed one before one could have even consented to its having spoken.[57]

Hatley is leaving it open that the face of the Other who addresses one is that of the murderer. Hatley is suggesting the frightful possibility that the Other to whom we are pledged with no possibility of abdication is not only the victim, but also the genocidaire.

I am responsible to Stojan Sokolović before he ever turns to face me, before he ever speaks, before I ever know, before I ever hear, see, or read about what he has done. This is the difficult – even impossible – consequence of the claim that the ethics of encounter is prior to ontology, which is to say, prior to my knowledge. Furthermore, in the Levinasian formulation, the temporal encounter with the Other is assymetrical to his encounter with other Others. His crime is thus not the prior condition through which I encounter him. The point here is *not* to suggest that Stojan Sokolović should not be called to account if and when it is demanded of him. It is not to absolve him of responsibility. Rather, the point is that if I take seriously the encounter with the face of the Other, then the moment in which that occurs I must recognize that my responsibility remains regardless of who it is that faces me. In this, there is no possibility of abdication. This does not negate my responsibility to the Third, with whom I am simultaneously, yet diachronously, faced. But neither does this assuage the fact that I am also faced with Stojan Sokolović. My response is thus not situated in a taxonomy of categories of identity, a metaphysics, an ontology of being or of criminality or of nationalism. If, in this moment, it is the case that I am fundamentally responsible for and to Stojan Sokolović, then I will not be able to synchronously excise him from the realm of those to whom I find myself responsible. I will not be able to forsake him, and though I am not called to forgive him, I am called to responsibility both for and to him, and for what he has done. The Other is thus also the Serb – the one who has been made intolerable on the basis of his intolerance. Indeed, the inability to reduce the Other to the Same should not mean that we locate in our neighbour a quality or turn of mind that we could never possess.

NOTES

1 Martin Buber, *I and Thou* (New York: Touchstone, 1996), p. 148.
2 Virginia R. Dominguez, 'For A Politics of Love and Rescue', *Cultural Anthropology*, Vol. 15, No. 3, pp. 361–393, 2000, p. 388.
3 For a full analysis of events leading up to the start of the air campaign, see my chapter and others in Florian Bieber and Zhidas Daskalovski, eds, *Understanding the War in Kosovo* (London: Frank Cass, 2003).

4  Throughout the bombing of Yugoslavia, NATO steadfastly refused to refer to the military operations as 'war'.

5  Interview with Canadian Forces press officer Paul Segunda, Ramići, Bosnia, 6 January 2001.

6  Emmanuel Levinas, 'Ethics as First Philosophy', in *The Levinas Reader*, Sean Hand, ed. (Oxford, UK and Cambridge, MA: Blackwell Publishers, 1989), p. 76.

7  William Paul Simmons distinguishes Levinasian thought from totalizing philosophies thus: 'Totalizing philosophies are grounded in an *arche*, usually a neuter term, like Being, spirit, reason, or history, which is declared to be the origin and guiding principle of reality. Philosophers desire to comprehend all experience through this neuter term. Metaphysics is reduced to ontology and thus philosophy is merely a battle between competing theories of being, literally an "ontologomachy". Even theologians subordinate the divine to a neuter term "by expressing it with adverbs of height applied to the verb being; God is said to exist eminently or par excellence". The transcendent can be subordinated because all objects are reduced to a thing, and as a thing they can be comprehended or grasped. Whatever is other can always be reduced to the Same; thus, there is nothing beyond the grasp of the Same. Although relative alterity, that is, qualitative differences between objects, may remain, radical alterity or transcendence is destroyed.' See 'The Third: Levinas' Theoretical Move from An-archical Ethics to the Realm of Justice and Politics', *Philosophy and Social Criticism*, Vol. 25, No. 6, pp. 83–104, 1999, p. 84–85.

8  Levinas, 'Ethics as First Philosophy', p. 78.

9  Simmons, 'The Third: Levinas' Theoretical Move', p. 85.

10  Levinas, 'Ethics as First Philosophy', p. 83.

11  *Ibid.*, p. 84.

12  Fyodor Dostoevsky, *The Brothers Karamazov*, Andrew R. MacAndrew, trans. (New York: Bantam Books, 1970), p. 347.

13  Levinas, 'Ethics as First Philosophy', p. 84.

14  *Ibid.*, p. 84.

15  Emmanuel Levinas, *Of God Who Comes To Mind*, p. 69. Judith Butler argues that: 'To be ecstatic means, literally, to be outside oneself, and thus can have several meanings: to be transported beyond oneself by a passion, but also to be beside oneself with rage or grief. I think that if I can still address a "we", or include myself within its terms, I am speaking to those of us who are living in certain ways beside ourselves, whether in sexual passion, emotional grief, or political rage.' See *Precarious Life: The Powers of Mourning and Violence* (London: Verso, 2004), p. 24.

16  *Ibid.*, p. 72.

17  *Ibid.*, p. 68.

18  *Ibid.*, p. 74.

19  Alphonso Lingis, 'Introduction' in Emmanuel Levinas, *Otherwise Than Being*, p. xxix.

20  Michael J. Shapiro, 'The Ethics of Encounter: Unreading, Unmapping the Imperium', in Michael J. Shapiro and David Campbell, eds, *Moral Spaces: Rethinking Ethics and World Politics* (Minneapolis: University of Minnesota Press, 1999), p. 63.

21  *Ibid.*, p. 63.

22  Levinas, *Otherwise Than Being*, p. 13.

23  See Luce Irigiray, 'The Fecundity of the Caress', in Richard A. Cohen, ed., *Face to Face With Levinas* (Albany, State University of New York Press, 1986).

24  Lingis, 'Introduction', *Otherwise Than Being*, p. xxiii.

25  Levinas, *Otherwise Than Being*, p. 157.

26  Simmons, 'The Third: Levinas' Theoretical Move', p. 94.

27 Jacques Derrida, *Adieu to Emmanuel Levinas*, Pascale-Anne Brault and Michael Naas, trans. (Stanford, CA: Stanford University Press, 1999), p. 33.
28 Levinas, *Otherwise than Being*, p. 86.
29 David Campbell, 'The Deterritorialization of Responsibility: Levinas, Derrida, and Ethics after the End of Philosophy', in David Campbell and Michael J. Shapiro, eds, *Moral Spaces*, p. 38.
30 Patricia Molloy, 'Face-to-Face With the Dead Man: Ethical Responsibility, State-Sanctioned Killing, and Empathetic Impossibility', in David Campbell and Michael J. Shapiro, eds, *Moral Spaces*, p. 232.
31 Campbell, 'Deterritorialization', p. 39.
32 Quoted in Campbell, *Ibid.*, p. 39.
33 Caputo, *Against Ethics*, p. 123.
34 *Ibid.*
35 See David Campbell's argument in 'Deterritorialization'; and in *National Deconstruction: Violence, Identity, and Justice in Bosnia* (Minneapolis: University of Minnesota Press, 1998).
36 Jacques Derrida, 'Force of Law: "The Mystical Foundations of Authority",' in Drucilla Cornell, Michel Rosenfeld, David Gray Carlson, eds, *Deconstruction and the Possibility of Justice* (New York: Routledge, 1992), p. 13.
37 Campbell, *National Deconstruction*, p. 86; italics in original.
38 *Ibid.*, p. 191. See also Caputo, *Against Ethics*.
39 Campbell, *National Deconstruction*, p. 176.
40 *Ibid.* p. 209.
41 *Ibid.*, p. 34.
42 *Ibid.*, p. 183.
43 Quoted in Hannah Arendt, 'Organized Guilt and Universal Responsibility' in Peter Baehr, ed., *The Portable Hannah Arendt* (New York: Penguin Books, 2000), p. 151; italics in original. It should be pointed out here that the death penalty to which the German is apparently headed does not solve the problem of ethics and responsibility that the enormity of his crimes opens up. Indeed, as will be argued subsequently, the prosecution and execution of Nazis in the aftermath of the war helped to create the illusion that the 'problem' of Nazism and mechanized extermination had been overcome.
44 Fyodor Dostoevsky, *The Brothers Karamazov*, pp. 284–297.
45 Caputo, *Against Ethics*, p. 29.
46 *Ibid.*, p. 119.
47 *Ibid.*
48 *Ibid.*
49 William Connelly, 'Suffering, Justice, and the Politics of Becoming', in *Moral Spaces*, p. 129.
50 *Ibid.*, p. 129.
51 *Ibid.*, p. 129
52 *Ibid.*, p. 129.
53 James Hatley, *Suffering Witness*, p. 104.
54 *Ibid.*, p. 105.
55 *Ibid.* p. 105.
56 *Ibid.* p. 106.
57 *Ibid.* p. 76.

**3**

# *Being there*

The camera makes everyone a tourist in other people's reality, and eventually in one's own.[1]

The last time I was in Belgrade, Stojan Sokolović brought me to the park where Ivan Stambolić disappeared. After the ousting of Milošević in 2000, members of the new Koštunica government admitted that Stambolić had been dragged away from the park on his daily jog and murdered. His crime had been to say that he had made a mistake in assisting Milošević's rise to power in the late 1980s. It happened not far from where Zoran Djindjić would later be shot and killed, not far from where the NATO cruise missile landed on the maternity wing of the Dragiša Mišović hospital in the spring of 1999, not far from where the fortress of Kalemegdan stands purposeful watch on the headland over the fortuitous juncture of two rivers.

In Sarajevo, in 2002 on the tenth anniversary of the beginning of the Bosnian war, I paused to look at the Zoran Filipović postcards for sale – black and white photographs of grave markers standing like sentinels on the outskirts of the city, the skeletal remains of the National Library, a gutted Catholic church, four bodies under four white sheets. I stopped to buy a brick of white honey *halva*. I stared into the shops that sold copper *džezve*, vases, coffee cups, wooden cigarette holders, and plates emblazoned with the skyline of Sarajevo.[2] I stopped at a restaurant. I ate *ćevape*, with peppery onions and soft *lepinje*. Then I went for an espresso.

Even if I didn't still have my plane ticket from Toronto in my desk drawer, even if my passport was not still marked by the now-dry ink stamp at the Karakaj crossing, and at Surčin, Mali Zvornik, Sitnica, Gradiška, Župći, one could not assert that I did not know what I was talking about. One could not assert that I had not *been there*, wandering long twilights down the bricked pedestrian mall on Gospodska in Banja Luka, the cobbled, narrow streets of Sarajevo, the tree-lined avenues of Trebinje, or the chalet-dotted hills of Pale. One could not say that I had not stretched out my very own body on the coast beside the sea, sinking my bones into the stones, looking for the moments that would secure my trips as successful explorations of the former Yugoslavia, seeking out the photogenic angle that would earn me an authentic place as a respectable researcher and regional expert. I photographed burned houses, Mostar in the thin light before morning, the old city at Kotor illuminated by the afternoon sun. I talked to many people, locals and internationals, some over coffee or cakes or fruit salad with no record made, some over drinks in smoke-choked bars with a pen and a notepad, some in their living rooms with a tape recorder, some with translators, some without.

Indeed, the artefacts I collected, the interviews I logged, and the photographs I shot secured my claim of *being there* because I have at my disposal the luxury of travel, the right of access, the time to locate informants, the money to purchase meals, transportation, and lodging. I have not one, but two passports (an American and a Canadian) for which visas are seldom required. No one is concerned that I might be trying to migrate, to steal away local jobs, to make a refugee claim at the Bosnian border. I have academic credentials, funding from the appropriate institutions, permission from the ethics committee, the respect of (some of) my colleagues. I have the luxury of operating as a native speaker in a language that everyone else is expected to speak. In other words, I have purchased the right to access. I have purchased the right to experience, to observe, and to witness.

Acting as witness – seeking out the role of witness – is one implication of theorizing, which is in turn an implication of acting as a subject *at large* in the world, *at large* in the field, *at large* in the academy. Theorizing presupposes the ability – or at least the ability to attempt – to make sense of what one witnesses, observes, hears, intuits, desires, manufactures, or hopes. For the western academic, being at large in the rest of the world for the purposes of knowledge collection and dissemination is a relatively facile accomplishment. Movement is normally a circular phenomenon, involving a lateral and hierarchical shift from *here* to *there* and back again, requiring 'hardly more than a travel booking and permission to land; a willingness to endure a certain amount of loneliness, invasion of privacy, and physical discomfort; a relaxed way with odd growths and unexplained fevers; a capacity to stand still for artistic insults, and the sort of patience that can support an endless search for invisible needles in infinite haystacks.'[3] I have the resources to procure the travel booking. I have permission to land. In this regard, my circumstances are quite remarkable. Stojan Sokolović could not get a visa to interview me in my 'authentic' surroundings if his life depended on it. For Stojan Sokolović, having the money to visit me makes him all the more suspicious to consular officials. For Stojan Sokolović, the boundaries are fundamentally marked by rigidity and exclusion. So the notion of being at large does not necessarily coincide with the traversing or erasure of boundaries, although boundaries for western academics (and tourists) are rather porous.[4] Instead, being at large depends fundamentally on the *maintenance* of boundaries, especially for Others, which is the way in which we become aware of our own freedom of movement. Were it not for Stojan Sokolović's physical confinement to the territory on which he lives, my freedom to enter his world would be a non-issue, not even interesting enough to comment on. It is his incarceration, imposed by the poverty of his passport, that underwrites the range of my mobility. And so one still operates, even at large, in a state informed by confinement – confinement of the Self and of the Other which underwrites the notion of being at large.[5] As one professor in Novi Sad explained: 'If I had to fill out a form asking about my citizenship, I'd put "hopelessly Yugoslav" . . . the books I read, the literatures I teach, the languages I speak – [do] not mean a thing. My passport beats all. It shows that I can wander off only in my thoughts.'[6]

## Technologies

John Hutnyk argues that travel both embraces and constitutes a multitude of technologies that are deployed to make sense of the experiences that are the central purpose of travelling. The lens of the camera, the hastily scratched words on postcards, the sharing and reproduction of myths of the 'remote' and 'different', the poverty (both economic and moral) of the local population(s), which is documented and consumed as part of the 'authentic' experience, the cheap access to beaches, prostitutes, drugs, souvenirs, spectacular landscapes and prescribed sites bearing the 'must see' label all form a series of frames through which the experience of travel unfolds and is made to make sense.[7] The exotic smells, tastes, and other sensations, the rumour of past or present tragedy, of travesty, of trial and tribulation, the strange mystique of an unfamiliar language and alphabet help to constitute the 'machineries of traveller perception' – tools whereby capitalism 'transmutes all culture, emotion, identity, into a form open to exchange.'[8]

Technologies of travel involve far more than the unique collapse of time and space that modern travel possibilities afford, although they are also that. They are a mode of being – a way of forming and projecting the Self and consuming the Other for pleasure, profit, or some combination of these. As such, tourism has several minimally unifying characteristics. Tourism presupposes time as organized and regulated and the division of leisure and work into distinctive and regulated spheres. Tourism involves some measure of spatial movement and a period of stay away from home and from the realm of the everyday. The tourist journey takes place outside the normal places of residence and work and involves a clear intention to return home. Tourist destinations are normally not connected with work, and in fact they are understood to offer important distinctions from work and the everyday. Destinations are chosen on the basis of the anticipation of intense pleasures that are different from those normally experienced at home. Crucially, such anticipation is 'constructed and sustained through a variety of non-tourist practices, such as film, TV, literature, magazines, records and videos, which construct and reinforce that gaze.'[9] This gaze is 'then normally visually objectified or captured through photographs, post-cards, films, models, and so on. These enable the gaze to be endlessly repro-duced and recaptured.'[10] The gaze is also constructed through the use of signs, and much of the tourist experience is geared toward the 'image' of what is seen – i.e. images of the traditional, natural, pristine, authentic, historic, and so on. Finally, there exist a wide variety of tourist professionals whose primary concern is to enhance the tourist experience and to locate and reproduce new objects for the tourist gaze.

## Fieldwork

Unlike tourism, fieldwork is justified, legitimated, and underwritten by insti-tutions whose primary claim is to produce and secure what counts as know-ledge. Unlike the tourist experience, fieldwork is not separate from work, but is rather an extraordinary and important extension of work which is demarcated from other scholarly tasks such as achieving tenure and pro-motion, supervising students, compiling course readings, preparing and delivering lectures, and so on. However, the work of everyday research and the field experience are also very different, with fieldwork often conceived as occupying a more respected status than ordinary, text-based library (or, increasingly, internet) research. Like tourism, fieldwork involves spatial movement and a temporary period of stay in the target environment. While tourism is a mass-based phenomenon, that is, able to be experienced in some form or other by large numbers of people in the modern world, academic fieldwork is far more exclusive and exclusionary, which also helps to under-write the legitimacy of the act and to secure the expertise of the actor.

While fieldwork is not necessarily associated with the anticipation of touristic pleasures, the field researcher anticipates what she will encounter, not through postcards, films, photographs, and so on, but through schol-arly texts, field notes of other researchers, academic conferences and other media appropriate to the academy. The net effect of this is invariably the production and reproduction of expectations concerning what one will find upon arrival, making it surprisingly similar to the anticipation experienced by the tourist. Like tourism, fieldwork relies fundamentally on preconceptions and on the interpretation of signs and signifiers, which also include locating people and communities in their traditional cultures, natural surroundings, pristine habitats, authentic practices, and historic conditions. Finally, although there are clearly not as large a number of fieldwork professionals as there are tourists, the institution vests the field researcher as a professional with the authority to compile and determine what and who is important in any given political or social environment.[11] As discourses produced fundamentally in the western experience of modernity, tourism and fieldwork 'share the same visual "episteme", the power/knowledge system centred on a logic of cultural "spectacalization."'[12]

A further consideration involves what Hutnyk calls 'technologies of inscription and representation.'[13] Hutnyk understands that the ways in which technologies, typologies, topologies, and topographies are made to hang together constitute the basic rubric of narrative and optical engagement with respect to the tourist gaze. He argues that, 'the ways in which the world is "revealed" to us are conditioned by the use made of technologies which are instrumental in that revealing, and the ends – say, of the logistics of the commodity system – which that use of technology enables.'[14] This revelation is created and conditioned by the categories of representation which are manifest in the west: film, writing, scholarship, fieldwork, recording, and the depthless lens of the camera through which it is claimed that 'true' representation can be made.

Crucially, these gaze-based phenomena are institutionally based phenomena, requiring an environment with a means of replication for both predictable experience and organized study. The technology of the gaze allows for both the representation and the disciplining of the object of study, which is presented as lacking the agency required to articulate alternative, contradictory representations. Michel Foucault notes that: 'The clinic was probably the first attempt to order a science on the exercise and decisions of the gaze . . . the medical gaze was also organized in a new way. First, it was no longer the gaze of any observer, but that of a doctor supported and justified by an institution . . . Moreover, it was a gaze that was not bound by the narrow grid of structure . . . but that could and should grasp colours, variations, tiny anomalies . . .'[15]

John Urry employs this quotation from Foucault's *The Birth of the Clinic* in order to demonstrate that that the tourist gaze is 'as socially organised and systematised as is the gaze of the medic.'[16] Urry goes on to qualify his observation with the caveat that tourism does not enjoy the same kind of institutional support as does medicine. However, fieldwork research is not only supported, but also fundamentally legitimated by the academy and its attendant institutions, such as university presses, travel and research funds, and ethics review committees. There is an entire social value hierarchy in place in the academy which institutionalizes the phenomenon of the gaze, and which forms spectacles for academic consumption whose purposes are twofold and interrelated: the creation and transmission of knowledge, and the securitization of the researcher as 'expert' in the academic hierarchy. The scholar is called upon to 'make sense' of a particular place, people, or political or social phenomenon. To the extent that the fieldwork destinations of scholars and researchers are frequently places of political or social instability, or are recent conflict zones, the research experience appears on the surface to be quite different from that of the tourist. However, both the scholar and the tourist participate in the creation and experience of an 'authentic' vision of the Other whose objective existence can be verified through the technologies of the gaze. The difference is minimal – perhaps no more than that between the strictly bounded tour and the independent traveller's engagement with a more 'uncertain' locale. As Cheong and Miller note: 'The package tour is the extreme case of constrained movement, the self-guided tour the least. In the setting of the former, tourists can find themselves quite literally imprisoned on buses and boats, and in enclave resorts. In these moments, they depend considerably on guides, as well as other agents. *But the self-guided tour also shows the movements of tourists limited and structured by the guidebook, the agent, or the signpost.*'[17] Similarly, field researchers are oriented to the environment of study by the guidebooks, agents, and signposts of academic disciplines – thus, scholarly texts, other researchers, and written histories of the region to be visited are the basic currency of exchange that orients the researcher and often predetermines what or whom the researcher will investigate.

The similarity between fieldwork and tourism is perhaps most significant in the case of 'independent' or 'adventure' tourists. It is worthwhile to remember that anthropology as a scholarly discipline emerged from adventure tourism. In *Public Places, Private Journeys*, Ellen Strain undertakes a genealogy of tourism and ethnography to demonstrate how modern travellers engage in elitist activities that are very similar to the exclusivity enjoyed by the field researcher. Strain distinguishes between 'the traveler who seeks and knows how to recognize authenticity from the tourist who either gladly or unknowingly accepts Disneyland's versions of the world's wonders. The traveler designation in these tourist/traveler distinctions is reserved for the explorer of past eras or for intellectuals of the contemporary era.'[18] The avoidance of places considered to be 'overly touristy' had, by the 1920s and 1930s, already signaled the development of different types of tourism; some more mass-appeal oriented (Disneyworld or the Caribbean resorts of today) and others, more exclusive, less frequented – the preserve of intellectual and economic elites (contemporary nature hiking in Peru, temple-hopping in Nepal, Pacific crossings in privately hired yachts).[19] Increasingly, the sense of engaging with unmediated authenticity is one that coincides with travel to 'exotic', 'pristine', and culturally 'pure' or 'untainted' locales. Unlike the simulated world of Walt Disney or Club Med, the quest for direct contact with authentic cultures and peoples unmediated by the institutions of tourism (large hotels, western-style meals and accommodations, group activities) is one in which the traveller seeks immersion in the 'different' but 'real'. Of course, the traveller has still engaged with the institutions of tourism through the purchase of plane tickets, car rental, and the other activities associated with 'arriving at' the desired destination. Furthermore, in both cases, the tourist/traveller has already engaged in the consumption of images associated with their destination of choice prior to undertaking the journey.

Strain notes that: 'As a core component of the tourist gaze, the illusion of demediation offers the false promise of communion with authenticity and an escape from the very mediation that the semiotics of tourism unveils.'[20] But the touristic experience is always already mediated through the technologies that explore, apprehend, and reify the peoples and cultures that serve as the objects of the traveller's desire. 'The touristic vision is constructed by way of an oscillating series of objectifying strategies: reduction to surface spectacle; mystification; assimilation to Western structures of aesthetics, narrative, or scientific explanation; reduction to a simplistic surface/depth model demanding unveiling; totalization; essentialization; and synecdochic consumption, accumulation, and representation.'[21]

Strain's genealogy of tourism and travel reveals the collapse of the tourist gaze into the increasing professionalization of the adventure travel that later became legitimized as anthropology (and, by extension, evolved into fieldwork practices that leaked into other social sciences). Strain notes that 'anthropology moved from a hobby to a profession' wherein the anthropologist was employed in the construction of ethnographic visions and displays for museums and other exhibits, such as world fairs.[22] Through the legitimacy provided by the academy as anthropologists increasingly attained university positions, the discipline underwent a professionalization that would simultaneously 'enact an erasure of its roots in popular culture.'[23] Academic authority went hand in hand with the discovery and representation of authenticity with respect to other peoples and cultures. 'Once removed from the ranks of rich hobbyists and sideshow hucksters and set up as a noble figure pursuing knowledge in a mystically foreign landscape, the anthropologist could return to popular culture, but now in

43

the fictive form of a hero.'[24] The authority that is conferred on authenticity is reflected in the ability to say 'I was there' – I was witness through the immersion of my body in the field environment, in the immersion of my body in the culture of the Other. This authority allows for the production of knowledge, as opposed to the dissemination of gossip or rumour. It makes knowledge out of gossip and rumour by employing the advanced technologies of scientism: observation, testable data, the photograph, the audiocassette, and other instruments of truth.

The professionalization of the gaze laid the groundwork for the reconstruction, reproduction, and consumption of 'tourist places' as essentially knowledge productive through sociocultural processes seated in a strongly visual set of practices.[25] Williams observes that: 'We spend time in advance of a tourism trip attempting to visualise the experience by examining guide books and brochures, or in anticipatory daydreams; we often spend significant parts of the trip itself engaged in the act of sightseeing in which we gaze upon places, people and their artefacts.'[26] Moreover, the process through which the destination is constructed is a highly selective one, characterized by hyperattention to some aspects of some places, and the virtual erasure of others (i.e. those elements that are perceived as uninteresting, mundane, or simply unappealing). In fieldwork, what is disregarded are those things considered to be unimportant for the purposes of the research agenda, that which is considered to be 'inauthentic', and things which might disrupt the narratives that have already been established back in the university research setting. 'In the process, we are inventing (or reinventing) places to suit our purposes. The gaze is also a detached and superficial process, as the term itself suggests. This superficiality increases the role of cultural signs within the invention and consumption of tourist places ... places or actions that represent, through simplification, much more complex ideas and practices.'[27]

For example, in the fieldwork setting, particular cultural signs and simplifications have already coded the peoples of Bosnia as victims and perpetrators, respectively. This, in turn, frames the researcher's approach to, and interest in, the objects of research. That Muslims in Bosnia are primarily the victims of Serbs frames and mattes the research narrative, which in turn governs the kinds of information the researcher is interested in obtaining. Narratives outlining mass, targeted rape of Muslim women, for example, caused a surge of researchers to come looking to interview only those women who had been gang-raped.[28] Often, researchers press exceptionally hard to either get where the 'action' is, or to find those who have experienced the 'action' themselves. This is also about the relentless pursuit of authenticity – the closer one gets to the 'real' experience, the more authentic one's finished research product becomes.

Furthermore, it is possible to identify what can be termed a 'controlled immersion' into the host environment. As Williams argues, the 'traveller does not experience reality but thrives instead upon "pseudo-events" – commodified, managed and contrived forms of provision that present a flavour of foreign places in a selective and controlled manner.'[29] Physical isolation from the host environment is possibly the most insidious form of mediation. In the fieldwork setting, this may seem oxymoronic and contrary to the purposes of fieldwork, which are ostensibly to become immersed in the local culture in such a way as to say something intellectually mean-ingful about it on the way out. However, the field researcher who contrives to become physically, intellectually, and emotionally immersed in the field experience becomes the victim of Strain's 'illusion of demediating mediation', wherein the researcher believes that there is a possibility of authenticity in the local environment, and that this can be apprehended and juxtaposed to the 'mythic' or 'inauthentic' environment. As Strain argues: 'The myth of demediation produces the illusion that certain types of experience can strip away the typical mediations that intervene in the experience of reality, or that certain technologies, through their radiant powers of representation, can somehow reverse the postmodern eclipse of authenticity.'[30]

## Adventure tourism

Debbie Lisle argues that the phenomenon of war tourism undermines the general assumption that tourism takes place only in zones of security where conflict or danger is not a real threat, even as it fractures the binary distinc-tion that lies at the core of the discourse of separation. War tour operators in post-conflict Sarajevo provide one such example. War tours in Bosnia are geared toward representing the conflict to the layperson – the tourist – while NATO briefing tours in Bosnia are geared toward representing the conflict and NATO's subsequent intervention to the scholar and the researcher. Tourists and scholars alike are craning their necks behind the smoky glass of air-conditioned buses to gaze on the 'authentic' Bosnia: bullet holes in the gypsum walls of houses and apartment blocks; the 'splash-marks' in the surface of the asphalt where grenades have fallen; the casings of artillery shells for sale on street corners as flower vases and planters. (I admit, I considered buying one.) The danger may have passed, but it has only recently passed, and other, conflict-related perils are still in place, for example, landmines and other unexploded ordnance as well as uncertainty in the political sphere and potentially dangerous, anti-western Serbs with hair trigger tempers and homicidal tendencies.[31] Thus, far from occupying zones of distinction on either side of a conceptual dividing line, tourism and fieldwork share a good deal in common and in some cases have actually been collapsed in on each other to the point where it is difficult to make a significant distinction at all between them. Increasingly, the destinations and itineraries of adventure tourists are remarkably similar to those of field researchers. Consider the following examples:

The Ukrainian 'SAM' travel company offers an exclusive Chernobyl day-trip travel itinerary at a cost of US$193 per person. Upon arrival, tourists visit the Chernobyl nuclear power plant and observe the sarcophagus that shelters the radioactive masses and debris from the 1986 disaster. The itinerary includes experiencing the 'peace and quiet of the ghost-town Prypyat – all 47,000 inhabitants had to abandon their homes the next day after the accident.' The visitor will 'explore the deserted apartment blocks, schools, hotels, and kindergartens.' After lunch (the quality of the food is guaranteed), visitors will have the opportunity to attend a briefing by specialists who will answer questions about the accident, its aftermath, and the long-term effects of the fallout and contamination on the surrounding environment. Following the briefing, visitors will set off to explore Chernobyl's surrounding villages, where local residents – mostly the elderly – still live inside the exclusion zone.[32]

Tours of the Cuchi tunnel system in Vietnam are also designed to provide the authentic experience so tourists might experience how fighters involved in the resistance to the US invasion lived. After exploring the tunnel system, Anne Dimon remarked, 'I don't know how they did it. These tunnels are narrow and confining ... I had to edge along slowly in a crouched position through the network of tiny passageways burrowed through the earth in three levels like an underground condo. Here and there, tunnels connect to full rooms – some with original furnishings like bamboo beds, another with medical instruments on display.'[33] Dimon's exploration is one in which time stands still as the tourist's sense of temporality is disrupted. Writes Dimon: 'That sense of another time became even more palpable when I met up with Cuong, my Hanoi-born and educated guide who led me up to Lac, one of the country's many hill-tribe villages.'[34] One commentator on travelling in India notes that one must enjoy India without guilt: 'Yes, there are poor people in rural villages and city slums; yes, life is hard, but relatively few are starving and there is growing promise of a better future combining old and new worlds.' Once that's out of the way: 'A visit to India is an adventure. Every day is different and you can't help but be moved. Because it is such a vast country, many recommend that to truly experience it, a visitor should focus on one area or one facet at a time.'[35] The travel writer advises visitors to: 'Spend 24 hours on a hired rattan-covered boat for you alone taking a leisurely backwater lake and river cruise. You'll sleep aboard in a bedroom with a private bathroom and be attended by a crew and a fine cook. The cruise allows cool breezes and unusual views of rice paddies, mud huts and river people who live on 10-metre-wide strips of land with a small house, a garden and animals.'[36] One is left with the distinct impression that the 'river people' are simply interesting fixtures on display for the enjoyment of the Western tourist – they appear to be indistinguishable from their stilted houses and interesting animals.

Adventure tourists are also eager to get to Afghanistan. 'The main reason to go is the bragging rights', says one traveller. 'Mostly it's just cool to be in a place called "Kandahar".'[37] The Afghanistan-based Kabul City Tours assures its visitors that they will see 'breathtaking scenery, the beautiful faces of the people, [and] the unbelievable destruction',[38] while British Airways spokesperson John Lampl describes the increasing demand for a commercial London-Baghdad flight: 'I've already had people calling me: travel writers wanting to go because it's exotic, the war's going to end and they're going to write about it . . . a lot of people that have been everywhere, that want to go somewhere exotic and want to see what's left of Baghdad.'[39]

The spectacle of violence as spectacle constitutes a violence further to the prior violence before it was packaged and resold as spectacle. Tours to the sites of catastrophe – to Chernobyl, Rwanda, Dachau, Auschwitz-Birkenau, the genocide sites of Cambodia, Vietnam's Ho Chi Minh Trail, Sarajevo, Srebrenica, Kosovo, Iraq, Afghanistan, and Angola – are all destinations of increasing interest to adventure tourists. The catastrophe is purchased with the strange currency of the media image – television, photography, film – and this image is almost always one of disaster. After disaster, reconstruction and the simulation of reconstitution draws the tourist faithful in pursuit of the authentic. After colonization, enslavement, genocide, and the annihilation of African lifeways in favour of the politically, religiously, hierarchically European, safari tourists still seek out the 'pre-colonial', the pristine, untouched tribesmen in their native dress and with their accompanying animals and wares. Because there is no possibility of finding the pre-colonial – indeed if the pre-colonial exists is it precisely because it remains outside the experience of the west, eluding the gaze of the west – the postcolonial is revis(ion)ed, re-fabricated, re-articulated as the pre-colonial for the pursuit of touristic pleasures.

Kenneth Little argues that, 'on safari', local peoples are displayed in ways such that they 'become symbols that stand in for themselves; they are exotic signs of themselves, representations of otherness, marked categories, labelled and framed by mechanical media forms such as film, tape, and print through which tourists have their African experience.'[40] Alongside the desire to train the tourist gaze on the exotic animals which are the object of the safari, 'indigenous people become objects of tourist manipulation . . . It is this 'traditional', read 'primitive', culture that tourists come to see, and because it does not exist, it is made for them.'[41] Thus, it is the very disaster of colonialism, enslavement, and murder that lays the groundwork for the (western) tourist desire to seek out and experience the pre-colonial – the authentic.

If tourism attempts to be the epitome of personal fulfilment through its ability to produce and package a world of pleasure or danger (or pleasurable danger) for the tourist, then academic fieldwork is a clearly intentioned variation of this. Academic fieldwork is specifically engaged in representation for the furtherance of knowledge and knowledge production. It is specifically about providing a package which will be presented back home to other scholars through conferences, seminars, and publication, to policy communities and, through university outreach programmes, to the general public. In the university and, by extension, in the academic presses, fieldwork serves to underwrite and legitimate the authenticity of scholarly research and research claims. *Being there* is the first claim to authenticity but this does not solve the first order problem (though it heralds the problem) of representation that *being there* entails.

## Immersion

In Canada, the Department of National Defence's (DND) Security and Defence Forum offers annual 'field excursions' to sites of NATO occupation. The tours, which sometimes include trips to Bosnia, are 'designed to expose . . . academics and students to NATO structures and operations', in the field.[42] Upon his return, Holger Herwig at the Centre for Military and Strategic Studies at the University of Calgary described his impressions of Bosnia as falling into 'three major categories: the land, the UN/NATO presence, and the role of Canadian Forces in NATO's Stabilization Force (SFOR) operations.'[43] For Herwig, 'Bosnia is a land left behind by modernization: there exists not a single modern highway and rail service has virtually come to a standstill.' The country's rivers are 'choked' with refuse – the 'flotsam and jetsam of a dysfunctional society'. The UN occupies a 12-story, 'permanent palace' in Sarajevo, its international staff of 'well-heeled bureaucrats' travelling about the city in Mercedes, Land Rovers, and Toyotas, while local 'professional cleptocrats . . . Sarajevo's professional and political criminal class of former Communist functionaries turned capitalist entrepreneurs' prefer Mercedes or BMW. Canadian troops, described as 'young, dedicated, professional soldiers, operate under near impossible conditions. At Velika Kladuša, the Canadian contingent is housed in the midst of the town, ringed by Bosnian houses, with a heliport within 50 metres of potential snipers.' In Drvar, Canadian soldiers are exposed to local flour mill employees, who 'are a primary source of human intelligence for the local war lords.' Herwig notes that '[u]nfortunately, we were not able to interact with the [local] people, for both linguistic and security reasons.' It goes without saying that Herwig's 'post-war tour' of Bosnia took place behind the tinted windows of an air-conditioned bus while he and his colleagues gazed out at the 'rugged splendour' of a country inhabited by pre-modern, cleptocratic, side-arm sporting, post-communist criminals with whom he could not interact for 'linguistic and security reasons.' In Herwig's article, which appears in the *University of Calgary Gazette*, Herwig can be seen posing in front of an armoured personnel carrier dressed in a military flak jacket and helmet. It is hard to avoid the impression that Herwig has gone on safari. Another frame depicts four local women standing on the pavement in front of a ruined block of shops and apartments. These locals, with whom Herwig has had admittedly no contact, serve as woeful props against a backdrop of Bosnian destruction. The use of photographs produces far more than simply the evidence associated with *being there*, although they are also that. For Gillian Rose, 'photographs are not simply mimetic of the world they show. Rather ... the production, circulation and consumption of photographs produce and reproduce the imagined geographies of the social group or institution for which they were made.'[44] Thus, photographs of local women standing in front of ruined buildings are reproductive of specific understandings about the differences between 'our' world and 'theirs' – 'theirs' being an extraordinary one of destitution, decimation, and destruction.

On holiday, photographs are usually taken in order to capture images that are outside of the photographer's ordinary experience because their subject matter is considered particularly interesting or intriguing. Herwig has not included, for example, photographs of contemporary condominium buildings, Bosnians riding in modern buses in city transit systems, or other everyday activities that do not highlight the recent conflict. Such images would not make interesting souvenirs, but more importantly, they help to perpetuate the image of Bosnia as an essentially abnormal society that can never experience the relative peace and calm of the contemporary 'everyday'. If one follows the images and narratives associated with field trips to Bosnia (academic, journalistic, or otherwise), the entire country becomes a metaphor for violence, destruction, and poignant – or repellent – human tragedy.

Participants' photographs are not the only souvenirs that can be brought home to use as slideshows in undergraduate lecture halls. NATO tours in Bosnia include access to a souvenir coffee mug available at NATO bases in Bosnia with the NATO logo and the English words PEACE STABILIZATION FORCE transliterated (not translated) into the Cyrillic alphabet: ПЕАЦЕ СТАБИЛИЗАТИОН ФОРЦЕ.[45] The mug serves as a souvenir, a cultural artefact of the NATO occupation which fetishizes Bosnia (and particularly Serbs) as exotic and foreign through the use of the Cyrillic alphabet to spell out a phrase that makes no sense in either Cyrillic or Serbo-Croatian. The Cyrillic is employed to provide NATO's Bosnia Tour coffee-drinkers with an image of their desire; of exoticism, cultural and political foreignness, and as a reminder of the heroic subduing of the Serbs. The Bosnia Tour participants can thus enjoy their morning coffee back in the comfort of their homes or offices while being reminded in a number of ways of Bosnia, NATO, and their NATO trip. First, the souvenir mug serves as a keepsake for remembering the trip through Bosnia. In this way, the NATO mug serves a similar purpose as any souvenir picked up on holiday would – to remind both oneself and one's colleagues that one has *been there*. Second, the NATO mug reminds the participant of the 'service' that NATO provides in protecting Bosnians from one another. This helps to secure the justificatory subtext of NATO's occupation and the ongoing foreign administration of Bosnia. A third function of the mug, beyond the thinly veiled attempt at authenticity through the use of the Cyrillic alphabet, is the reminder it serves to the participant of the progress and security of his or her own nation, which is not in need of peacekeeping, peacebuilding, or international administration and whose sovereignty is not in doubt.[46] A fourth function of the mug is its alibi function for the violence associated with the Bosnian war and the exercise of power on the part of NATO as critically instrumental in the securing of peace. The very appropriation of the Cyrillic alphabet and its manipulation to spell out a specifically English language/Latin alphabet phrase provides an incisive illustration of the exercise of Western cultural and military power in Bosnia, and specifically with respect to Serbs.

## Thanotourism

Tourism necessarily invokes the desire for difference because tourism is also essentially a quest for the extraordinary – for the extraordinarily exterior.[47] Therefore, there is a constant dialogue of negotiation in place between the *extraordinary* and *security*, wherein the safety of the tourist must be constantly weighed against the sites of the desirably extraordinary. As Debbie Lisle notes: 'When the safety of the tourist is perceived as compromised, or can no longer be guaranteed, the site in question is often removed from the repertoire of tourist destinations.'[48]

However, it is precisely the compromised safety factor that acts as a draw for a new kind of tourist. What are we to make, for example, of the thriving 'war tourism' firms in Sarajevo? Or of the thousands of journalists and researchers who have descended on the region in the last fifteen years, armed with cassette recorders and university ethics review committee guidelines concerning how best to 'protect' informants from the perils of their research.[49] Justin Doebele noted in 1997 that: 'The newest kick for jaded tourists who have hit all the world's hot spots is to hit the world's really hot spots. The idea behind what some are calling terror travel or extreme tourism is basically to take the US State Department's travel advisory warning list and make an itinerary out of it.'[50]

The inherent tenuousness of the lines between war, tourism, journalism, and fieldwork, and between fiction, fact, and fantasy, is well illustrated by the autobiographic narrative of Anthony Lloyd, an adventure traveller and freelance journalist who worried that he was 'a sluttish dilettante day-tripping into someone else's nightmare'[51] while searching for the authentic Bosnia during the 1992–1995 civil war. Lloyd was not officially institutionally affiliated, nor has he been laid claim to by media or academic departments. He subsisted in Bosnia by selling the occasional freelance photograph to European media, and he subsisted after Bosnia by writing a book about his experiences there. The question of authenticity figures squarely in Lloyd's narrative. He is constantly on the lookout for new, authentic experiences of the 'real' Bosnia through which to seek personal and professional fulfillment. In Lloyd's formulation, Bosnia was characterized by 'unfolding and limitless adventure', where the most basic reason for 'being there' was 'to watch'. Lloyd's narrative is marked by an orgy of killing, mutilation, irony, and comradeship, where the memory of action has a narcotic effect which delivers a 'hit' that can be obtained by visiting 'old war haunts'.[52] Local women are uniformly characterized by Lloyd as 'beautiful', 'long-legged', 'lithe', 'unobtainable', and in at least one instance, 'vampiresque'. What is also unobtainable for Lloyd, at the end of the day, is the authenticity of Bosnia. Although he complains about those who 'had not been in the war voicing their opinions on it',[53] he also acknowledges what he sees as the fundamental degree of separation between the internal and the external, the internalized Self and the introspective Bosnian Other. Lloyd writes:

> You could have a good time in Stara Bila that summer, providing you had not been born in the place. Congregated there were every type and nationality of journalist, photographer, cameraman, writer, producer and engineer – the wild, brash, bold and bland, their egos often disproportionate to their talent, if not fame. The fighting spilled further into the hills around us; they glowed with burning villages at night and echoed with firefights by day. We sometimes watched it over barbecues.[54]

Lloyd does not want to be distanced from the war – he wants to be of it, as well as in it, but there is a barrier for Lloyd, who fears himself to be inauthentic and incapable of occupying the conceptual space of both the represented and the representer. The angst associated with being fundamentally unable to experience the total immersion in the local environment that would obscure or erase the boundary between Self and Other is precisely the reason for seeking out the next immersion experience. The quest to fully experience what is at stake for the Other is always foiled by the Self's ability to leave the conflict or other extreme environment for the 'safety' of home. There is, alas, a difference between the roasting of lambs for journalists' barbecues and the abject destruction of lives that is going on among Bosnians in the village below. Lloyd understands this at some level, observing that: 'Sometimes, it seemed the more I wrote the more distanced I became from the war, packaging it out to faceless men in a London office like the middleman in a business deal, handling the goods without consuming.'[55] The imagery of consumption is appropriate to an analysis of the self-initiated immersion of journalists, scholars, or tourists in a local environment marked by danger and uncertainty. And yet, Lloyd's voyeuristic front row seat over barbecued lamb provided him at least a certain degree of authority, the most obvious outcome of which is the existence of his book. Clearly, *being there* holds enormous sway when it comes to transmitting what one has seen and experienced in an environment which others have not had the benefit (or the inclination) to visit. Further, because sites marked by conflict and danger are not high on the travel itineraries for most people, the one who does visit for personal or professional purposes is likely to have his or her authenticity relatively unchallenged.

Lloyd is not alone in his pursuit of the 'high' associated with dangerous adventure tourism. In a volume that is described as 'the high octane guide to surviving hot spots, war zones, and the new hidden dangers of global travel', Robert Young Pelton lectures naive would-be tourists on the perils and survival strategies that Americans need in order to 'come back alive' from their exhilarating extreme tourism adventures. In one passage dealing with the Balkans, Pelton admonishes his readers not to 'stand on any part of the former Yugoslavia that you are not absolutely sure about – nobody really knows how many mines are scattered about the region, but all the estimates have a lot of zeros on the end of them, and you only have to tread on one for it to ruin your whole trip.'[56] For the traveller who gets to go home at the end of the trip, travelling through heavily mined regions may bring a feeling of exhilaration and provide a topic of boastful conversation with friends back home in the bar or the office. Of course, for people whose lives are daily affected by landmines and the other perils of conflict, it is loss and struggle, not exhilaration, which is more likely to be the norm.[57] As Lisle shows, contemporary tourism is an increasingly voyeuristic phenomenon wherein the consumer seeks to engage with what is considered to be both exotic and dangerous.[58] This phenomenon is not lost on national tourist boards: for example, Northern Ireland, Bosnia, Croatia, and Vietnam have all capitalized on popular images of their status as being or having recently been danger zones. The (recent) war zone and its inhabitants thus experience a kind of commodification in the representation of conflict and the adventure types of travel that conflict may give rise to.[59]

There is no consensus among academics concerning whether or how to explicitly admit authorial presence in the process of writing. But this conversation on ways of writing is beginning to unfold across the terrain of our disciplines.[60] However, any removal of the theorist from the process of theorizing in the field is juxtaposed with the inevitable physical immersion of the bodily self in the community to be observed. The paradox that is thus to be overcome is attempted through the universalization of observation and experience, as well as through the assumption that there is a universally possible iteration of human experience. As Geertz puts it with respect to anthropologists, practitioners of fieldwork 'need to convince us . . . not merely that they themselves have truly "been there", but . . . that had we been there we should have seen what they saw, felt what they felt, concluded what they concluded.'[61] In a discipline-wide attempt to maintain the myth of human objectivity, 'explicit representations of authorial presence tend to be relegated, like other embarrassments, to prefaces, notes, or appendices.'[62] Even those who are engaged in non-positivist or non-structural approaches to scholarship and fieldwork still have to address the fact that fieldwork is fundamentally implicated in representation, which is fundamentally implicated in relationships of power because it is the researcher who determines what counts in the narrative of the informant, and who interprets the objects of the gaze. The authority of the immersed researcher is necessarily achieved through the silencing or appropriation of local authority. What is needed, is a fundamental reconsideration of the epistemological and ontological commitments that inform most fieldwork.

The field researcher, then, occupies a role that hangs precariously between subjectivity and claims to authenticity, between immersion of the researcher-self in the communities and lifeways of the Other, and appropriation of the Other's authority to speak. While the question of authenticity is one that still hangs unresolved in a number of disciplines, there is a palpable sense, especially among regional specialists in International Relations, that fieldwork is absolutely fundamental to any claim of authenticity, even if the researcher and/or the fieldwork site is far removed either spatially or temporally from the event or the subject of study. Bourdieu cheerfully notes that: 'The researcher can only arrive after the show, when the lamps are doused and the trestles stacked away, with a performance which has lost all the charms of an *improvisation*',[63] but it may also be the case that being there 'before' carries the same sort of problematic authority (or lack thereof, as the case may be) as being there 'after' – a sort of pre-tourism. I was in Banja Luka when Zoran Djindjić was assassinated in March of 2003. In conversations with Belgrade colleagues over subsequent days, I was reminded that I had once enjoyed an espresso in the café beneath the window where the gunmen had been waiting for him. I tried to recall the café. 'It had pink umbrellas', my colleague prompted. Oh, yes. Pink umbrellas. I remember. My ability to share such a memory with students and colleagues in the university environment secured me as having *been there* and supplied me with the authority to comment convincingly on the event and its aftermath. Moreover, my sharing of a Serbian colleague's reaction to the assassination (*takav je život ovde* – that's the way life is here) with fellow 'regional specialists' secured my authority among fellow Balkanists, who tend to regard Serb reactions as politically juvenile, defeatist, and predictably repetitive. *Takav je život ovde.* We all laughed sadly over this 'typical Serb response' as at some inside joke.[64] It is precisely such 'inside jokes' that work to secure the authenticity of the regional specialist and field researcher – the kind of 'inside jokes' that cannot be challenged by those who have not been there.

NOTES

1   Susan Sontag, *On Photography* (New York: Farrar, Strauss, and Giraux, 1977), p. 57.
2   A *džezva* is a long-handled pot for making coffee.
3   Clifford Geertz, *Works and Lives: The Anthropologist as Author* (Stanford, CA: Stanford University Press, 1988), pp. 23–24.
4   Ease of movement for fieldwork, conferences, seminars, and the like is arguably the almost exclusive terrain of Western academics. It is almost unheard of for a Western scholar to be denied legal entry to the community of study. Conversely, a panel that I was part of at Rutgers University in New Jersey in 2001 ended up proceeding without my co-panelist, a Belgrade academic, whose visa was denied the day before after a three-month delay in processing. Counting on the delayed visa, he had purchased the plane ticket for the conference. This was almost an exact replay of the same situation with another Serbian academic in 2000 at a conference on Kosovo in Budapest.
5   States of confinement are not confined to the realm of the interstate. There are multiple sites of confinement, among them poverty, ability, sex, race, and age. But the state of being at large also indicates that somewhere, someone has issued a warrant for my proverbial arrest. It indicates that my own incarceration may be looming just around the next corner, in my next encounter, because I may be stopped in my tracks by the very boundaries that are the alibi for my own freedom. Stojan Sokolović retains the power to resist my arrival, my inquiries, my representations. He can choose to stop talking, to not talk at all, to misdirect or mislead. He can choose to stop serving me

coffee from his little metal cups. He has multiple ways of resisting at his disposal and I have found myself at his mercy on several occasions.

6   Commentary of an Assistant Professor of English and American Literature at the University of Novi Sad. See *War Correspondence* at the University of Pittsburgh's 'Jurist' website, a network of law professors: http://jurist.law.pitt.edu/email.htm#Ins35. For a history of the development and uses of the passport, see John Torpey, *The Invention of the Passport: Surveillance, Citizenship and the State* (Cambridge; New York: Cambridge University Press, 2000). Of course, there are a variety of ways in which movement and transactions are restricted for Western academics, but these tend to be enacted by one's own country of citizenship. Consider the travel and trade prohibitions outlined in US passports with respect to Cuba, North Korea, Iran, Haiti, and Serbia (1995 issue).

7   John Hutnyk, *The Rumour of Calcutta: Tourism, Charity, and the Poverty of Representation* (London; New Jersey: Zed Books, 1996), p. 21.

8   *Ibid.*, p. 21.

9   John Urry, *The Tourist Gaze: Leisure and Travel in Contemporary Societies* (London: Sage, 1990), p. 3.

10  *Ibid.* p. 3.

11  Of course, there are limitations to this, and knowledge production must still adhere to the parameters of acceptable scholarship.

12  Kenneth Little, 'On Safari: The Visual Politics of a Tourist Representation', in David Howes, ed., *The Varieties of Sensory Experience: A Sourcebook in the Anthropology of the Senses* (Toronto: University of Toronto Press, 1991), p. 159.

13  Hutnyk, *The Rumour of Calcutta*, p. 15.

14  *Ibid.* p. 19.

15  Quoted in Urry, *The Tourist Gaze*, p. 1.

16  *Ibid.*

17  So-Min Cheong and Marc L. Miller, 'Power and Tourism: A Foucauldian Observation', *Annals of Tourism Research*, Vol. 27, No. 2, 2000, pp. 371–390, p. 381; italics mine.

18  Ellen Strain, *Public Places, Private Journeys: Ethnography, Entertainment, and the Tourist Gaze* (New Brunswick, NJ: Rutgers University Press, 2003), p. 4.

19  *Ibid.*, p. 23.

20  *Ibid.*, p. 4.

21  *Ibid.*, p. 18.

22  *Ibid.*, p. 23.

23  *Ibid.*, p. 24.

24  *Ibid.*

25  Stephen Williams, *Tourism Geography* (London; New York: Routledge, 1998), p. 174.

26  *Ibid.*, p. 173.

27  *Ibid.*, pp. 173–174.

28  Elisabeth Rehn and Ellen Johnson Sirleaf, 'Women, War, and Peace: The Independent Experts' Assessment on the Impact of Armed Conflict on Women and Women's Role in Peace-building', United Nations Development Fund for Women (UNIFEM), October 2002. See www.unifem.undp.org/resources/assessment/index.html. This is also an issue of identifying 'victims' and speaking for them.

29  Williams, *Tourism Geography*, p. 178.

30  Strain, *Public Places, Private Journeys*, p. 3.

31  US State Department travel website advisories continue to describe Republika Srpska as anti-Western and potentially unsafe.

32  All information on the Chernobyl package tour is available on SAM's website, accessed on 20 June 2004: www.ukrcam.com/tour/tour_3.html.

33  Anne Dimon, 'Visiting Another Place, Another Time', *Toronto Star*, 10 April 2004, J14.
34  *Ibid.*
35  Vian Ewart, 'Images of India', *Toronto Star*, 3 April 2004, J1.
36  *Ibid.*, p. J22.
37  Jeannette Hyde, 'Ban the Extremists Says LP', *The Observer*, 17 November 2002.
38  Kabul City Tours website accessed on 14 June 2004: www.kabulcitytours.com/index.html.
39  Sascha Segan, 'Iraq: The Next Adventure Travel Destination?' *Frommer's News and Highlights*, 23 April 2003. Accessed on 10 January 2004: www.frommers.com/activities/article_print.cfm?destid=ADVENTURE&articleid=1045.
40  Little, *On Safari*, p. 153.
41  *Ibid.* pp. 152–153.
42  Department of National Defence, Security and Defence Forum Annual Report, 1998–1999.
43  This and all immediately following quotations are those of Holger Herwig, 'What Price Victory?' *University of Calgary Gazette*, 1 May 2000. Accessed October 1 2002. www.stratnet.ucalgary.ca/news_views/archives/2000/apr00/tours/Bosnia.html.
44  Gillian Rose, 'Practising Photography: an Archive, a Study, Some Photographs and a Researcher', *Journal of Historical Geography*, Vol. 26, No. 4, 2000, 555–571, p. 555.
45  I am grateful to Marie-Joelle Zahar of the Department of Political Science at Université de Montréal for allowing me to pore over her NATO souvenir mug for an untoward length of time.
46  And yet it is precisely the radical doubt associated with sovereignty and the nation-state more generally that evokes the performativity of the contributing states. As I have argued elsewhere, intervention serves as an alibi for sovereignty. See my 'International Intervention, Discourses of Representation, and the Production of Subordinated Sovereignties', in Kyle Grayson and Cristina Masters, eds, *Theory in Practice: Critical Reflections on Global Policy* (Toronto: Centre for International and Security Studies, 2003).
47  Here, Levinas asks, 'Can there be something as strange as an experience of the absolutely exterior . . .?' See 'The Trace of the Other', Alphonso Lingis, trans., in Mark Taylor ed. *Deconstruction in Context* (Chicago: University of Chicago Press, 1986), p. 348.
48  Debbie Lisle, 'Consuming Danger: Reimagining the War/Tourist Divide', *Alternatives*, Vol. 25, No. 1, Jan–Mar 2000, p. 95. It is also interesting to note here that places that have been removed due to perceptions of insecurity – Hong Kong because of SARS; Bali because of the nightclub bombings; Turkey because of the war in Iraq and 'bird flu', and perceptions of Middle Eastern instability in general – have been working double time to lure tourists back. Lisle refers to this process as 'sanitation', wherein the compromised tourist destination is (re)presented in markedly different terms than those that removed the site in the first place. Although Lisle specifically refers to conflict zones, destinations affected by other disaster phenomena, such as illness (Toronto and SARS) or natural disaster (Montserrat and the volcanic activity there) are represented as insecure in similar ways and with similar effects.
49  One of the most telling points of ethics review committee guidelines is their clear assertion that it is the ethics committee and researcher, not the local informant, who are empowered to determine what constitutes a meaningful risk.
50  Justin Doebele, 'Club Dead', *Forbes*, December 15, 1997.
51  Anthony Loyd, *My War Gone By, I Miss It So* (New York: Atlantic Monthly Press: 1999), p. 36.
52  *Ibid.*, p. 54.

53 *Ibid.*, p. 5.
54 *Ibid.*, p. 91.
55 *Ibid.*, p. 111.
56 Robert Young Pelton, *The World's Most Dangerous Places*, 5th edn (New York: Harper Collins, 2003), p. 417.
57 The International Campaign to Ban Landmines reports that there were 1,167 land-mine deaths in Bosnia in the four post-conflict years from 1996 to 2000. See *Landmine Monitor Report*, Human Rights Watch, 2000.
58 Lisle, 'Consuming Danger', p. 106.
59 *Ibid.*, p. 107.
60 The recent 'Ways of Writing' workshop at the International Studies Association Annual Convention in San Diego in 2006 is a case in point. I am grateful to have been invited to participate.
61 Geertz, *Works and Lives*, p. 16.
62 *Ibid.*
63 Pierre Bourdieu, *Homo Academicus*, Peter Collier, trans. (Cambridge: Polity Press/ Blackwell, 1988), p. 160.
64 Of course, Bosnians and Serbs return with their own jokes about themselves, though the effects and purposes of their circulation differ dramatically. For an analysis of how humour operates across the Bosnian cultural landscape, see Srdjan Vučetić, 'Identity is a Joking Matter: Intergroup Humour in Bosnia', *Spaces of Identity*, Vol. 3, No. 2 (July 2004), pp. 1–28.

# 4

# *On representation*

The hostage is the nonconsenting, the unchosen guarantee of a promise he hasn't made, the irreplaceable one who is not in his own place. It is through the other that I am the same, through the other that I am myself: it is through the other who has always withdrawn me from myself.[1]

Pinned up on the wall above my desk at the University of Manchester is a newspaper print black and white photograph of a young Orthodox priest standing on the flagstones against the wall of a Kosovo monastery. It is early summer, 1998. He wears a black cassock under a quilted black vest. His hair is tied back. A prayer rope is wound around his left hand. On the ground beside him kneels a penitent in a striped polo shirt, his whole body bent over as though in some terrible, terminal pain. The priest's eyes are fixed on the ground in front of him. I have stared at this photograph for the last eight years, but the expression on his face never changes; it is, in my estimation, at least, an unmistakable expression of mourning. The photograph, shot by a Belgrade-based Reuters photographer named Petar Kujundžić, bears the caption: 'A man prays next to a Serbian Orthodox priest yesterday at Kosovo's Gracanica monastery, near Pristina.'[2]

It is not clear whether the priest and the penitent know they are being photographed. Neither is looking in the direction of the camera. Nor, of course, do they see me outlining their forms now, tracing the edgeless outline of their bodies over and over again in the grainy image of the photograph. They remain there in the summer sun, exposed by Petar Kujundžić to be commented on, to be analyzed, to be assigned their place in the narratives on Kosovo, to be preserved in one of the largest archives in the world for the future reference of whomever comes to find them – for example, myself. The young priest at Gračanica has become a copyright – a fetish – the intellectual property of Kujundžić, protected by Reuters and it is they, and not the priest, who must provide permission for the reproduction of

the image. And yet, there is no copyright or trademark or licensing agreement in place that explains why he is standing there on the flagstones,
that explains the complexity of his thoughts and of his memory, that
explains why the penitent came to the gates of the monastery, whether he
came from near or far, whether he asked for this priest or another, whether
he left with his soul restored or with his faith shattered.

Here we find the saying passed into the said – the unfixed passed into
the immobilized; we find the ethical passed into the political. I do not believe
that Petar Kujundžić intended for me to stare these eight years at the
mournful countenance of the young priest at Gračanica. I do not think
that Kujundžić intended for him to remain immobilized all this time, represented in the same simple way, without recourse, standing in the summer
sun with his long, lean body shrouded in the same black cassock forever.
The photograph seizes the form of the priest and the penitent, it renders
them timeless, ageless, changeless. Every day, caught in the frame of the
photograph, the same mournful expression, the same sense of despair. They
will never have the chance to present another face but if I write only about
their grief I will have destroyed them.

Kujundžić's photograph, like all representation, is not outside the
sphere of intentionality and of ethics. It has a context. In the summer of
1998, with the international community threatening armed intervention
against Serbian military and paramilitary forces in the midst of a looming
war, Kujundžić has not photographed the twisted bodies of the latest victims
of fighting or massacres. He has not sought out the line-up of men and
women outside the morgues waiting to identify the brutalized body of a
son or daughter or parent. He has not attempted to capture: 'The ultra-
familiar, ultra-celebrated image – of an agony, of ruin – [which] is an
unavoidable feature of our camera-mediated knowledge of war.'[3] He has
gone to Gračanica, not to Drenica. He has photographed a young priest in
the summer sun, not a massacre scene. Here, in the folds of the priest's
cassock, against the walls of the monastery, we find the space of the political – of the contested – unfolding without fail. The potential affinity of the
photographer for the priest, or of the priest for the photographer, does not
negate the struggle over representation that plays out in the space between
them. The priest is immobilized in the film, his intentions are lost, his name
is denied, the sound of his voice and the content of his conversation
destroyed. Photography is a hostage-taker. Devoid of any core meaning
outside of the unknown intentions of the photographer, the politics of
imaging seeks to naturalize particular interpretations of meaning, and the
photograph becomes a tool in the service of other goals.[4] Politics may be
read into and mapped onto the skin of the film with very real consequences,
but the photograph has still destroyed any sense of dimensionality that the

priest and the penitent could have hoped for in such a representation. The photograph has denied their complexity; the sounds of their voices, the content of their conversation, the movement of their bodies; it has muted the sunlight in their hair, the shadows they cast on the flagstone path; it has denied them their names. Why did Kujundžić deny them their names? Naming provides both access and obstacles; it is both an asset and a liability. For Kujundžić, it probably did not matter. The caption reads that the priest is a Serb. He will bear a Serb name. The penitent will also bear a Serb name, because what man who is not a Serb will come to prostrate himself on the ground beside a Serbian priest?

Here, in this inevitable moment of identification, which is marked by the entry of the third party – for example, myself – the mobility of the saying is ontologized, politicized, burned into the realm of the said. I and others like me see the photograph. We project our own intentionality – we overwrite and rewrite the captioning to suit our own needs – the needs we project onto bodies, borders, and the boundaries of nations. The caption is needed, argues Susan Sontag: 'And the misreadings and the misrememberings, and new ideological uses for the pictures, will make their difference.'[5] This would be so even if there had been room in the image or time in the caption for Kujundžić to situate himself explicitly as the architect of this photograph; to explain why he is at one of Serbia's holiest monasteries on Vidovdan, one of the most sacred and politicized feasts on the Serbian Orthodox calendar. This would be so even if Kujundžić admitted, for example, to having travelled to Kosovo because he expected to capture some instance of violence; a rally, a protest, an armed standoff, perhaps, and left instead with this photograph, which he did not intend to shoot.[6] It would be so if he came on his own pilgrimage to the gates of Gračanica, and if the photograph was thus an aesthetic byproduct of form and content that came together unexpectedly – fortuitously – after days of fasting and prayer. Here, the intention of the photographer, the affinity he feels for the priest, would be destroyed in the move from that instant of connection to the distribution of the image and the entry of the priest's countenance and all that surrounds him to the realm of the third person – the consumer of the image. Things never just 'are' but are rather made to be; they are vested with meaning and significance through the identification of their relationships with other things, events, people, and places. The reason why Petar Kujundžić snapped this photograph is less important than its effects, which are independent of his intentions.

Does not the photograph of the young priest with his mournful face corroborate and memorialize for many Serbs their sense of besiegement in Kosovo? Here, Gračanica becomes the fortress wall behind which the emblematic Serb – the Orthodox priest – is uniquely secured as a figure of sublime grief, of timeless loss, of exile, and sacrifice. Widely considered to be the most important endowment of the Nemanjić dynasty in Kosovo, surrounded by medieval frescoes, the stone-smooth sound of Old Slavonic *a cappella* ringing through the nave of the church, Gračanica is quintessentially Serb, forming the very cornerstone of Serb political and religious claims to existence. The relationality in which this reading is made possible is not pictured in Kujundžić's photograph, but every Serb who sees the priest and the penitent knows in 1998 that the Other is the Kosovo Albanian who has taken up guns in the hope of securing independence; the Kosovo Albanian whose broken body represented through film and photography became itself emblematic of war and ethnic cleansing – a fetish and a reason for intervention. Indeed, mourning the pain of the priest and the penitent, as Susan Sontag points out, 'should not distract [us] from asking what pictures, whose cruelties, whose deaths are not being shown.'[7]

Irrespective of the reason Petar Kujundžić chose to photograph the young priest at Gračanica – if there was any conscious reason at all – the images seared onto the film stored at Reuters take on a life and consequence of their own. Seen in Belgrade, the image might be doing some political work to secure the identity of Kosovo as Serbian and to affirm the feeling of suffering and martyrdom. Outside of Serbia, and in the Balkanist scholarly imaginary, the image might work to reinforce the sense we have of Serb paranoia, and of the pathologies associated with their historico-political claims to Kosovo. Perhaps a third reading involves the denial that Serbs are singularly responsible for wholesale death once again. Here, one sees that the lovely, mournful face of the priest and the prostrate penitent cannot belong to a people capable of only murder and outrage. Here, the priest and the penitent seem to assume a guiltless responsibility in the measure of their grief, their fear, and their uncertainty. After all, the fortress walls of Kosovo monasteries would be no match for the NATO cruise missiles which would damage and destroy many of them almost exactly one year after the photograph was taken. And they would be no match for the battalions of young men who later came surging through breached walls to set the churches and the icons alight.[8]

The reason why the priest looks so troubled cannot be conveyed by the photograph, and I cannot purchase the right to access it. There is no sense of what it is that he has seen or heard or dreamed; there is no sense of rumour or fact or revelation, even though the photograph itself is certainly choked with rumour, fact, and revelation. Indeed, Petar Kujundžić knows many things that his photograph cannot express and to which intellectual property laws cannot secure access. Kujundžić knows, for example, that the prayer rope wound round the left hand of the priest is measured out in sets of thirty-two knots which are separated at the end of the set by a single black bead, which forms the thirty-third repetition and symbolizes the traditional age of Yeshua at his death. He knows that the priest has innumerable folds and secret pockets sewn into his cassock in which he carries these ropes, perhaps a bit of frankincense, or a banknote with which he might buy his life in a bribe at a later date, or which he might give to a stranger who does not have enough change to pay for all the beeswax candles he needs to light for the souls of his family and friends. Kujundžić knows, but there is no place for him to describe how, in other circumstances – in the thin light of morning, for instance – the young priest regards the stone-vaulted nave of the Church of the Assumption as the sun slants through the windows, or the way he chants the psalter from the sacred, unseen places behind the iconostasis to which neither Kujundžić's press pass nor the purity of his best intentions can provide him access. Kujundžić surely knows – but he cannot convey – the way the priest's lungs fill with the acrid, smooth scent of frankincense, how his heart fills with immanence, how his hands tremble with ecstasy. His ecstasy cannot be copyrighted any more than his life can be represented by a photograph.

Kujundžić knows that ducking out of the hard summer sun and into the stone-cold monastery with its medieval, faded, frescoed walls is as refreshing as diving into a cold spring when one's skin is sweat-soaked and itchy with exhaustion. Kujundžić knows these things. He has not come out of nowhere to photograph the priest and the penitent without speaking their language, without knowing their customs, without keeping his distance. He did not photograph the priest inside the nave or the sanctuary, but on the grounds outside. It is even quite possible that Kujundžić, the priest, and the penitent had a conversation at some point before the photographer headed back north on the road that leads to Belgrade. It is possible that the priest served coffee, or that he sliced up some early green apples for them to share as they talked. It is likely – though not certain – that they laughed together over something trivial at least once. Indeed, while being there does not confer authority, what one knows and expresses is often mediated by where one stands, by the language one speaks, by the name one bears, by whose trust one can earn, by whether or not one is capable of making an admirable cup of coffee. Who knows the measure of affinity the priest felt for Petar Kujundžić, or Petar Kujundžić for the priest, if any at all?

Not only would there be too little time to formulate the words and too little space in the place where the caption must go, but an attempt to report on the state of the soul of the priest at Gračanica would not be relevant to any properly social scientific endeavour in either its form or its content. As Susan Sontag observes, the facts worth knowing: 'Are expected to be transmitted tersely and emphatically.'[9] *The Globe and Mail*, from which I snipped this photograph, has room and time for only this: 'A man prays next to a Serbian Orthodox priest yesterday at Kosovo's Gracanica monastery, near Pristina.' The photograph conveys only mourning in this instant, which drags on forever, and we cannot make sense of it. The caption makes the attempt to convey what seems to be necessary. Without the caption, I could not report, for example, that the photographer is Petar Kujundžić, that the distributor is Reuters, that the monastery is Gračanica, or that the priest is in Serbia at all (which is different politically, temporally, and spatially, than saying that the priest is in Kosovo or Kosova, near Priština or Prishtinë). Indeed, without the caption, the priest could be an Albanian, and this would change the political character of the photograph as well as the possibilities corresponding to its appropriation, interpretation, and dissemination. In the case of Kujundžić's photograph, the evident grief of the priest and the penitent seems emblematic of the war that would soon overtake them. Yet, the photo predates the generally accepted understanding among scholars of when the 'real' war began – that is, when NATO launched its own attacks – one year later at the end of March 1999. The priest and the penitent are mourning there in 1998 over whatever it is that has come to pass in that moment; they cannot know how bad things will be in another year. And so my own sense of this photograph – informed now by the *post facto* knowledge of how bad things became – has altered the image after the fact, has conferred a retrospective meaning upon it that would not have been recognized by the priest and the penitent on Vidovdan in 1998. Indeed, I did not recognize it myself.

The photograph, even with the caption, even with the date, even with the location, expresses no necessary fact or event or meaning. In this sense, 'the photographic act is a duel; that is to say, it is a challenge to the object and the object's defiance of that challenge. Where that confrontation is ignored, there can only be escape into technology or aesthetics – that is to say, into the most facile of solutions.'[10] The priest defies this rendering. He defies all rendering. In Baudrillard's formulation:

> there is a kind of symbolic murder in the photographic act. But the object isn't the only thing that disappears; the subject also disappears on the other side of the lens. Every press on the shutter release, which puts an end to the real presence of the object, also causes me to disappear as subject, and it's in this reciprocal disappearance that a transfusion between the two occurs. It isn't always a successful act, but when it is, this transfusion is the sole condition of success. It is, in a sense, an invocation – an invocation to the Other, the object, to emerge from this disappearance, and so create *a poetic situation of transference or a poetic transference of situation*. Perhaps in this reciprocity there is a glimmer of a solution to the problem of our notorious 'inability to communicate', to the problem of the non-response of the Other.[11]

All we can say about the priest and the penitent now is that they have awakened to find themselves at war. Who knows where they are now? Who knows if they are even still alive? And that is all that matters in the age of the catastrophe, even if it is not all that mattered to Petar Kujundžić, to the priest, or to the penitent on Vidovdan in 1998.

## Naming

The power to designate people, places, and events as mattering, or as mattering in a certain way or, by omission, as not mattering at all, is grounded in the practices of representation. The power to produce truths through the privileging of particular narratives at the inevitable expense of others is grounded in the practices of representation. Representation, in turn, relies on witnesses; it relies on naming, signifying, and (re)producing events in value-laden ways – in ways that capture, reify, and spectacalize.[12] Representation frames narratives, it dictates their content, but it is also the Damoclene sword that threatens in every perilous moment to destroy the particular claims to coherence and sensibility that are the basic features of narratives. The textuality of events means that there is no necessary correlative meaning; rather, meaning is produced in the realm of relationships and in images. The production of meaning involves operations that link events and incidents into a coherent framework – into an intelligible matrix of understanding that is reproduced through performance and text (and through performance *as* text). The production of meaning is made possible through the mass distribution of images and explanations, through the situating of events into particular teleologies of history or progress. It is produced through the archive at Reuters.

The power to designate is grounded in cultural positionality, in the privilege accorded to professionalization of what we do and in the reasons associated with observation and empirical study. In the pixels of the digital print, the priest at Gračanica can ever only mimic the reality it claims to capture: a man of flesh and bone and blood. Yet this observation in itself conveys nothing; it conveys nothing about *why*, or *how*, or *in what measure*. At the same time, it destroys the possibility that he is a man of flesh and bone and blood because it makes him a fetish, a representation of himself that causes his own disappearance in the reproduction. The identification and subsequent naturalization of meaning rests on a system of representation in a logic of symbolic exchange. Baudrillard argues that: 'Any system invents for itself a principle of equilibrium, exchange and value, causality and purpose, which plays on fixed oppositions: good and evil, true and false, sign and referent, subject and object. This is the whole space of difference and regulation by difference which, as long as it functions, ensures the stability and dialectical movement of the whole.'[13] Here, we find the fundamental need of the Other in a system of exchange designed to justify and underwrite the Self – designed to assuage the anxiety associated with the possibility of meaninglessness – of valuelessness – of non-existence. The first-order paradox lies in the fundamental discontinuity – the absurdity of the hyper-non-sensical, which is the simultaneous need of the thing that one must also destroy. Holger Herwig needs the lawless, dangerous Bosnian to underwrite and justify himself on safari. Petar Kujundžić needs the Kosovo Albanian if the Serbian priest is to occupy a place of emblematic loss. And this is true even if Petar Kujundžić intends no emblem at all, because it is not Petar Kujundžić that reads the photograph. He submits it to be read by others. In this way, the photograph also marks what it does not contain within the frame of its image. Whether or not he appears in the photograph, the Other is the alibi for our existence, the identification of which commands that the Other also needs to be destroyed, reformed, stamped out. This is not a logic of opposition – a logic of difference – that works in an enclosed, discreet system of mutual exchange. Rather, this is a system that is under-written by the very destruction it seeks to avoid. 'The subject deprived of all otherness collapses into itself, and sinks into autism. The elimination of the inhuman causes the human to collapse into odium and ridicule.'[14]

Because we cannot identify a universal schematic of value, there is no possibility of absolutes (or, indeed, of absolution); everything becomes a function of relativity and therefore, every act requires an equivalent in order to assess its value. The question of equivalence is the question of what an act is exchangeable for, and therefore, the indicator of its relative value.[15] Regardless of Petar Kujundžić's intentions, of the intentions of the priest, or of the pentitent, or of the distribution at Reuters, the editor at the *Globe and Mail*, and the editors of every other periodical in which the photograph appeared, the effect remains both integral to intentions and radically anterior to them. And from the radical uncertainty that dwells between intentionality and effect, entire narratives unravel, their 'meaning' is catastrophically undermined – fundamentally betrayed by the opacity, the undecidability, and the inscrutibility of fixing meaning in time, space, and temperament. It is difficult to determine where justice lies here. Is it just that all I have to do to secure permission to reproduce the image of this man, who can effect no binding protest, is to call the New York office at Reuters and simply pay a small fee? Does not the very silence of the priest pose its own challenge to whatever strategy I may devise for the use of his image? Does not the silence of the priest contest me in the very fact that the priest is most certainly *not* silent, but only silent in a representation that has been imposed upon him, only silent because the photograph has made him so? Does not the very life of the priest defy the logic of the immobility of the photograph? Has the photograph thus not destroyed him, and he, perhaps, the photograph?

Relying on an interpretation (a representation) of intent that can actually never be verified, cries for justice are levelled in injury and in outrage – they proceed from those who have been wronged, and who still have the voice – as though that were all that remained – to demand what is due them. The charge itself does not rely on the response that can(not) be formulated. The charge does not require a symmetrical response; it does not ask for reciprocity. For example, response may include the possibility of standing silent before the charge; of standing silent in the silence after the charge has been laid so that the charge might simply stand – unchallenged; to let it ring out, unopposed and unopposable. Response might involve finding the money to track down the photographer, to purchase the plane ticket, to translate the text, to find the priest, to close the distance between us so that I might hear his challenge, so that he might have a chance to say *no*.[16] Thus, our attempts to secure and securitize image, meaning, and objectivity, to deny things their mobility, are always met by contest and challenge, whether we choose to hear it or not. As Kujundžić's photograph securitizes the young priest so that I and others might inspect and display him, so the priest also stands in defiance of this and every project. Just as Herwig's representations immobilize Bosnians and reify their society as one of eternal danger and lawlessness, he is also exposed for inspection as he stands in his flak jacket, wandering through the Bosnia of his imagination. For Baudrillard, this is expressed in the formulation that 'the uncertainty of thought comes from the fact that I am not alone in thinking the world – that the world, in its turn, thinks me.'[17] Herwig, who watches, is also watched. Herwig, who gazes, is also gazed upon. Herwig stands contested; the reason for his visit: contested; the photographs he shot: contested; the explanations he gave: contested; his characterizations of people, places, and events: contested.

This is the charge levelled by the timeless, ageless, changeless form of Petar Kujundžić's photograph of the priest and the penitent. Here, I stare at the form of the priest in his wrinkled cassock, at the crumpled form of the penitent. The priest and the penitent contest me. They contest my reading of them, of their intentionality, of the intentionality of Petar Kujundžić in the framing of the photograph. They defy any reading of them as emblematic of Kosovo, as any man must deny a reading of himself as emblematic of anything. There is no quintessential Serb. There is no quintessential Serb position. There is no emblematic Serb loss or sacrifice. In this photograph, there is only a young priest in possession of the only things that remain his own: the body beneath the cassock, the hands through which he passes the thirty-two knots of his prayer rope, the eyes which are trained on the flagstones, the hair pulled casually back to the nape of his neck, illuminated in the summer sun. This is the charge of my responsibility for the representation that I have made, which stretches out across time and space; the expression of a moment which is neither measurable nor contestable nor verifiable, because we can never replicate the moment that the representation claims to have captured. The moment comprises a third dimension. The moment is always past, never present, from the millisecond in which the image is burned onto the film, or captured by the pixels of our digitized machinery. Here, there are only moments now; moments in which our well-intentioned movements are shattered in a single instant – in the frame of a single image. Whether or not the charge can be answered is a question that arises only later and which requires attention to questions of ethics and responsibility. But those things happen in time, synchronously in the Levinasian *said*. The laying of the charge demands of me *in that instant* a payment that I cannot make because I cannot return or reneg(otiat)e. It contests me diachronously in a space which is otherwise than temporal, which is the space occupied by the image of the priest and the penitent. Herwig and I cannot undo the conduit of violence that we opened up. Kujundžić cannot undo his decision to expose the priest at Gračanica to my merciless stare – made possible in black and white through the distribution at Reuters – made possible in high resolution and in colour by a telephone call to the archive in New York. Responsibility demands of us a currency that we are simultaneously unable to possess, a movement that we are simultaneously unable to make because there is no possibility of pure gift, of pure forgiveness, or of payment in full. The payment will always be dissymmetrical in relation to the charge. Levinas notes that: 'The Other who expresses himself is entrusted to me (and there is no debt with regard to the Other – for what is due cannot be paid: one will never be even).'[18] One is not indebted who can never pay. In the world of economics, one simply declares bankruptcy.[19] Even after I have arrived at the gates of Gračanica to ask the priest permission to use his image, I will still have assumed that he feels the same things at stake as I do. I will still have assumed that my intentions can be unproblematically conveyed, that he will see them as I want him to, that a priest in a Kosovo monastery and I can communicate in the framework of the intentionality of this text and its assumptions. We speak no common language, even if I can improve my *ekavica* to the point of expressing the sublime.

Stojane Sokoloviću!
Holger Herwig!
Petre Kujundžiću!
*Pope!*[20]
I am declaring bankruptcy.

The problem of representation is further exacerbated by the question of who is the represented – who is made to lay still – and who does the representing. This is a problem of determining who is the hostage of whom, which demands at least the minimal recognition that we are all hostages in some form or another, though some of us are more so than others. When I look at you, when I have you in my sights and in my sites (but not in my cites, because you are to be only observed and commented on, not permitted to speak with your own voice and in your own language) I have already taken you hostage. This is so because, in the gaze, I am already formulating an idea – a systematization – of who it is you are, where you are going, what you are doing. I am already weighing you before you ever turn to face me, and before we ever speak – if we never speak. I am already wondering what I should write, how it can be expressed, who will read it, what they will think of me. And of you. I am already wondering if I should take the lens cover off my camera, if I should focus that cold eye on the warm surface of your skin, your face, your smile, the delicate curve of your hands.

Representation is also this visuality, and thus finds repose in descriptions of bullet-studded apartment blocks, hollow, rusting factories, the whistling memory of mortar rounds and bodies piled up in the centres of burned villages. The value – which is the meaning – that is identified in and by the representation depends on the description as well as on the systematization and on the situating of the representation in a framework whereby it becomes exchangeable for something else. Alphonso Lingis claims that 'as we speak, I progressively identify [the Other] and his or her intentions and attitudes. I interpret what he or she says and how he or she stands and moves with my own codes and categories.'[21] This is the development of familiarity – of the potentiality of familiarity – which is not yet on the horizon as the Other turns to face me. 'For in facing me, calling upon me, summoning me, the other presents him or herself not as something identifiable, but as other.'[22] This is the impossible space between expression and interpretation, marked on the face – in the trace – of the Other. The face of Stojan Sokolović. The face of the priest at Gračanica. The face of Holger Herwig.

The 'I' who gazes in from the comfort of my office at the seemingly endless signs and signifiers of the former Yugoslavia makes just such a representation. There is little interest in the reception our representation receives on behalf of the represented. Did Kujundžić ask the priest whether he wanted to become the copyrighted material of Reuters?[23] Herwig writes for the *Calgary Gazette*, not for *Oslobodjenje*.[24] Which of us feels that she must answer to the priest behind the broken walls of Gračanica? The Other has seen me; he addresses me, but I am gazing over at him, at her, at them, and I am busy putting their respective forms to print, stringing together words to make sentences, to make paragraphs, to make chapters, which in turn make claims and assign characteristics. This is Yugoslavia, Serbia, Bosnia, Kosovo; a tragedy, an inferno, a dissolution, a disaster, a slaughter-house, a bloodbath.[25] I am gazing over 'there', I am watching, and I have appended their characteristics, aims and goals, tactics and strategies, outcomes and possibilities, legitimacy and the lack thereof. They do not see me looking. The priest at Gračanica does not see me tracing the lines of his cassock; he does not see me tracing the contours of his face with my eyes, over and over again. Yet he faces me, and I am caught, as Lingis claims, with my eye at the keyhole. There are a whole division of us 'Balkanists' in the corridor, waiting our turn to see, so that we can say something. But we are still talking to ourselves. I trace the form of the priest, the folds in his cassock, the contours of his face. I watch him – this image of him – this image that he does not see me seeing.[26] As Susan Sontag observes, 'the other, even when not an enemy, is regarded only as someone to be seen, not someone (like us) who also sees.'[27]

In similar fashion, Stojan Sokolović turns round in his tracks on the street and he watches the air-conditioned tour bus drive by – a huge, lumbering bus, too large for the narrow roads, its windows darkened with shaded glass so that the occupants can see out, but so that Stojan Sokolović cannot see in, cannot see who is watching him, taking notes on him, or photographs of him, capturing the form of his body in the frame of the print that will turn up on a slide in an undergraduate lecture hall with a caption in another language that reads: 'Sarajevo Man Waits for Bus In Front of House with Bullet Holes.' Here, we are all hostage-takers, staring out at the objects of our desire, the alibis for our careers. Stojan Sokolović exposes me as a hostage-taker. My very bones are exposed for inspection and I am compelled to answer for myself. I do not know how to do so. 'A man prays next to a Serbian Orthodox priest yesterday at Kosovo's Gracanica monastery, near Pristina', explains the caption beneath the photo of the young priest with his hair pulled back and his prayer rope wound round his hand. But the *Globe and Mail* typesetter cannot even insert the accent marks required for the proper pronunciation of the Serbo-Croatian consonants.

Alphonso Lingis argues that it is the speaking with another that allows us to increasingly categorize, but it is also simultaneously the case that the more we speak, the *less* I understand, the *less* I can organize the space, the place, and the charge of Stojan Sokolović with my own systematized categories because individual human lives necessarily defy the orderly cate-gories devised to contain them. The boundaries of their bodies and of their souls are incongruous with systems of organization and hierarchies of type. This is the myth of order. 'I present to the other the representation of [him] that I form. But in facing me, contesting or confirming that identity I have assigned to [him], the other arises apart, beyond the representation – other. [His] move in facing puts the trace of this removal in the visible.'[28] As soon as I tell my itinerant colleagues that I have heard a man speak, and that his name is Stojan Sokolović, I have represented him. He should elude me, if he can. I am unstable.

Here, though, instability becomes an imperative; it moves from the realm of things uncontested to the realm of things ineluctable. It moves from that which demands denial of difference to that which can no longer be denied. Instability becomes the basic form and content of that which is marked fundamentally by fragmentation. Our representations are fictions of stability underwritten by the drive to identify and fix the stable subject in time and space, into the firmament of identity and being; a project propelled by fear of meaninglessness. Does not the photograph capture and reify, framing the myth of the stable subject, framing the priest and the penitent in the timeless pose characteristic of priests and of penitents, framing the way we see them in relation to one another; the one on his knees, the other with his downcast eyes standing against the fieldstone walls of the sanctuary? Does not the photograph convey the reality that we perceive prior to the viewing, which in turn confirms what we already know about who they could be? Photographs appear to convey truths, to secure consensus, to simplify events through the apparent designation of victims and perpetrators, to inscribe meaning in expressions; in the way that the priest has tied his hair back, in the clasped hands of the penitent; to inscribe meaning in locations, on a flagstone path against a fieldstone wall attached to a building steeped in historical significance, behind the gates of a monastery in the embattled territory of Kosovo whose undulating green hills have been identified as *in dispute* for seven hundred years, which is the age of the stones in the foundation walls of Gračanica. Here, the fragmented subject is made to appear unitary, stable, predictable, sensical, conveyable and, in its turn, representable. Here, the fragmented event is memorialized into a single iteration of experience, and of experientiality.

## Fragmentation

The inherent fragmentation of events is already always a cause for anxiety, but here it is more pronounced, a feast for visceral realities that want to stake their claims as facts beneath the smooth river flow of the progressive trajectory of history. Technologies of print and satellite-relayed, real-time imagery stake out the ground on which such representational monuments are built. In Moscow's Victory Park, for example, the bas-relief images carved into the spire of victory depict even the tendons on the necks of men and women representing the resistance, destruction, and ultimate reconstituted resurrection of Russian cities over the German armies in 1945. The sculptures evince a determination in the face of chaos, a steely sort of suffering, and a resignation that is symbolized as timeless, frozen, and future-oriented even though the observer knows that the representational imagery recalls the past: the battles at Minsk, Kursk, Stalingrad.[29] The sculptures represent a past of past events; past struggles, past deaths, past thoughts of a future that is itself now past, past thoughts of a reconstruction that is now complete. These forms of recollection help to constitute knowledge and the knowledge of memory with their exchangeability. The spire stands in for the war, serves as its alibi. We, born of parents born after the war, are certain that the war took place because the monuments and commemorative ceremonies that serve as its alibi are there; corporeal. Each bas-relief figure stands in for an embattled city.

Beneath the spire in Victory Park there is an underground museum with dioramic re-enactments of battle scenes. In the staging of the battle scene, events disappear behind their representations; they melt into simulation. The frozen faces of plastic men cause the disappearance of the Stalingrads, the Kursks, the Minsks because the Stalingrads and Kursks and Minsks are cities and not men or women, and because their faces are plastic and changeless and because they belong to no one. But the underground museum also has an enormous room whereupon the names of the war dead are stamped into the round walls. From the floor to the ceiling, the names, patronymics, and surnames of tens of thousands of war dead (the ones that are remembered and thus represented) stand in two-inch high, gold leaf letters; a wall of proper names that feels absurdly disconnected from the representations of the battles behind the dioramic glass. It is not in front of the dioramas, but in front of the proper names that one's knees begin to tremble and threaten collapse. It is in front of the proper names that one is confronted with silence, with the inability to respond, with the inability to find the edges of meaning.

Proper names provide relationality in ways that plastic men in dioramic boxes cannot. The immediate connection between proper names and individuals is salient; it draws the threads between our lives and our relationships. Our names are given to us, bestowed upon us, by particular others; by parents, grandparents, siblings, communities, immigration officers, by photographers, or by the omissions of photographers. These names provide a place, however fleetingly, from which to speak, to contest, to testify. For John Caputo: 'A name gives a victim an idiom, at least the start of an idiom, and a chance to sound an alarm. The best monument to victims is just to write down their names, one by one, to make a long detailed list of the proper names.'[30] It is thus that the reading of names at Yom Shoah expresses that which replicas of Auschwitz cannot. Auschwitz can show us *what*, but not *who*. Auschwitz can suggest that human beings were trapped inside its gates, but it cannot tell us who, exactly, even if it can tell us *Jews*. Only the reading of the names provides the intimate awareness of *who* was taken to poison showers, of *whose* weight the stark, fetid bunks bore, of *whose* drawn countenance turned to face the firing squad. In other words, Auschwitz as a proper name – as the name of an event and of a place which is a central node in a matrix of death – subsumes within its frame the proper names of the people whose lives were lost there. Similarly, images of nameless Bosnians standing in front of bombed out buildings, or of women grieving at gravesides, or of children's torn bodies after they have inadvertently taken their play into minefields suggests that the loss is a universal one; it suggests that those who are nameless can be displayed in a universal image of grief and mourning and death. These images become iconic representations of individual lives which are stretched out and taken from the bodies of those who bear the pain so that they can serve as representations of other categories.

Here there is also an ever present danger in the politics of naming – the danger of names that are liabilities, or of namelessness. Does not the name of Petar Kujundžić already lead me to assume at least a minimal degree about his positionality; about the ease with which he might pass through the gates of Gračanica? Susan Sontag argues that to deny the suffering their names demotes them to 'representative instances of their occupations, their ethnicities, their plights.'[31] The individual loss – the grief that seeps into the skin of the individual – is lost. And yet, in other instances, names may be liabilities – the name of Stojan Sokolović, for example, who cannot be a victim in the context of our own political imaginaries when he bears the name of the perpetrator.

Proper names are nevertheless both expressable and repeatable, and are uniquely particular in that they summon individual lives and deaths. As such, proper names serve as testimonies in the system of human meaning. But proper names are also muddy, messy, and murky. Proper names are an impassability – an impossibility – because they harbour the possibility of a universal system of identification and meaning, while simultaneously summoning the impossibly particular: the unique relationships between women, men, children, parents, siblings, lovers, brothers, sisters, victims, perpetrators, bystanders, researchers, photographers, and informants. There is no singular way to read, interpret, and map events; the proper name is mobility lodged in a field of immobility. It is the ephemeral lodged in the discourse of the tangible. It is possibility lodged in an apparently impossible position. It is the narrowest of fissures carved in an otherwise impassable stone face. Proper names, places, and events signify specificities, but cannot capture or contain them. People disappear beneath the very signifiers which are intended to capture and embrace them. Women and men become nameless as proper names themselves are occluded by other proper names. Individual men and women and children are subsumed beneath the proper name of Bosnia, or Kosovo, or Srebrenica. 'Bosnia' tries to capture those individuals who were made to succumb to murder and dispossession, but it does not make room for proper names on its own. The experience of 'Bosnia' is not the same for Stojan Sokolović as it is for another man, for a woman or child, for a priest or an imam, for any person who is not Stojan Sokolović. Indeed, Stojan Sokolović was not forced to surrender his body to a mass grave. And yet: 'The fields of disasters are marked with dates and proper names, which are so many alarms sounding, so many sounds of warning and calls for help. Proper names are so many points on the map of disasters. They are the stuff on which ethics comes to grief and which launches the search for another idiom for disasters.'[32] The name of Stojan Sokolović is enough to crack the edifice of ethics.

In Victory Park, the battles disappear within their representations, as for Baudrillard, 'the extermination of the Jews disappeared behind the televised event *Holocaust*.'[33] The cinematographic version of the Holocaust allows one to find its parameters, allows one to assign it meaning – even if the meaning we struggle with is actually its *meaninglessness* – it allows for narrativization to provide order and benchmarks, and touchstones in ways that the names of individuals cannot. As Levinas argues, in the staging of the said, the saying is destroyed. Or in Baudrillard's formulation: 'One no longer makes the Jews pass through the crematorium or the gas chamber, but through the sound track and image track, through the universal screen and the microprocessor.'[34] In Auschwitz-Birkenau, visitors pass through the ordeal of *the Jews*, who are made to lay still as they are observed – as their bunks, their workplaces, the walls against which they were executed, the soot from the ashes of their bodies on the crematoria walls, their hair clippings, their shoes, their suitcases, and the manner of their extermination are made to lay still so that the perfect gaze of an eternal, memorialized future can persist. At the Tuol Sleng museum in Phnom Penh, visitors pass through torture chambers and gaze at bloodstains that have long since dried over and faded almost imperceptibly away. Thousands of photographs of the murdered stare back, more passive than any passivity, made to lay still – to stay frozen in deaths which have become representations of death in a representation of a past that is preserved for an endless present. And yet, giving women and men their proper names, allowing them that microcosmic identification bears testimony to the fact that their deaths are uniquely theirs, that their lives were uniquely theirs – and not anyone else's – to lose. As Derrida notes: 'If death . . . names the very irreplaceability of absolute singularity (no one can die in my place or in the place of the other), then all the *examples* in the world can precisely illustrate this singularity. Everyone's death, the death of all those who can say "my death", is irreplaceable.'[35]

Events are swallowed up into representations of events – into simulations of events such that the distinction between what we have done and what we say about what we have done is so profoundly fractured that the difference between them is difficult to make with any confidence. 'Nächste halt . . . Dachau', announces the conductor.[36] Even at Dachau, the first operational concentration camp in Germany and a major contemporary tourist attraction, most of the site has been reconstructed from the ground up after having been destroyed by American soldiers in 1945. David O'Donoghue notes that: 'Even the watchtowers had to be rebuilt, and the iron gate [at the entrance] is a reconstruction.' In short, 'it's not always easy to tell reality from replica.'[37] For Baudrillard, the (non)event lives on in altered form, in form altered for consumption through the ultimate Technicolor tube of hyper-visuality: the simulating screen. In other words, it is the signs, or representations, that we increasingly associate with 'reality', on screen and in text. The reproduction absorbs, subsumes, and refracts the event it claims to copy, until the event is nothing more (can never be more) than a copy – a copy upon a copy – a signification upon a signification, where what is signified is both simulation and simulacra. The more disastrous an event, the more it is disciplined into simulation, because ours is a society drawn to catastrophe, claims Baudrillard.[38] We simulate and reproduce catastrophe at every turn, until the event itself is lost forever beneath the simulation that replaces it. For Baudrillard, for example, this means that '*Holocaust* is *primarily* (and exclusively) an event, or rather, a *televised* object . . . that is to say, that one attempts to rekindle a *cold* historical event, tragic but cold, the first major event of cold systems, of cooling systems, of systems of deterrence and extermination that will then be deployed in other forms'[39] – in multiple forms, multiply, even as they are yet fractal and fragmented, clear and unclear, calculated and stumbled upon. In Bosnia, it can be said that the events, which were broadcast in 'real time', facilitated the representation of consumption and the consumption of representation. We (re)kindle (c)old events 'through a cold medium, television, and for the masses who are themselves cold, who will only have the opportunity for a tactile thrill as well, which will make them spill into forgetting with a kind of good aesthetic conscience of the catastrophe.'[40] The men and boys of Srebrenica are un-covered and re-covered, but their deaths disappeared behind the televised event *Genocide*.

## Trust

The realm of representation is deeply bound in trust, and in its lack. Representation supposes that behind the sign dwells a coherent reality to which the sign attests; it supposes that the dioramic men at Victory Park represent the battles whose names are emblazoned on the descriptive, commemorative plaques. The axiom of representation asks us to trust the equivalence posited there. Similarly, the field researcher asks us to suppose that her work reflects the objects and communities of her study. She asks that her experience be read – as it claims to be produced – as a faithful reproduction of what she saw, heard, and otherwise sensed.

When we realize that representation is essentially the production of an apparently uncontested reality, when we realize that representation can never be a faithful signifier of that which it claims to have captured, when we realize that all representation is simulation, then we can identify a fundamental incongruity. As Baudrillard argues, '[a]bstraction today is no longer that of the map, the double, the mirror or the concept. Simulation is no longer that of a territory, a referential being or a substance. It is the generation by models of a real without origin or reality: a hyperreal. The territory no longer precedes the map, nor survives it. Henceforth, it is the map that precedes the territory – *precession of simulacra* – it is the map that engenders the territory and if we were to revive the fable today, it would be the territory whose shreds are slowly rotting across the map.'[41] In other words, the account provided by the representation becomes indistinguishable from the reality which it claims to represent; the weight of our faith and our trust lies in the simulation, in monuments to wars and famines, in photographs of priests and penitents, which eventually stand in as alibis for themselves and not for any other event or experience. There is no longer a correlation between the spire at Victory Park or its underground museum with its dioramic battle scenes and its wall of proper names and the events that these are intended to alibi. Victory Park is its own simulation, its own reality, which is independent of the long, intangible years its architects intended it to represent. The connection is irretrievably lost because it was never there. As Baudrillard notes, 'representational imaginary, which both culminates in and is engulfed by the cartographer's mad project of an ideal coextensivity between the map and the territory, disappears with simulation.'[42]

Representation attempts to accommodate simulation by positing it as a false representation, and this is precisely its bankruptcy; there is no representation in a world that can no longer claim an affinity between the observer and the object of observation. The distance between these is dimensional – delusional; one ascribes meaning, produces reality, even when one believes that one is only discerning or distilling or discovering it. Holger Herwig's inability and unwillingness to interact with Bosnians during his tour of Bosnia provides the very basis for the implicit presentation of culture, of Otherness and of language as threat. Indeed, the attempt to securitize language is the mark of all expertise; it is the attempt to cordon off the terms of engagement from other iterations, Other ways of knowing, Other languages. It is only this sanitization – this radical, traumatic excision of the Other from his own land – that provides the space for representation to identify, codify, and reify narratives. The priest at Gračanica has little choice but to trust Petar Kujundžić – to trust his representation even as he defies it. Petar Kujundžić and the priest at Gračanica are not exchangeable for one another; they are not parallel to one another, they cannot change places, even though they also cannot be understood as wholly Other to one another. The priest cannot capture Kujundžić, cannot hold him to account under any law or regulation any more than he can hold me. Yet, are we not equally immobilized before him? Are we not equally commanded to answer to him precisely because there is no legal mechanism in the world which would force this from us? Are we not equally implicated in the manufacture and consumption of other people's pain – of other people's lives displayed in the unidimensionality of a single sentence of captioning?

Trust, if such a thing can be said to exist at all, is that absurdity which surrenders the Self to what is unknown, yet which retains faith that all will be well; it is the surrendering of the Self to the possibility of destitution and destruction; to abject despair. It is the Abrahamic formulation that God would not demand Isaac, even though this was precisely what was required. Trust is faith by virtue of the absurd; it is faith in the face of the radically unknown, the radically different, the absolutely Other. There is no currency or formula for exchange. The balance of reciprocity is blown apart. I am the hostage of the priest, as the priest is the hostage of the penitent. Lingis points out that:

> to *trust you* is to go beyond what I know and to hold on to the real individual that is you . . . When we leave our home and community to dwell awhile in some remote place, it happens every day that we trust a stranger, someone with whom we have no kinship bonds, no common loyalty to community or creed, no contractual obligations. We have no idea what he said, what are his family, clan, and village coordinates, the categories with which he represents for himself society, nature, and the cosmos. We attach to someone whose words or whose movements we do not understand, whose reasons or motives we do not see. Our trust short-circuits across the space where we represent socially defined behaviors and makes contact with the real individual agent there – with *you*.[43]

76

It is this space of radical possibility, stretching to the limits of existence, which engenders the fear associated with uncertainty. It is this limitless space across which all of the Others and all of the other Others are
speaking and moving in ways that are unintelligible to the systems of
exchange we have devised. Because they do not conform to our expectations, because they cannot be represented, assimilated, or totally destroyed,
they are left to dwell on the other side of the shaded glass, which separates
them from us on the air-conditioned bus on the tour through Bosnia. They
are disallowed, disqualified, disinvited, relegated to the pavement where
they are observed and commented on.[44] Here, representation bleeds into
simulation and is thus made incontrovertibly suspect.

We trust that representations are true – true equivalence – that they
are exchangeable for the realities which they purport to image. Yet, that
trust is shattered in the simulation, as 'simulation envelops the whole edifice
of representation as itself a simulacrum.'[45] Mediated by those who represent, we consume the pain of others. But what of the production of that
pain, which is its mediation? What of its manufacture as still-shot, video,
audio, text, and so on? The organization of suffering, or of any condition,
into a coherent set of images or narratives is always achieved through the
essentialization of that image, and comes at the expense of the image that
is not captured or broadcast. For example, Youssou N'Dour has observed
that our knowledge of Africa is divided into three images: poverty, AIDS,
and war. Within that triad of this apparently quintessential, transconti-
nental African condition, other conditions and experiences, for example,
love, devotion, respect, compassion, assistance, forgiveness, spirituality,
health, joy, and celebration are subsumed or sidelined by the exclusive
focus on suffering and conflict.[46] The production of such impressions reifies
pain, and makes voyeurs of us all in the process. We regard the pain of
others – others' disasters – as spectacles.[47] And it is the pain of others that
provides the skeletal structure of our research agendas. We organize it carefully into a series of events, into a teleology of meaning, into an archive of
information, into a war which is given a proper name and a span of dates
like a human life: 1939–45, for example. There, the nameless man on the
street turns round as the tour bus lumbers up the side of a hill on a road
that is an infamous destroyer of transmissions. He turns to regard the
shaded window behind which the scholars stare at him with impunity. It
is the hottest summer on record. Sweat courses down his back. Alphonso
Lingis remembers:

> Facing me, the other exposes to me the defenselessness of his or her eyes. I
> saw the other's look, agile and penetrating, measuring the distances, surveying
> the obstacles, disengaging the objectives – the dominant and wary eyes of
> someone protecting, supplying himself or herself. But when they turn to me,

their direction wavers and their objectives disappear. They turn to me like a liquid pool waiting for unforeseeable disturbances. They are more naked than the flesh without pelt or hide, without clothing, divested even of their initiative and position. ... The eyes turned to me are denuded even of any information they had picked up and which could be scrutinized, of any form I could manipulate. Their nudity exposes them to whatever message I may want to impose, whatever offense I can contrive.[48]

The bus arrives at the top of the hill, and turns onto the road that leads to Mostar. The famous bridge is the next stop on the agenda. People dwell in there, it is said. The bridge over the Neretva River whose destruction became emblematic of the war in Bosnia was reopened with great fanfare on 23 July 2004.[49] For Chris Patten, external affairs commissioner for the European Union, the reopening of the bridge was 'a symbol of hope for the future, which [he] passionately believe[d] will see Bosnia-Herzegovina as a full member of the family of the European Union.'[50] A number of European dignitaries were on hand at the reopening ceremony. Prince Charles was there. But the Canadian Broadcasting Corporation reported that: 'Most citizens of Mostar were barred from the site. They watched the festivities at home on television.'[51] The Bosnian man on the street, who had been momentarily distracted by the lumbering tour bus, moves on into his day, unaware that his countenance will appear in a slide show on another continent in just a few weeks. His name will not matter. He will not be invited to celebrate the reconstruction of the bridge that spanned the breadth of his own river. He has been disqualified from attending the ceremonies because of his untrustworthiness and his violence. He is not (yet) European enough.

The issue of trust here is not that which asks whether the representation being made is an accurate one – whether an instance of reality can be captured and transmitted in any kind of faithful way. Rather, the issue of trust raises questions of ethics; it asks us to understand that our representations can never be more than what is said of them – that they can never be more than how they are received, regardless of whether or not they are haunted by the soul of the represented in some intangible way. I cannot represent you because you lie outside of my experience – outside of my skin – there is no possibility of drawing you with ink or with words. To paraphrase Alphonso Lingis, when I leave your presence, I cannot reinstate you in a representation because my visit has taken nothing from you.[52] My representation of you is thus not a representation at all, but a simulation masquerading as you – a skin with no soul. My estimation of you remains marked by an inescapable violence. The reason I snipped Petar Kujundžić's photograph out of the *Globe and Mail* on 29 June 1998 and carried it around with me all these long years is not outside of violence just because I did it out of love.

# On representation

NOTES

1   Maurice Blanchot, *The Writing of the Disaster*, Ann Smock, trans. (Lincoln, NE: University of Nebraska Press, 1995), p. 18.
2   Photo by Petar Kujundžić, *Globe and Mail*, 29 June 1998, p. A10.
3   Susan Sontag, *Regarding the Pain of Others* (New York: Farrar, Straus, and Giroux, 2003), p. 24.
4   I should include my own goals in this analysis. My reasons for cutting this photograph out of the *Globe and Mail* on 29 June 1998 and my discussion of it here are not outside of the violence of representation.
5   For a discussion of the need of the caption, see Sontag, *Regarding the Pain of Others*, p. 29.
6   Kujundžić would have been well-advised to travel through Kosovo on Vidovdan if his goal was to capture an instance of political violence on film. The day marks the anniversary of the now infamous battle of Kosovo in 1389, which is identified as the beginning of the fall of medieval Serbia to the expanding Ottoman Empire. It was on Vidovdan in 1989 that Slobodan Milošević, attending a rally on the 600th anniversary of the battle, cloaked himself in the Serb nationalism that is widely regarded as an important political mile-marker on the road to war in Yugoslavia.
7   Sontag, *Regarding the Pain of Others*, p. 14.
8   In March 2004, a widespread riot in Kosovo resulted in the razing of several monasteries and the murder of more than 30 people.
9   Sontag, *Regarding the Pain of Others*, p. 20.
10   Jean Baudrillard, *Impossible Exchange* (London; New York: Verso, 2001), pp. 145–146.
11   *Ibid.*, p. 144.
12   For a full account of the politics of spectacle associated with war photography, see Susan Sontag, *Regarding the Pain of Others*.
13   Baudrillard, *Impossible Exchange*, pp. 5–6.
14   *Ibid.*, p. 12.
15   See Baudrillard, *Impossible Exchange*.
16   But the point here is that the distance between us cannot be closed. In the translation of the text, I am still assuming that the priest can give permission for my own ethical intention. The impossibility of this possibility haunts me, because I have to choose, and I do not know which way to decide.
17   Baudrillard, *Impossible Exchange*, p. 8.
18   Levinas quoted in Jacques Derrida, *The Work of Mourning* (Chicago: University of Chicago Press, 2001), p. 204.
19   This is also reflective of the fundamental bankruptcy of meaning more generally – with the radical emptiness of all signifiers and all signification.
20   Priest!
21   Alphonso Lingis, *Foreign Bodies* (New York: Routledge, 1994), p. 175.
22   *Ibid.*, p. 175.
23   Kujundžić may have. I cannot know from here. Whether or not he did, however, does not void the value of the question.
24   A Sarajevo daily.
25   See David Campbell's literature review in *National Deconstruction*.
26   It is somewhat ironic that I, the voyeuristic consumer of images of other people's bodies, am immersed in a culture where making eye contact with strangers is restricted to the perverted, the ill-intentioned, and the insane. It is a particularly interesting phenomenon that I, acculturated not to stare under any circumstances, stare so shamelessly

at the bodies of others whom I feel sure cannot see me looking. Is this not also the promise of pornography? That one may shame without shaming?

27  Sontag, *Regarding the Pain of Others*, p. 72.

28  Lingis, *Foreign Bodies*, p. 175.

29  So past is past that Stalingrad has even reverted to the use of its earlier name: Volgograd – although we might be able to appreciate that there are good reasons for this reversion.

30  Caputo, *Against Ethics*, p. 69.

31  Sontag, *Regarding the Pain of Others*, p. 79.

32  Caputo, *Against Ethics*, p. 30.

33  Jean Baudrillard, *Simulacra and Simulation* (Ann Arbor, MI: University of Michigan Press, 1995), p. 53.

34  *Ibid.*, p. 49.

35  Jacques Derrida, *Aporias*, Thomas Dutoit, trans. (Stanford, CA: Stanford University Press, 1993), p. 22.

36  David O'Donoghue, 'Holocaust Tourism', *Sunday Business Post*, January 13, 2002.

37  *Ibid.*

38  Baudrillard, *Simulacra*, p. 50.

39  *Ibid.*; italics in original.

40  *Ibid.*, p. 50.

41  Jean Baudrillard, *Simulacra and Simulations*, in Mark Poster, ed., *Selected Writings* (Stanford, CA: Stanford University Press, 2001), p. 169.

42  *Ibid.*, p. 170.

43  Alphonso Lingis, *Trust* (Minneapolis, MN: University of Minnesota Press, 2004), p. ix; italics in original.

44  Some might object on the grounds that it is the scholar imprisoned on the tour bus that is the outsider moving through the Other's territory, space, politics, and culture. One might remember that Security and Defence Forum (SDF) tour participants are prevented from 'entering' the unmediated Bosnia by their own tour guides, and not by locals. In other words, the scholar/tourist is welcome to exit the bus. The Bosnian, however, is not welcome on the bus, which has thus become a notable site of exclusion.

45  Baudrillard, *Simulacra*, in Poster, p. 173.

46  Youssou N'Dour, comments at Harbourfront, Toronto, 6 July 2004. This is not to suggest, however, that suffering, including poverty, AIDS, and war, should be ignored.

47  Sontag, *Regarding the Pain of Others*.

48  Lingis, *Foreign Bodies*, p. 171.

49  That the Mostar bridge became symbolic of 'the senseless violence of the war in Bosnia' is interesting and interestingly incongruous considering that the bridge was destroyed by Croat tank fire and that the war in Bosnia is widely viewed in retrospect as having been most violent between Serbs and Muslims. See 'Historic Bridge Reopens in Bosnia', CBC Online, 23 July 2004: www.cbc.ca/story/world/national/2004/07/23/bosnia_bridge040723.html accessed on 23 July 2004.

50  *Ibid.*

51  *Ibid.*

52  Lingis, *Trust*, p. 198.

# 5

# *On responsibility*

What [causes] my unease [is] not the implicit claim that denial itself is an understandable response to evil (this is something that Primo Levi and others have reported to be a fact about the camps), but rather the notion that doing so actually works, and without remainder: Auschwitz will disappear if only we close our eyes and laugh hard enough.[1]

In the December 2003 International Criminal Tribunal for the Former Yugoslavia (ICTY) judgment against Stanislav Galić, Trial Chamber Judge Rafael Nieto-Navia offered his dissenting opinion on the question of whether the Tribunal possessed the jurisdiction to determine whether the charge of 'inflicting terror on a civilian population' was, in fact, an actual, documented crime for which the accused could be legally prosecuted and convicted. Nieto-Navia explained that, before reaching a verdict, he had expected 'the Trial Chamber to confirm whether such an offence existed as a form of liability under international customary law, attracting individual criminal responsibility under that body of law.'[2] Nieto-Navia's findings indicated that the charge exceeded the legal framework within which the Tribunal understood itself to be operating. In this finding, the question of whether the actions of Stanislav Galić had caused feelings and experiences of terror in the civilian population of Sarajevo (the ethical issue) was subordinated to the question of whether the ICTY had the appropriate precedent in place to convict the accused for a crime whose juridical facticity was in doubt (the legal issue). Nieto-Navia's dissent on the issue of legality was based on the observation that 'the Tribunal cannot create new criminal offences, but may only consider crimes already well-established in international humanitarian law.'[3] Thus, in Nieto-Navia's statement, we see the trace of a murky grey zone emerging between ethics and law; we see the incongruity between what can count as established fact and what cannot – between the formed and the formless. Nieto-Navia's point is that it is not alright for the ICTY to develop prosecutable offences as they go, that this undermines the possibility of a fair trial, at least insofar as Galić could not have understood his actions as crimes if those crimes were not identified somewhere in the constitutive texts of jurisprudence before he committed them.[4] Thus, the question of whether Galić indeed contributed to experiences of terror among Sarajevans and that of whether he could be held responsible for this highlights the fissure that runs between the issues of jurisprudence and those of ethics; it points to the incongruity, the contingency, the tenuous relationship between them. It points to the fact that law cannot contain ethics, nor ethics law, for these overreach and displace one another; indeed, they may at times even betray one another.[5]

For Giorgio Agamben, there is a fundamental distinction which arises clearly 'every time the borders that separate ethics from law are traced.'[6] This is in part because law is not at its core concerned with ethics or even with order; rather, law at its core is concerned – preoccupied, one might venture to say – with *judgment*, which is its overriding purpose: 'Judgment is in itself the end and this, it has been said, constitutes its mystery, the mystery of the trial.'[7] The fissure that runs between ethics and law is not simply a separation of the concepts and practices that are associated with each, but points rather to the ways in which each has contaminated the other, such that those practices that are associated with law (i.e. the trial of Stanislav Galić) are simultaneously equated with the pursuit of the ethical. An exploration of this fissure, then, reveals not a neat division between binary positions, but rather the existence of a dwelling space in contravention of the logic of binaries that has got us this far in law and in ethics in the first place. For Derrida, this is expressed as the asymmetrical relationship between law and justice. Law is not justice because it provides prescription for action and is structurally incapable of taking into account the contingency – the particularity – of justice. Justice is fundamentally reliant on undecidability and on *différance* – the paradoxical imperative associated with both the requirement to defer the decision, and the simultaneous urgency that calls for an immediate response.

For Derrida, undecidability is precisely the condition of decision because it draws attention to the simultaneity of at once needing to make a decision and not being able to. Here there is an aporia – a virtual impasse – between the requirement to decide and the inability to know what to choose. Derrida argues that: 'The undecidable remains caught, lodged, at least as a ghost – but an essential ghost – in every decision, in every event of decision. Its ghostliness deconstructs from within any assurance of presence, any certitude or any supposed criteriology that would assure us of the justice of a decision, in truth of the very event of a decision.'[8] Undecidability, then, is not the oscillation between two possibilities, two

potentialities, two oppositional choices with discrete and unique consequences – for example, the choice between upholding universal principles
concerning the commission of war crimes and of allowing for particularisms
and contingencies to get in the way of that. Were this the case, then a
decision as such would not be a decision at all, but rather the application
of a rule or principle – an automatic, technological server-side application
that 'might be legal; [but] would not be just.'[9] Rather, undecidability points
to the impossibility of decision without ordeal – without suffering – without
that any number of possibilities may be chosen and may injure, or may be
ignored and injure worse. The problem for Nieto-Navia lay in his observation that the equation did not add up.

When the application of rule – when the law – is recognized as contingent and is loosened, the terrain becomes radically undecidable and the
moment of decision becomes a madness that has no anchoring rationality.
The legal precedent has flown out the window and we are left, empty-
handed. For Derrida, the idea of justice is always what is just beyond reach,
but which is always reached for. It 'seems to be irreducible in its affirma-
tive character, in its demand for gift without exchange, without circulation,
without recognition or gratitude, without economic circularity, without
calculation and without rules, without reason and without rationality.'[10]
At the same time, there is a need to resist locating the idea(s) of justice
along a continuum of metaphysical preordination – it cannot be reduced
to law and regulative ideals (i.e. in the Kantian sense), or to a Jewish formulation of messianism or a Christian eschatological vigilance. For Derrida,
justice is always 'to come' – it is always in the process of arriving, yet it
does not arrive. If, having arrived, justice grows complacent and is made
to work for the law alone, it ceases to be justice. This is why justice, like
democracy, is always in transit, always on its way, arriving in a future
that is never present. If it is said to have arrived it is reduced to the realm
of bounded political practice, rather than announcing an ethos of politics.
But justice, even if always 'to come', is not a bounded, true-but-veiled
phenomenon awaited in fear and trembling. Justice is precisely that which
takes place in the pain of the undecidable. Reading the undecidable as pain,
as suffering, as a madness that bathes the decision in human sweat and
tears, illustrates the urgency of the need for decision – the need for justice.
'Not only *must* we calculate, negotiate the relation between the calculable
and the incalculable . . . but we *must* take it as far as possible, beyond the
place we find ourselves and beyond the already identifiable zones of morality
or politics or law.'[11] We must take it beyond and despite where we find
ourselves. Moreover, the urgency of decision means that we must begin
calculating where we are. Deconstruction pays no homage to the mystical
authority of beginning. We are urged to begin where we are; in the middle

of a sentence, in the middle of the street, in the middle of a war or a trial proceeding. Beginning where we are indicates that there is no teleology of existence but only moments that are characterized by their urgency in the present – that are characterized by their vocal awareness of 'now'.

For Derrida, in order for a decision to be 'just', the law must be simultaneously preserved and suspended. We might say that instead of simply subjecting the case to the law, the law must also be subjected to the case; the law must also be reinterpreted and reinvented, reconstituted and reconstructed in each instance. For Derrida, 'you can't simply call for justice without trying to embody justice in the law. So justice is not simply outside the law, it is something which transcends the law, but which, at the same time, requires the law . . . [s]o even if justice is foreign to the process, it nevertheless requires the process, it requires political action, rhetoric, strategies, etc.'[12] Yet law sometimes requires suspension, not because it will always marginalize some people some, or even all, of the time (it will), but because 'law' itself claims an ultimacy that comes at the expense of what it sees as falling under its power, which is essentially everything and everyone. The law is a principle that lives for itself – it is always the law that needs protecting, upholding, and not the individual who is trapped by, beneath, and within the law. If the individual is what is upheld, then the law finds itself in another position, or at least needs to engage in a competition of justification. The concept of difference/deferment implies both a deferral of decision – a detour or delay – and the heterogeneity of difference associated with the ethical demand that politics proceeds immediately, without delay. Here, the aporia lies in the ultimate impossibility of the simultaneity. For Kierkegaard, the law must be suspended in order that faith can enter in, and the Other must be regarded with perfect faith – faith that he will not destroy us *even though he may*. The law is its own power, reposing on its own manufactured authority, which is reproduced through the successful, and even the unsuccessful, exercise of that authority. In this system, the transgression serves as an alibi for law, just as evil stands in as the faithful alibi of good.

It is one of the basic philosophical tenets of Western thought that 'good' and 'evil' are discreet, mutually exclusive categories of being. This is reflected in the very structure of our legal systems where complainants are usually understood as victims and defendants as the perpetrators of crimes. This correspondence between victim and perpetrator equally suggests a set of discreet categories which does not readily allow for ambiguity, though it may allow for a degree of mitigation with respect to the crime committed in a legal sense. Indeed, everything from humanitarian relief to the constitution of tribunals such as the ICTY relies fundamentally on the ability to identify and demarcate victims from perpetrators. This must be achieved definitively and purposefully, and must immobilize the categories that it constitutes.

Similarly, the law recognizes a clear distinction between perpetrator and victim; it holds that neither bleeds into the other. It requires a binary logic that insulates both good and evil from the excessive scrutiny that would reveal the presence of the grey zones. It would have me obscure or deny the fissures that appear between the (front) lines, the lack of clarity that is inherent in the reading of events and in events themselves. And while the fissures are the beginning of the recognition of the unfolding of politics, they are also the herald of danger, because it can be pretended that there are, in fact, no gaps at all, or, it can be accepted that there are gaps, but they can be filled in as power politics would have them filled in – the filling of a vacuum, a void for the reinscription of the 'line in the sand' between killers and killed.[13] Voids and vacuums are heralds of danger. When we start talking of voids and vacuums, we answer with the language of occupation, penetration, filling up – with the language of ontology – of 'thingness'. The widening of the fissures in the plaster edifice of law provides the space for undecidability; it is the beginning of politics, of ethics, but it is also a site of danger. It is the same inherent possibility that democratic processes can pave the way for absolutism, internment camps, and annihilation. It is the fundamental paradoxical fate of democratic thinking: there is always danger lurking just inside the space of the possible.[14] So the issue is not that of whether the law can ever give justice (it can, but at the expense of other justices), but of whether the law provides justice because it is law, or because it, like other applications, may sometimes deliver what one would not imagine of it and which would thus exceed our expectations of it. Law, then, is not in simultaneity with justice – justice may happen under the law, despite the law, but it does not always require law to unfold and, in fact, law may hinder its coming. Nevertheless, the relationship between law and justice may also lay the groundwork whereupon one is destroyed by the other. Thus, the violence in Bosnia is subsumed by the Tribunal which was set up in very specific ways to prosecute very specific iterations of it. Law has the potential to destroy justice by suggesting that justice has been served by the legal application of a rule or principle. Agamben notes that, at Nuremburg: 'Despite the necessity of the trials and despite their evident insufficiency (they involved only a few hundred people), they helped to spread the idea that the problem of Auschwitz had been overcome. The judgments had been passed, the proofs of guilt definitively established.'[15]

It is the very ordering of Auschwitz into a trajectory of 'meaning' that creates the 'problem' as a singular thing that can be, and thus is claimed to be, overcome. 'May it never happen again' is the watch phrase while 'it' happens again all over the place, all the time, everywhere, as the basic form and formulaic of our contemporary political existence. The distillation of the events associated with the Shoah and other instances of mass murder into coherent, teleological narratives subsumes both contingency and undecidability beneath the technologies of inevitability as it works to normalize experiences of trauma.[16] It is precisely this which leads us to understand the frenzied need to frame the disaster in comprehensible terms – the need to reconcile the disaster with the knowable, the calculable, with that which can be analyzed and overcome. The Hague, the trials at Nuremburg and in Arusha evince the need to arrange events into a historical narrative that can be thus exceptionalized so that ethics does not founder on the shore of absolute ruin. It also poses a binary in the assignation of 'good' and 'evil' associated with specific groups of actors. It requires victims and perpetrators, prisons, prosecutors, spectators who can serve as witnesses and give testimony. These categories cannot be too messy, lest the story become so confused that it can no longer be told in any reasonably comprehensible way. One might be, yet cannot be, relegated to silence.

The recognition that there is a fundamental lack of clarity in the space between victim and perpetrator leads to an appreciation of the inadequacy of both ethics and the legal frameworks which are said to embody them. In the case of the Shoah, for example, camp inmates were implicated in their own destruction through their incorporation into administrative apparatuses, 'thus confronting them with the hopeless dilemma whether to send their friends to their death, or to help murder other men who happened to be strangers, and forcing them, in any event, to behave like murderers.'[17] Here, in the moment, 'the distinguishing line between persecutor and persecuted, between the murderer and his victim, is constantly blurred.'[18] It is the very reduction of the individual to an abject state of universality, to 'bare life', to one who can be killed, but not sacrificed, according to Giorgio Agamben, that characterizes both the persecutor and persecuted.[19] It is thus that Hannah Arendt identifies in Adolf Eichmann what she has referred to as 'the banality of evil'.[20] The identification of banality in this sense is not that which would trivialize the camps and the politics that gave rise to them, but is rather the mind-numbing realization that Eichmann was himself simply an unthinking 'cog' lodged in a machinery of total domination. The identification of Eichmann as the automatonic agent of totalitarianism par excellence confirms for Arendt her earlier recognition of the superfluity of men that emerges from systems of total domination. If individuality is undermined to the extent that all men can be replaced in such a system, each with another, then Eichmann's 'evil' is not unique to him as a moral agent in the midst of a machinery of horror. Indeed, if, as Hannah Arendt argues, all men in totalitarian systems can be replaced, each with another, then Eichmann's deeds might just as easily have been committed – as they were – by countless other men, who can be thus understood simultaneously as both everyone and no one. As Arendt notes: 'Men insofar as they are more than animal reaction and fulfillment of functions are entirely superfluous to totalitarian regimes. Totalitarianism strives not toward despotic rule over men, but toward a system in which men are superfluous.'[21] For Arendt, this bare fact constitutes the attempt at normalization; it is the reason why Eichmann defies the ethical categories of good and evil that are designed to exceptionalize his deeds. In this liminal space, the relationship between murdered and murderer blurs, the executioner becomes the victim and the victim the executioner, and both together become fundamentally otherwise than what they appear to be before the law as intentioned agents and objects. For Agamben, this is the place where: 'A gray, incessant alchemy in which good and evil and, along with them, all the metals of traditional ethics reach their point of fusion.'[22]

For Berel Lang, the sense of Eichmann's unexceptionality is a herald of danger – a warning that those who do not stand vigil against racism, anti-Semitism, and hatred of all types will fall into complacency as whole peoples fall under the machinery of elimination. But, as Arendt so aptly notes: 'The insane mass manufacture of corpses is preceded by the historically and politically intelligible preparation of living corpses.'[23] For Lang, if these processes are seen as unexceptional, then there is no way to stand guard against them politically – there is no reason to highlight them as any more or less problematic than any other political processes. However, the identification of such processes as unexceptional does not in itself trivialize those processes. Indeed, the normality and even predictability with which these processes take place are precisely the grounds on which the everyday needs to be opposed. To illustrate this, Giorgio Agamben recalls a passage by Primo Levi wherein the 'special teams' at Auschwitz were engaged in a soccer match against members of the SS. For Agamben, this match is not to be read as 'a brief pause of humanity in the middle of an infinite horror.' Instead, Agamben views the match – a moment of normality – as the 'true horror of the camp.'[24] It is precisely this desire to normalize, to incorporate that which defies incorporation, that attempts to insulate us – the spectators – from all of the horrors that we have perpetrated, witnessed, continue to witness, and dismiss. For Agamben, this is the very iteration of the 'shame of those who did not know the camps and yet, without knowing how, are spectators of that match, which repeats itself in every match in our stadiums, in every television broadcast, in the normalcy of everyday life. If we do not succeed in understanding that match, in stopping it, there will never be hope.'[25] And so, while the Shoah is exceptionalized through a range of narratives intended to cordon off and spotlight 'the event' as fundamentally unique, events such as those which took place at Tuol Sleng and in the cities and villages of Rwanda continue to take place with little commentary and no intervention. The political and mechanical technologies of death that made possible the Shoah are not exceptional. They make possible the camp, the gas chamber, the killing field, the torture chamber, the electric chair, the firing squad, the tenuous, torturous limbo of Guantanamo Bay and Abu Ghraib. We are part of the politics of normalization with respect to mass violence and the normality of our everyday lives bears witness against us to that effect.

Yet, even as I strive to escape it, at the same time, I have followed the letter of the law – I am implicated in power and power relations simply in the act of writing, and of representing. I am implicated in occupation, penetration, filling up the democratic void in the former Yugoslavia – in the identification of that space as a fundamental lack – lack of democracy, lack of humanity, lack of compassion, lack of love. I forge into that space marked and marred by the clarity of what has already been decided. I project myself into that space – that politically bankrupt and ethically empty space. Trinh Minh-ha proceeds with the painful awareness that her writing – the luxury within which her ability to write unfolds – is always made possible by another woman's labour. [26] My writing was made possible by my estimation of Stojan Sokolović's moral bankruptcy, and that is a price that he subsequently pays. This is why the law is not enough – it stretches too thin to accommodate what it claims to represent and in many cases leaves its Others (and thus its Selves) painfully exposed to injustice despite the rumour of its best attempts to mitigate or even overcome this.

The law is also a representation – a representation of justice that is painfully simulated – the 'real' subsumed and obliterated beneath the simulacrum. Indeed, all writing is representation, and there is no better organized writing than that undertaken by the law or by the academy. But this should not be mistaken for a successful species of authenticity. Stojan Sokolović could not provide a more authentic representation of that of which he spoke than could I, even though different positions empower different people to say different things. While the problem rests on the question of who is empowered to speak and about what, the putative claim to have an authoritative interpretation that marginalizes other narratives and accounts and that is subsequently called upon to legitimize certain actions, which are also presented as responses to particular 'realities', remains equally suspect.

But somewhere along the way, decisions have to be made. How shall we proceed? It is, to be sure, a difficult question, but one in which I am aware that I have comparably little to lose. If the ethical moment is in fact in that liminal space, does my ability to engage ethically within the interpretations of Stojan Sokolović's narrative depend on his own ability or failure to engage ethically with that of which he spoke? There is confusion and peril here, because I cannot know and because Stojan Sokolović is himself implicated in power relations in the inevitable selection process in which he engaged and through which he certainly must have forgotten, privileged, or marginalized something just as I am sure that I must have forgotten, privileged, or marginalized something in my own interpretation of his accusation. The task of navigating this question turns on the understanding that one does not speak for always and forever – that one does not speak authoritatively, with authenticity or certitude, but rather that one speaks only for the moment, from a nameable place that is always implicated and contained within a particular space and time. At the same time, one does not have the right to lay claim to that particular position as one of authenticity, or to suggest that what one says from one position encompasses all that can be said, in perpetuity. My position is always fractal and fragmented, always subjected to ambiguity and ambivalence, always just a moment away from disaggregation and dissolution. I respond here, now, from this position. I pause, I back up, I look elsewhere, I move on, I try again.

## Identification

The identification associated with identification – with naming – underwrites claims to exceptionality. There are inevitable fissures between witnessing, experiencing, feeling and thinking and what can be said about that witnessing, experiencing, feeling and thinking – what can be meant by it. These fissures yet widen between Stojan Sokolović's representation and my interpretation of that representation (my own representation of that representation, as it were), as they widen yet further between my interpretation and my rendering. However, the identification of these series of gaps does not need to presuppose the existence of an *in situ* narrative wherein each telling and retelling constitutes a *telos* of movement further from the 'truth'. In other words, Stojan Sokolović is not once removed from the truth so that I am twice removed from the truth so that the one who reads this text is thus thrice removed from the truth. Rather, we have entered into a sphere of radical indeterminacy, where the sign or symbol can never stand as a faithful representation of the real; there is no longer a billboard announcing the substance, a shorthand for marking, pointing to, and communicating reality – a paid advertisement for the 'is', 'has been', or 'will be'.

For Baudrillard: 'The irruption of radical uncertainty into all fields and the end of the comforting universe of determinacy' is not a problematic phenomenon awaiting eradication through the application of a security rule or principle, but is rather the fundamental rejection of security itself – the awareness that continuity-based thinking announces and thereby betrays 'the theological form of our superiority.'[27] In other words, the apparent teleological, seamless progress of knowledge and narrative is made so only because it is the replacement God of our post-politico-Christian faith. The gaps between narratives herald the instantiation of new narratives that may or may not have anything to do with one another; even if they share the same name, the naming itself does not indicate that there is a necessary commonality between them beyond the correlation inevitably produced by the act of naming and the meaning that is accordingly assigned thereto. But even this is fraught with trouble.

For example, the adjective *post*, Rene Girard points out, cannot be used independently in English. It can only modify that which it purports to describe as coming 'after', and so the referent of *post* is always the thing that we strive to overcome, but which ever remains in our sights, sites, and cites – serving to keep ever-present the noun which it simultaneously both rejects and fundamentally relies on for signification and meaning.[28] The English (derived from the Latin, as opposed to the Greek, or the Sanskrit, or the Hebrew) word *post* keeps us in line, quite literally; it keeps us in line and in continuity with linear conceptions of history, culture, and time, even as those modified nouns strive to overcome that which still signifies and defines them. The *post* holds the line as fence posts and signposts and mile-markers. Postmodernism, poststructuralism, postcolonialism, post-Christianity, and so on, seem thus ever unable to shed the remnants (the nouns) which are their legacy and which continue to frame the debates within the parameters set out by proper scholarly practices. Despite our attempts to overcome, resist, subvert, and reconstitute the world of these nouns: 'The past is the substantive part of the recycled label, the hated referent which stubbornly reasserts an independent existence.'[29] Ironically, this labelling legitimizes precisely that which it claims to have moved beyond. For Michael Shapiro, 'while speech can counter the violence of language by disrupting language's pretension to conceptual mastery, it must inevitably, to remain intelligible, do some violence and thereby affirm aspects of what it resists.'[30]

In Serbo-Croatian, the word *post* means *fast* (as opposed to *feast*) – as in a religious fast, constituted and marked by a set of ritualistic restrictions concerning what one must do (such as reciting certain prayers) and/or what one must avoid doing (such as eating certain foods). The verb *to fast – postati* – indicates a restriction of action wherein one consciously limits oneself –

restrains oneself – denies oneself – in deference to the doctrinal require-
ments of a particular canon – a 'law' that is teleologically and universally
(that is, intercommunally) understood. The concept of the fast is a useful
one for exploring those very disciplinary practices that are visited upon us
by that which precedes the Anglo-Latin *post*. The language of scholarship
is a ritualized language of fasts – a language of *posts* – a language of self-
imposed sparseness and scarcity that regards the world of human politics
and interactions as a phenomenon that can be apprehended, nailed down,
dissected while living, and rendered as a knowable whole – as a phenomenon that can and must be squeezed into the narrow confines associated with meaningful narrative form – with history. The social scientific
project – the methodological project – regards difference as deviation, non-
adherence as theoretical and methodological blasphemy, and blasphemy as
profoundly threatening to our ability to identify what counts as knowledge.
Both social science and Christianity have their core canons – their ritualized languages, forms, and formulaics, and both promise what amounts to
essentially the same thing: epistemological salvation through certainty.[31]
The image of the religious fast evokes images of piety, devotion, and self-
discipline. In most cases, it also invokes the imagery of power, position, and
influence: the keepers of the canon – the priests and the scholars – set an
example (ideally) for others to follow: self-denial with the greater goal of the
institution and maintenance of a like-minded or same-oriented community,
which is in turn canonized and cryogenized into cold systems – into cooling
systems. The power to discipline is supplemented crucially by the power
to excommunicate – by the power to excise an offending member from
the spiritual and political community. As William Connelly notes:

> There are, indeed, parallels between sixteenth-century Christian definitions of
> internal otherness and the range of contemporary orientations to academic
> otherness among secular social scientists. There have been shifts in the locus
> of faith, in the degree to which faithfulness is demanded, and in the treatment
> of new heretics, but the discursive strategies by which the core elements of
> faith are protected reflect a certain consistency. . . . [t]hese microstrategies of
> academic containment, like their world-historical predecessors, reveal how
> fragile the established structure of faith is, how compelling its maintenance is
> to the identities of the faithful, how difficult it is to keep the faith by demon-
> stration, reason, and evidence alone, how indispensable a discursive field of
> contrasts, threats, and accusations is to its internal organization.[32]

*Postati* – derived from a solely ecclesiastical form – governs behaviour in
a strictly enclosed and circular repetition of time in an identically idealized
space. Both the Latin *post* and the Slavic *post*, then, set up in a temporal
way the terms of engagement as a relationship with a rigid, linear past
that has already laid out its plan for the future. In this way, the Latin *post*

is set against the signifier of the Slavic *post* – the post against the post, so to speak – the possibility against the possibility or, in this case, the possibility against the signifier and, by extension, against the signified.

Derrida employs the French word *glas* – invoking a death knell, a tolling bell (*never send to know for whom the bell tolls*) – a coming in and a going out. In Serbian, *glas* translates as *voice*; it invokes tone and intonation, phonemes and morphemes, inflection; the signifier against the signified. It invokes voice and language, publications, like *Glas Srpski*[33], the *Serbian Voice*, as though there is only one, and that it should bear a proper name. The *glas* of *glas* is the death of voice – the mourning of the death of voice – and the death of voice is death indeed.

The danger of naming involves attributing characteristics, but it also reifies, thereby excluding what the name (necessarily) cannot capture. The Serbian name *Stojan* means that he will stand fast. The name *Holocaust*, signifying a particular techno-ideology of mass murder perpetrated against the Jews of Europe, does not readily pull into its sphere of signifiers the mass murder of Serbs, who could not stand fast, whose own bodies faltered and collapsed beneath the killing machines at Jasenovac and in mobile gassing vans – the reason why women name their sons *Stojan* – both because and despite.

The grey zone that obscures victim and perpetrator – that effects their merger into one superfluous product of totalitarianism – muddles the possibility of responsibility, which is itself a muddled conception of how to respond, as though there were only one way, to the traumas of which we are inevitably a part, though we are spatially and temporally removed from some of them. Responsibility must be more and other than the juridical category which it also implies. Responsibility reconstituted is a feeling that comes over one – awash with urgency – marked by trauma and ruin. We are all already damaged, already broken and glued back together with varying degrees of success. It is because of this shared ruin – the universal particularism of our fragmentation – that we find ourselves responsible, on first glance because of the hiding of the cracks, and on second glance because of their revealing. Responsibility takes place at a moment's notice – it grabs hold of me by the throat – it shakes me a bit – assaults me when I'm not looking (when I'm struggling not to look) – it traumatizes me absolutely. But what is required in the response is ultimately unidentifiable in any universal sense. I do not know what is asked of me, or what I should do. I cannot make a formula – a list of commandments or guidelines – that will serve as the groundwork from which obligation is able to proceed without contestation. Responsibility takes place in the here and now – right now – at this moment – and it is unrecordable as anything other than a pure event in an ever-reappearing 'now':

In appealing to me as to someone accused who can not challenge the accusation, responsibility binds me as irreplaceable and unique. It binds me as elected. To the very degree to which it appeals to my responsibility, it forbids me any replacement. As unreplaceable for this responsibility, I cannot slip away from the face of the neighbor without avoidance, or without fault, or without complexes; here I am pledged to the other without any possibility of abdication.[34]

For Levinas, responsibility to the Other takes place in the face(ing) of the Other – in marking the trace of the Other. I undergo a 'guiltless responsibility, whereby I am none the less open to an accusation of which no alibi, spatial or temporal, could clear me.'[35] I fear for the one who will be killed, who is and has been killed, but that fear also extends to the one who will kill, who has killed and who is killing still. The killer denies the face, the voice, the very existence of the Other. It is this denial which haunts the one who kills, who aids and abets, who makes possible – those of us who remain. It is the guilt of denial, the denial of guilt, which sticks in the throat of the one asked to account for the Other. It is this line of questioning that takes account of the Other as perpetrator, which provides him with the opportunity to embrace the human in the choice of his response. As James Hatley points out, God does not approach Cain after the murder of Abel in outrage and accusation. Rather, God simply asks Cain 'Where is your brother?' thereby giving him the opportunity to confess, to embrace the humanity of both his murdered brother and himself *as a murderer*. 'Where is the Other?' But the murderer, faced with the question that would provide him the opportunity to say what he had done 'pretends and then pretends that he does not pretend.'[36]

Thus answers Cain, 'Am I my brother's keeper?' Here, though, is the split second before Cain answers, wherein he is made to lie still under the question. And there is also a moment in which Stojan Sokolović is made to stand still under the accusation of, for example, the exhumation at Srebrenica, or in the midnight glow of Luminol in the detention centre at Omarska, or in the internment camps near the Karakaj crossing where the soldier in his greatcoat smoked my cigarettes in the pouring rain. Stojane, where are your neighbours? What became of them? Which of us is responsible before he who is responsible? For Levinas, it is as fearful to contemplate the persecutor as it is the persecuted. For Levinas, one must fear not only what one might do to the Other, but also what the Other might do to oneself. This is not to fear for oneself, however, but rather to fear for the other *as persecutor* in the commission of the violence. I remain responsible to the Other even as he cuts me down, because of the unbearable measure of his irresponsibility, for which I remain responsible.

## Dilemmas

Here, we find that the aporia of exclusion raises its head again. We should recall that Levinas excludes the Palestinians from the sphere of those to whom the Israeli self is responsible through his identification of their violence and their irresponsibility. Here, Levinas is making space for the particular over against the universal. For him, as for Berel Lang, the juridical state of Israel is necessary for the protection of the Jews. But once that move has been made, juridically, then persecution is solidified into a category of permanence marked on and by the performative 'body' of the state.[37] This requires the continued identification and reification of a danger and it thus instantiates the binary between which the categories of good and evil are arrayed as fundamentally oppositional. Recall the explanation provided by Levinas: '[I]f your neighbor attacks another neighbor or treats him unjustly, what can you do? Then alterity takes on another character, in alterity we can find an enemy, or at least then we are faced with the problem of knowing who is right and who is wrong, who is just and who is unjust. There are people who are wrong.'[38] For Campbell, this formulation of the Other is 'restricted to the neighbour in such a way as to keep the Palestinians outside of the reach of those to whom the "I" is responsible.'[39] One would not want to deny that this is so, that this is indeed the logical conclusion of Levinas's commentary. But Levinas here demonstrates the ease with which the Other is excised from the community of neighbours and of brothers on the basis of violence and irresponsibility. Similarly, the epithet *genocidaire* appended to the Serbian body politic serves to exclude the Serb from the list of those to whom the western, academic, inter-governmental, policy-conducting *I* is responsible. As the Bosnian Muslim undergoes a radical, violent excision from the imaginary collective of the Serbian body, so the Serb undergoes a radical and violent exclusion from the civilized community of acceptably behaved peoples. As the Jew undergoes a radical, violent excision from the European body politic, so the Palestinian is excised from the realm of those to whom the state of Israel is responsible. It is precisely this which highlights the ambiguity between perpetrators and victims, but the more important point is that in order to retain and remain within the categories of good and evil, the evil must be excised from, *and thus fundamentally supportive of*, the conception of the good. The identification of what is evil draws the cloak of goodness around the body politic ever tighter, attempting to leave no fold – no wrinkle – in which ambiguity might be seen to be dwelling.

Attention to the violence of the Other obscures the violence which is inherent in the Self and in its very construction. Furthermore, attention to particular violences obscures violences that are seen as tangential or secondary. Thus, identifying Serbs as perpetrators in Kosovo reifies both Serbs and Albanians, and it trivializes the subsequent murders of Serbs since the entry of peacekeepers in 1999. Similarly, the identification of Serbs as bearing the greatest measure of responsibility in Bosnia trivializes the forced expulsion of Krajina Serbs by Croat forces in the summer of 1995. This is not to suggest that the clearly systematic violence committed by Serbs should be ignored in favour of seeing Serbs as victims. Such a move would reproduce the binary that I am trying to disturb (because of my own sense of disturbance). Rather, the point is to recognize that categories of perpetrator and victim are not unambiguous, that the grey zone which Agamben identifies means that we cannot unproblematically elevate the particular into the universal. To do so is to recognize that none of us is wholly innocent, that there is no pure non-violence, that we are all participants in political and social practices that reify frontiers and excise what does not fit into the narrative that constitutes the myth of the righteous Self.

Attention to the violence of a singular Holocaust means that we can sometimes miss other holocausts, smaller ones, perhaps, or ones that take place in parts of the world that no one who matters cares about. The exclusive focus on one thing always marginalizes another. As Derrida notes, 'I can respond only to the one (or to the One), that is, to the other, by sacrificing that one to the other. I am responsible to any one (that is to say to any other) only by failing in my responsibility to all the others, to the ethical or political generality. And I can never justify this sacrifice, I must always hold my peace about it. Whether I want to or not, I can never justify the fact that I prefer or sacrifice any one (any other) to the other.'[40] My love for one or the other is always at the expense of one whom I have not had the opportunity to love – of one whom I have not seen. My feeding or clothing of one is made possible by my failure to do so for an-other. Levinas notes that 'to approach is to be the guardian of one's brother; to be the guardian of one's brother is to be his hostage.'[41]

In the seconds after the charge is laid (as though there is a temporal limit to undecidability), before any order could be identified and systematized and the value added calculated with the staid certainty of science, I have become a hostage – a prisoner of the prisoner I have taken.[42] Levinas stands vigil over the Holocaust, an event with a proper name which resulted in the annihilation of countless Others who bore proper names. The unwavering focus on the Holocaust also serves as a justification of the existence of the Jewish state – the pressing need for Jews to not be victims – for Jews to be secured as well as is humanly possible to be secured. It is for the protection of the Jews that the Palestinians in the Chatila and Sabra camps are exposed to their deaths. It is for the protection of Americans that Muslim men are fingerprinted, investigated, detained, deported. It is for the protection of the Serbs that the Muslims must die. It is for the protection of the internationalized narratives on Bosnia that the Serbs be virtually exclusively responsible for what happened there. Levinas has truly been called to account for his statement on the Palestinians, but he also says that '[a] person is more holy than a land, even a holy land, since, faced with an affront made to a person, this holy land appears in its nakedness to be but stone and wood.'[43] I would not sacrifice one Palestinian for the whole of the holy land. Neither would I give one Serb for Bosnia.

It is on this discourse of the 'one' – this discourse of the individual – that the edifice of ethics begins to crumble. Decisions on 'Serbs' and 'Bosnians' (as though Bosnians can't be Serbs nor Serbs Bosnians) do not take into account the proper names of those who were murdered for the perpetuation of the myth of these realities. Stojan Sokolović is subsumed and silenced beneath the narratives on Serb war crimes. Sead Sinanović and Osman Osmanović are subsumed and silenced beneath the cover of several thousand dead at Srebrenica.[44] For Sead and Osman, the identification of events in July 1995 at Srebrenica as 'the worst massacre in Europe since the Second World War' means nothing. Those are labels we add for ourselves posthumously, so to speak, to categorize and order. Men and boys hunted down and shot to death in and around Potočari did not attribute their impending violent deaths to something identified as 'the worst massacre in Europe since the . . .'. And yet, while 'Serbs' and 'Bosnians' can fit nicely into the taxonomies that designate and identify 'peoples' and 'nations', Stojan Sokolović, Sead Sinanović, and Osman Osmanović defy and subsequently destroy those categories. John Caputo argues that: 'The individual – who is, after all, very small, no more than a bit or a fragment – is more than metaphysics can handle. Philosophy founders on something quite small; it chokes on a small fragment, a bit of microeconomics.'[45]

Standing responsible to the victims of Serbs is perhaps shameful for us because of the failure of our response, but it is not philosophically or ethically difficult. Of course, we say, Kosovars are victims of ethnic cleansing; Bosnians are victims of genocide; this is a facile gesture. It costs nothing for us beyond the vague sense of guilt we feel for our ultimate lack of interest while at the same time insuring us against our own violence through the identification of Serbs as the perpetrators of violence par excellence. Our ability to identify victims as victims absolves us from further responsibility, because they are not the victims of *our* violence. Our sensibilities are moved by victimhood. It is when I become responsible to Stojan Sokolović – when I become responsible to the Serb, even in the face of what the Serb has done to the Bosnian Muslim – that the trouble begins. It is when I look into the liquid eyes of the one who has killed and recognize that my responsibility to him is as great as it is to the one who has been killed that the labyrinthine vertigo of that position spins me around. I fear for him, for what he has done, for the suffering he has caused and causes still, for the sickness he has visited upon himself and upon others.

What is responsibility? I cannot definitively say. I have been reflecting on this for several years now, and have come no closer to a conclusion. Perhaps responsibility is simply itinerant. Responsibility might involve, for example, learning to speak the language that the one who addresses you is most fluent in. Derrida sometimes complains that the first order require-ment of his texts (his responses) is the need for him to address himself to his audience in English. 'Je dois, donc, c'est ici un devoir, m'addresser à vous en anglais.' To speak the language of 'the majority', he claims, makes good juridico-ethico-political sense. English is just, for example, because it gives the foreigner the right to speak, to engage in politics (or at least in the politics of English). The right to speak and the use of the language of the majority then places us – speakers of English – on equal footing through the ability to speak with other speakers of English and, by exten-sion, to be heard and understood. Speaking the language of the majority is the law, claims Derrida, 'but it's hard to say if the law we're referring to here is that of decorum, of politeness, the law of the strongest, or the equit-able law of democracy.'[46] Stojan Sokolović and I spoke English. Almost all of our conversations were conducted in English with a few interjections here and there directed at Serbian waiters in Serbian (which is different, politically, spatially, and temporally, than saying that they were directed at Yugoslav waiters in Serbo-Croatian or Bosnian waiters in Bosnian). *Dajte kafu sa šlagom.* Bring us coffee with sweet cream. The Serbian borrows the German, which makes one to wonder whether the Serbs have their own word for sweet cream; perhaps they do but no one uses it, which is effec-tively the same thing as saying they don't have one, or that it doesn't matter whether they have one, because in any event, they don't use it. They use the German loan-word – *schlag*. (I don't know of German words that are lost in place of 'better' Serbo-Croatian ones.)

Stojan Sokolović can speak English better than I can speak Serbian, and so he, like the Serbo-German word for cream, is 'on loan' to me, seeking justice through another idiom and in a language that uses concepts, cries, and cases (*padeži*) that are not his. I ask Stojan Sokolović to explain himself to me in English, without giving him the opportunity to demand of me that I explain myself to him in Serbian. This is not an issue of purity, but of power. He is transformed from a speaker of Serbian to a speaker of English, while I remain on my side of the table, on my side of the balcony, on my side of the train compartment, untransformed and uncompromised, my place of privilege untouched and unaffected. One can say that it is just to speak the language of the majority – and Derrida tries again in English. But here, where I am writing these lines, the language of the majority is Serbian – Bosnian – Croatian. And the vast majority of my interviews were conducted in English. That is the language of power. That is power at work, masquerading as justice. To paraphrase Derrida, how can I justify my presence here speaking one particular language, rather than there speaking to others in another language?[47] How can I justify the expectation that Stojan Sokolović will (be capable of and willing to) engage with me in English? Right now, the only people who listen to Serbs speaking Serbian are other Serbs. For Derrida to stop speaking French for a moment in favour of English is not without cultural implications. For Stojan Sokolović to stop speaking Serbian in favour of English is steeped in relations of power. 'And so we have already, in the fact that I speak another's language and break with my own, in the fact that I give myself up to the other, a singular mixture of force, *justesse* and justice.'[48]

## (Finding) the Other in time

John Caputo argues that the terra firma of ethics – the clear, orderly lineage and the firm foundations that underpin western understandings and portrayals of ethics – is actually a form of fiction that is able to masquerade as truth because it has annihilated what does not fit into the teleology of the stories it tells. These stories need to be deconstructed in order to show not only where the justifications come from, but also to allow for a cutting of the net that binds conceptions of ethics so tightly. In order to provide a space for other conceptions, attempts, and approaches, there needs to be a recognition and exposure of the gaps that appear within these conceptions. These gaps are not created by deconstruction, but are already there beneath the spackling in the edifice of ethics.

For Caputo, obligation is neither beholden to nor reliant on a higher order of ethical principle, but is rather what happens between people here and now, with no discernable grand narrative connection to the history of being in philosophy. In this formula, ethics cannot contain the conception of obligation – obligation, as it were, is the undoing of ethics, in which deconstruction is also implicated. The process of deconstructing ethics unbinds obligation from ethics – liberates it from the system of ethics, which is the condition for the ability to respond to the demands of obligation. As Caputo notes, 'obligation is not anything I have brought about, not anything I have negotiated, but rather something that happens to me. Obligations do not ask for my consent. Obligation is not like a contract I have signed after having had a chance to first review it carefully and to have consulted my lawyer. It is not anything I have agreed to be a party to. It binds me. It comes over me and it binds me.'[49]

This formulation of obligation is a move that cuts through the fortress walls of ethics because it undermines ethics as the philosophical temple – as a specific sort of orientation in human interaction. When I am obligated not because the law has ordered me to be, not because there is a universal imperative to care for others, not because the social contract ordains me to be an agent of reciprocity, but because *I have been personally bound by an address in a way that cannot be escaped*, several things happen. First, I have shed the cloak of the universal language of ethics. Slipping out from underneath the universal allows me to escape the totality of representation that is involved in responding to the Other. Conceiving obligation as a feeling of responsibility empowers me to forget about understanding the Other in any universal sense, wherein I can substitute myself for the Other, while still allowing me to maintain the language of response and of responsibility. As Caputo notes: 'I cannot send myself an obligation. I find myself obliged but I cannot oblige myself, no more than I can tell myself something I do not know.'[50] In other words, obligation comes upon me and I am left undecided with the need to decide yet pressing in on me from all sides – undeferrable. Second, and related, obligation opens up and highlights the cracks in the fortress walls between the universal and the particular; it throws out the roadmap, and when there is no roadmap, we move or stand still in the dark on the basis of faith alone. We dwell, in other words, in the cracks. Third, the personal cry suspends time. It undermines the linear sense of time that forms the metaphysical foundation of western metaphysics because the cry and the response are simultaneous – and simultaneously impossible in their simultaneity. There is no possibility of cognition, interpretation, calculation, and no amount of time allotted to the 'problem' will overcome it. The impossibility is built into the call. What is more, the progression of time as a linear phenomenon is implicated in violence and in justifications for violence. As Caputo asks: 'Does it not belong to the very essence of the logic of violence that there is always already a prior, older, past offence that requires retribution, that there is no originally innocent party?'[51]

In the suspension of time – the teleological suspension of Kierkegaard's de-universalizing ethics – what emerges is only ever 'now'. Kierkegaard notes that time is a fundamentally relative temporality – an interiority. The three days it took Abraham and Isaac to get to Mount Moriah may be infinitely longer than the several thousand years that separate Kierkegaard from Abraham.[52] For Kierkegaard, the suspension of the teleology of the ethical is also the suspension – the rearticulation – of time. The ethical, then, has no immanent teleology but is itself *telos* for what lies outside of or beyond it. Ethics reposes on itself, immanently; it has nothing outside of it to justify it, and yet it serves as the universalizing basis for all human interaction. Ethics, in other words, constitutes the law. For Kierkegaard, the law must be suspended so that faith can enter in. There is no faith under the law or within the teleology of the ethical. Faith requires a stepping outside of the ethical, a teleological suspension of the ethical, a suspension of the law in favour of faith because faith is always outside the law, despite the claim of our longstanding faith *in* the law. For Kierkegaard, human calculation must be suspended in order that faith can enter in – faith in what is incomprehensible and in what is otherwise impossible. Faith enters in by virtue of the absurd. The philosophical fissure between knowledge and faith is the place where I reside – I cannot get ahead of either of them and both of them crush me down mercilessly. The relationship between knowledge and faith, however, is not dissymmetric, not oppositional, even though one must be suspended so that the other can arrive.

The identification of a cry – a particular cry – that binds me to the neighbour who has uttered the cry is taking place even as I formulate these sentences, even as you read them. The call for justice moves between time and being, between mimesis and aesthetics, between Self and Other, between truth and fiction, between scholarship and rumour, and between the possible and the impossible. The suspension of time as *telos* and trajectory – the opening up of time as an immediacy, which is its corresponding urgency – provides the framework of engagement with the Other because it retains the urgency of the need to respond without postponing it into an ever-more-distant future. The suspension of time as *telos* and trajectory does away with the messianic promise of tomorrow and leaves us only today – here – now – to respond.

But here, I cannot make the movement of faith. I can only make the movement of resignation; I can only ever be resigned but I cannot act out of pure faith, that is, out of the absurd or the preposterous. Don't I cling still to the safety net of knowledge? But faith is needed when dealing with others. We cannot know the Other's intent, or what it is that we are actually obligated to (do). The moment of the incoming of the Other – the space between the arrival of the Other and her address – is a moment of fear and trembling because I cannot know what the Other wants, or who the Other is, yet I must receive the Other with perfect faith else I will destroy the possibilities that the Other presents. And since there is no possibility of perfect faith, there is no possibility of non-violence.

The Other calls for justice just out past the water's edge. Particular Others call out – they cry out – sometimes without speaking or articulating anything at all – sometimes just with the expressions on their faces or the moisture in their eyes or the way their hands reach out before them – to supplicate, to grab hold of, to balance their fragile bodies as they run – to throw their exhausted, salt-soaked faces down on the earth – to get there before they are gotten. The cry of the Other is equally a speaking; it is equally a string of profanity in a throat full of rage. It is not the call of the Infinite that makes me sleepless, but of the particular – of those who bear proper names. The call comes only in the here and now, over a particular event, it proceeds from human throats – from living flesh and dead – from bound and binding agents. There is only a moment to respond before the ability to respond has ceased forever, but the call itself never dissipates. As Caputo argues: '[o]bligation happens. It is a fact, as it were, but it is not a necessary truth. Obligation calls, but its call is finite, a strictly earthbound communication, transpiring here below, not in transcendental space (if there is such a thing). Obligation calls, and it calls for justice, but the caller in the call is not identifiable, decidable. I cannot make it out.'[53] The caller is just past the water's edge – incoming.

## Poetics

Kierkegaard maintains that he is not a philosopher, not a scholar, not a keeper or maintainer of knowledge, not a writer nor a benefactor of any system, but rather a 'supplementary clerk' in a 'poetic and refined' sort of way. This is a task and a vocation, exclaims Caputo, that is actually manageable, and 'to which [he] was summoned by neither Being nor the Spirit, but by a pseudonym.'[54] (And I by the pseudonym of Stojan Sokolović.) The task of a supplementary clerk, reckons Caputo, is to simply add a few things here and there – a few phrases, a few lines, a few addenda and postscripts, brief essays, a few columns and scraps of poetry – to the idea of obligation, and of disaster.[55] Calling on the Derridean treatise to begin wherever we are, Caputo finds himself 'here, now; here I am; *me voici*. In the middle of a text, on the receiving end of a command, in the midst of multiple obligations. I begin from below, having lost all communication from on high. Under obligation, under a host of obligations, aswarm with them.'[56]

The simple suggestion is that ethics has been permanently suspended in favour of obligation, of obligation without ethics, of responsibility without reason, of justice without law. Here we find that: 'Deconstruction settles gently into the uneasy space between these two, quivering between the universal and the singular. It lives *inter-esse*, being-in-between, in the margins – and negotiates the difference between them.'[57] Does it quiver between the universal and the singular, or does it tremble with trembling, which reacts to 'something which has already taken place . . . and [which] threatens still[?] It suggests that violence is going to break out again, that some traumatism will insist on being repeated. As different as dread, fear, anxiety, terror, panic, or anguish remain from one another, they have already begun in the trembling, and what has provoked them continues, or threatens to continue, to make us tremble.'[58]

Faith is just this paradox, claims Kierkegaard: that judgment (the point of the law, according to Agamben) be suspended in order that we can judge – that the individual be justified over against the universal, which is a 'paradox that does not permit of mediation.'[59] The inexplicability of faith is what separates it from the law. It cannot be systematized or ordered or catalogued or tried under the law for treason. It simply comes, an obligation which I did not seek, and with which I made no deal.

> *Stojane!*
> *evo me!*[60]

The response is a form of faith because one does not know to whom or to what one is responding to. The response takes place in the moments before we know who the Other is, what she wants, and who will be injured by it. Thomas Keenan writes of the opening scene in *Hamlet* that the 'who's there?' with which the play begins betrays only that someone has arrived, but not the identity of that person or what, if anything, he wants. 'The sentry . . . seeks to make the other appear, [to] present himself. And the other has up to this point concealed himself, has arrived in the dark as an apparition, a moving question, closed in upon himself . . . wrapped in the night, hiding himself in the folds of the dark and of the question . . . The sentinel asks for an opening, for the other to unfurl and to unfold *as self*. [However, t]he double imperative – to stop and to unfold – is virtually tautalogous: to stand is to unfold, to appear as a unitary subject.'[61] The identification, and thus the constitution, of the Other as a unitary subject brings her into the realm of the law through the stabilization of the Self.[62] Before the stabilization takes place through the appearance of the Other and the sentry's inevitable identification and representational processes, the gap between the sentry and the arrival is apparent, and it constitutes a moment of faith. The sentry does not know what the arrival wants – why he has come, what he is looking for, and to whom he is beholden – yet he stands with a not-yet-formed Other in his sites. The sentinel has become a hostage to the possibility of the Other in this decision, to the possibility that the Other may require something of him that he cannot refuse.[63] For the sentinel, the arrival of the Other is the possibility of possibility – the very frontier of possibility and of responsibility. For Keenan, in turn, the frontier is 'a chance for politics, the chance of the political. It is the idiom and the possibility of the other, of the one who arrives. But it is also something terrifying, since perhaps we are – indeed, we cannot not be – the sentinels.'[64] And it is always under the cover of darkness, without the benefit of knowledge that the politics and ethics of our responsibilities are exposed as a matter of risk and of undecidability.[65]

To attempt to negotiate this frontier is to negotiate an aporia, where undecidability figures prominently. For Caputo, the clarity of decisions are obscured by a 'film of undecidability', warning that the way is not safe and that we need to proceed with caution.[66] The irruption of alternate possibilities – of alternate narratives – contributes to the dismantling of the fortress walls – of the breaching of the firewall behind which rests only chaos and disorder where we expected order and symmetry.

*Stojane!*
*evo me!*

Here I am, but only for a moment – a unitary being for only the split second in which I answer, presumably for myself, which is no coherent entity at all.

NOTES

1 Espen Hammer, 'Adorno and Extreme Evil', *Philosophy and Social Criticism*, Vol. 26, No. 4, pp. 75–93, 2000, p. 75.
2 Judgment in the Case of the Prosecutor V. Stanislav Galić, ICTY Press Release, The Hague, 5 December 2003.
3 Prosecutor V. Stanislav Galić: Separate and Partially Dissenting Opinion of Judge Nieto-Navia, para. 109.
4 While, in the absence of other mechanisms, the ICTY might be a necessary instrument for the punishment of crimes against humanity, there are a range of problems that can probably never be addressed; for example, the Tribunal has already identified who counts as a criminal as a result of the politics of representation associated with the Bosnian war. The question of whether men already 'indicted' by the international media as war criminals can hope to receive an impartial trial highlights another fissure between justice and jurisprudence. See Geoffrey Robertson, *Crimes Against Humanity: The Struggle for Global Justice* (London: Penguin-Allen-Lane, 1999), p. 282.
5 At issue here is the question of how/if the Tribunal can do justice to both Galić and those whom Galić is claimed to have terrorized. At the very least, the Tribunal should itself be answerable to he whom it demands answers of.
6 Giorgio Agamben, *Remnants of Auschwitz: The Witness and the Archive*, Daniel Heller-Roazen, trans. (New York: Zone Books, 2002), p. 22.
7 *Ibid.*, p. 19.
8 Derrida, 'Force of Law', p. 24.
9 *Ibid.*
10 *Ibid.*, p. 25.
11 *Ibid.*, p. 28.
12 Jacques Derrida, 'Hospitality, Justice and Responsibility', in Richard Kearney and Mark Dooley, eds, *Questioning Ethics: Contemporary Debates in Philosophy* (London: Routledge, 1999), p. 72.
13 The notion of a 'line in the sand' necessarily invokes the very fluidity that I am trying to query here; indeed, there can be no 'line in the sand' – sand as a medium is inherently mobile, subject to winds and change that easily shift or erase 'lines' entirely.
14 See David Campbell, 'Post-Cold War Conflict and the Failure of Democracy', in Shawna Christianson and Robert Dick, eds, *Order and Disorder: Domestic Sources of Regional*

*Instability*, Occasional Paper #31, Centre for Defence and Security Studies, University of Manitoba, February 1995. Campbell argues that: 'The uniqueness of democracy lies in the fact that the locus of power becomes an *empty* place: popular sovereignty is a ground for authority, but it is a ground that is not permanently "grounded", as no person, group, or other authority can permanently appropriate the place of power (p. 116) . . . [and while] political indeterminacy can be hijacked by fundamentalist strategies and movements, it is also what allows for the disturbances and denaturalisations of the ethos of democracy.' (p. 135)

15  Agamben, *Remnants*, p. 19.

16  See Jenny Edkins, *Trauma and the Memory of Politics* (Cambridge: Cambridge University Press, 2003), especially Chapter 1.

17  Hannah Arendt, 'The Origins of Totalitarianism', in Peter Baehr, ed., *The Portable Hannah Arendt* (New York: Penguin Books, 2000), p. 133.

18  *Ibid.*

19  See Giorgio Agamben, *Homo Sacer: Sovereign Power and Bare Life* (Stanford, CA: Stanford University Press, 1998).

20  See Hannah Arendt, *Eichmann in Jerusalem: A Report on the Banality of Evil* (New York: Penguin, 1964).

21  Arendt, 'Origins of Totalitarianism', p. 137.

22  Agamben, *Remnants*, p. 21.

23  Arendt, 'Origins of Totalitarianism', p. 128.

24  Agamben, *Remnants*, p. 26.

25  *Ibid.*

26  Trinh T. Minh-ha, *Framer Framed* (New York: Routledge, 1992), p. 73.

27  Baudrillard, *Impossible Exchange*, pp. 8–9.

28  Rene Girard, 'Literature and Christianity: A Personal View', *Philosophy and Literature*, Vol. 23, No. 1, 1999, pp. 32–43, pp. 32–33.

29  *Ibid.*, pp. 32–33.

30  Shapiro, *Ethics of Encounter*, p. 67.

31  It is interesting to note here that the word 'post' is virtually identical in nearly all modern Slavic languages, rooted in the Old Church Slavonic – the originary bearer of all Slavic languages, if we can speak of such a thing – but Old Church Slavonic, unlike Latin, is at its heart an ecclesiastical language, its written Glagolitic script formed specifically for the Christian conversion of the Slavic speaking peoples of east Europe – an ecclesiastical gift and curse from two nomadic brothers on a mission.

32  William Connelly, *Identity/Difference*, p. 39.

33  *Glas Srpski* (The Serbian Voice) is a Banja Luka based Bosnian Serb newspaper.

34  Levinas, *Of God Who Comes To Mind*, p. 71.

35  Levinas, 'Ethics as First Philosophy', p. 83.

36  James Hatley, 'Beyond Outrage: The Delirium of Responsibility in Levinas's Scene of Persecution', in Eric Nelson, Antje Kapust and Kent Still, eds, *Addressing Levinas* (Evanston, IL: Northwestern University Press, 2004). Accessed on 20 June 2004 at: http://faculty.ssu.edu/~jdhatley/delirium.htm.

37  See Cynthia Weber, 'Performative States', *Études Internationales*, XXIX, 1 (1998), pp. 77–95.

38  Levinas, 'Ethics and Politics', p. 294.

39  Campbell, *National Deconstruction*, p. 180.

40  Jacques Derrida, *The Gift of Death*, David Wills, trans. (Chicago: University of Chicago Press, 1995), p. 70.

41  Levinas, *Of God Who Comes To Mind*, p. 72.

42  Johnny Clegg, *Jericho*, Capitol Records, 1990.
43  Levinas, 'Ethics and Politics', p. 297.
44  Sead Sinanović and Osman Osmanović were among the dead identified in the 2002 summary of forensic analysis associated with the exhumation of graves at Srebrenica.
45  Caputo, *Against Ethics*, p. 73.
46  Derrida, 'Force of Law', p. 5.
47  Derrida, *The Gift of Death*, p. 71.
48  Derrida, 'Force of Law', p. 16.
49  *Ibid.*, p. 7.
50  *Ibid.*, p. 26.
51  John Caputo, 'Reason, History and a Little Madness: Towards an Ethics of the Kingdom', in Richard Kearney and Mark Dooley, eds, *Questioning Ethics: Contemporary Debates in Philosophy* (New York: Routledge, 1999), p. 102.
52  Søren Kierkegaard, 'Fear and Trembling', in Hong and Hong (eds/trans.), *Fear and Trembling/Repetition* (Princeton, NJ: Princeton University Press, 1983), p. 53.
53  Caputo, *Against Ethics*, p. 15.
54  Caputo, *Against Ethics*, p. 20. The pseudonym mentioned here is Kierkegaard's – the author of *Fear and Trembling* penned the work as Johannes de Silentio – John of Silence.
55  Caputo, *Against Ethics*, p. 21.
56  *Ibid.*
57  *Ibid.*, p. 106.
58  Derrida, *The Gift of Death*, pp. 53–54.
59  Søren Kierkegaard, 'Fear and Trembling', in Robert Bretall, ed., *A Kierkegaard Anthology* (Princeton, NJ: Princeton University Press, 1936), p. 134.
60  Me voici!
61  Thomas Keenan, *Fables of Responsibility: Aberrations and Predicaments in Ethics and Politics* (Stanford, CA: Stanford University Press, 1997), p. 9.
62  *Ibid.*, p. 9.
63  There are always multiple readings. Keenan has not considered that the Other is equally the hostage of the sentinel; he has not considered that sentinels are usually armed, and that the approach of the Other also places the Other, and not just the sentinel, in mortal danger.
64  *Ibid.*, p. 11.
65  *Ibid.*
66  Caputo, *Against Ethics*, p. 4.

# 6

# *The one for the Other*

> The question concerning the disaster is a part of the disaster: it is not an inter-
> rogation, but a prayer, an entreaty, a call for help.[1]

In October 2003, the International Criminal Tribunal for the Former
Yugoslavia at The Hague brought an indictment against Dragan Nikolić
for crimes against humanity, including the murder, rape, and torture of
prisoners at the Sušica detention camp in eastern Bosnia. The list of Nikolić's
crimes reads like a litany:

On or about 6 July 1992, **DRAGAN NIKOLIĆ** took Ismet DEDIĆ out
of the hangar at Sušica camp and closed the door behind them. Detainees
inside the hall then heard Ismet DEDIĆ scream. A few minutes later,
**DRAGAN NIKOLIĆ** directed two detainees to drag Ismet DEDIĆ inside the
hangar, where the other detainees could see that Ismet DEDIĆ's body was
covered in blood. His body was barely recognizable and he appeared to
have suffered serious injuries. Ismet DEDIĆ died shortly thereafter. His body
was placed in a plastic bag and removed by other detainees.

From about the second week of July 1992, over a seven-day period,
**DRAGAN NIKOLIĆ** beat Galib MUSIĆ, a 60-year-old detainee by, among
other things, kicking him and beating him with a metal pipe. During the
beatings, **DRAGAN NIKOLIĆ** accused Galib MUSIĆ of asking a Muslim
organization to come to expel the Serbs from Vlasenica. Each time
**DRAGAN NIKOLIĆ** beat Galib MUSIĆ, MUSIĆ lost consciousness and, after
approximately seven days, Galib MUSIĆ died.

From early June until about 15 September 1992 many female detainees
at Sušica camp were subjected to sexual assaults, including rapes and
degrading physical and verbal abuse. **DRAGAN NIKOLIĆ** personally
removed and otherwise facilitated the removal of female detainees from the
hangar, which he knew was for purposes of rapes, and other sexually
abusive conduct. The sexual assaults were committed by camp guards,
special forces, local soldiers and other men.[2]

**Indictments**

Here, in the form of an indictment, we find an ascription of responsibility. It is not that something terrible happened to Ismet Dedić and Galib Musić – rather it is that Dragan Nikolić murdered them. Now, the referent is the one who killed, the one who kills. It is fearful to approach Dragan Nikolić. It is easier to approach Ismet and Galib. It is easier to approach Sead Sinanović and Osman Osmanović, who were killed at Srebrenica. It is easier to approach them – to approach their murders – because, while we can stare with sympathy when we see their skeletons unearthed at Srebrenica, we fail to see ourselves in those remains. We don't imagine ourselves in such a shameful position, all tangled bones and broken pelvises, all shattered skulls and battered ribs. It is because we can project ourselves into the space occupied by Dragan Nikolić – after all, he is not all tangled bones and ruin – that we need in some way to exceptionalize his acts and separate ourselves out from him. This is harder to do, because we who live are also always killing.

For John Caputo, the history of philosophy is one that is marked by originary ethics – by firm Greco-Germanic erections of Being, which are concerned with producing and sheltering Truth from the storm of heterodoxy.[3] On the steps of the temple, the refuse awaits its own sweeping away by the certitudes of time and the erectitude of the edifice of ethics itself – the temple guards – philosophers. Yevgeny Zamyatin's *We*. We will prosecute Dragan Nikolić, but Ismet and Galib had better stay buried, lest they return to point their fingers at the history of our philosophic systems that call for sacrifice to the ideal state – a sacrifice that is always made by someone Other, by someone to whom we do not have to answer, because he is conveniently dead. But here, it is the bodies of the dead which themselves raise the cry voicelessly; the broken body *itself* issues the command in the place before the matrix of language and sense begins, and before meaning is produced by situating Bosnia in an already intelligible matrix of war crimes and international law. It is the body collapsed, the body losing life, the body betrayed, that commands the approach. In the fractal space between the killing and the dying lies the command to respond. This command is not a phenomenological utterance. It is otherwise than phenomenological. This command does not allow us 'to remain in a mode of declarative discourse, *as if* one could simply talk about the structure of this command *as command, as if* one had the time and leisure to engage in a phenomenological reduction of the command in order to uncover its *eidos*, [which] utterly misses the commanding aspect of the command. The command is not given in order to be appreciated and questioned but to be listened and followed.'[4] In other words, the structure of the command defies the desire to locate it and explore its meaning in a specific cultural context or in the intellectual or cognitive character of the place from which it emanates.

It is the very ability of death to be meaningful after the event that gives testimony to the survival of those who were not killed, and who are thus left to interpret the meaning of the death. Kierkegaard notes that the tragic hero is such because others remain to mourn him (or those he has killed) and thus, to assign meaning for the death(s): death is summoned in order to save a nation, to appease angry gods, to assure victory, peace, security. Meaning is fundamentally dependent on the survival of those who will mourn and who will subsequently interpret the death as a meaningful event – as a sacrifice, for example, or an act of bravery. In other words, death can be made meaningful because it can be narrated by those who survive it. In 'Death in the Nuclear Age', Hans Morgenthau argues that death in an era of nuclear weapons – in an age of massive, nameless destruction – can have little meaning when there is no one left to mourn or to assign meaning to lived – and lost – lives.[5] It is also for this reason that James Hatley and others refer to the Shoah as a total loss, irrecoverable and irreparable. The destruction of all the generations on such an enormous scale attempts to ensure that there are no survivors to mourn the murdered. It is as if the murders themselves never happened, or happened only in a simulation of themselves – unreal – the crematoria swallowing up the millions who in their numbers become the nameless. We witness the dying of millions of Others at Srebrenica, at Biafra, at Bergen-Belsen, Auschwitz-Birkenau, Sobibor, Hiroshima, Dresden, Tuol Sleng. These dead bodies still speak. Their silence and the silence of the empty spaces where their children and the other marks of their existence should have been is precisely the evidence of their destruction. Thus, the silence itself bears witness to the destruction that is always present but which cannot be made up for outside its past. The silence persists, generations later, parallel to our own existence – that silence which is the alibi for our own speaking. The absence of the dead is our infinite parallel, the silent testimony to the destruction of the generations that haunts our present and which marks all our politics with the brushstrokes of trauma.

Being elsewhere in time and space, how shall I respond to the command of the dying body? How shall I respond to the murdered of Bosnia? How can I respond when I am too late? How shall I respond to the vocative cry that has passed into oblivion, but which remains the historical legacy that I have inherited, and to which I remain constantly attenuated and responsible? One cannot contemplate the victim from the comfort of one's office – in fact, the very comfort of one's office serves as an indictment against the neat, in-line textual analysis of the event that I attempt to narrate. As

James Hatley notes: 'The very comfort in which I live, my assumption that friends and food are a normal course of my existence is held up as evidence against me.'[6] And yet, the comfort of our offices is also all that we have. I am left with the simultaneity of the command to approach – to respond – and the impossibility of ever doing so. One therefore dwells in the fissures between these possibilities which are not possible. Therein lies the paradox of needing to respond and of not being able to respond because the Other has already been crushed. Within this paradox: 'The struggle to remember the death of other humans in spite of their annihilation remains the last possible human act of ethical resistance against their desolation.'[7]

## Bearing witness

There is a fundamental disjuncture between survival and testimony. For Agamben, 'The Shoah is an event without witnesses in the double sense that it is impossible to bear witness to it from the inside – since no one can bear witness from the inside of death, and there is no voice for the disappearance of voice – and from the outside – since the "outsider" is by definition excluded from the event' of which he would testify.[8] The one who survives the camp, the refugee and detention centres, does so because others could not. Again, 'the value of testimony lies essentially in what it lacks; at its center it contains something that cannot be borne witness to and that discharges the survivors of authority. The "true" witnesses, the "complete witnesses", are those who did not bear witness and could not bear witness. They are those who "touched bottom" . . . the drowned.'[9]

The enormity of the scale of loss has led us into a realm where events have no acceptable meaning, where the scale of death and violence is such that it cannot be justified in any meaningful way; it cannot be reasoned about. Yet the ability to bear witness and to interpret events remains insofar as anyone survives with their senses intact, and sometimes because no one can survive with their senses intact, because to survive with one's senses intact is not to survive at all, but to have escaped. Testimony and survival extend across time and space; testimony takes place in the in-between spaces, in the disjunctures – the disconnects – between being and time, between 'facts' and fictive or cathartic expression, between the poetics of justice and the narratives that emanate from, and thus legitimize, the rule of law. Testimony convicts or exonerates through the witness's ability to translate image, sentient feeling, expressions that cross the skin, twisting facial muscles, sighs, and cries of pain that are other than, but not exterior to, language. And yet: 'The distance between what has been witnessed and what can be committed to testimony – what was seen and what can be said – is often wide and always palpable: not only in the witness's statements but in the shrugged shoulders, the winces, the tears, and the silences that punctuate written and oral testimonies.'[10]

There is an unbridgeable distance, in other words, between the experience of the witness and what the court stenographer can commit to paper in his limited shorthand and which requires him to begin sentences with capital letters and end them with full stops, which requires him to follow the grammatical rules of subject-verb-predicate in the active voice and to choose a tense and stick with it. In the courtroom, there can be no metaphor and expressions of pain can only be formulated as facts related to events.

> I would need a distance of a hundred years
> To learn all the horrors I was contemporary to.[11]

The temporality, the proximity, of witnessing before the courts is unambiguous: the witness was there, the witness *saw*, the witness *heard*, the witness *experienced*. The witness must reproduce, faithfully, the substance of the testimony on demand, with no inconsistencies, no paradoxes, no intuition, or counter-intuition. Derrida argues that: 'When I commit myself to speaking the truth, I commit myself to repeating the same thing, an instant later, two instants later, the next day, and for eternity, in a certain way. But this repetition carries the instant outside itself. Consequently the instant is instantaneously, *at this very instant*, divided, destroyed by what it nonetheless makes possible – testimony.'[12] This committing to repeat the same things in the same ways cannot take into its purview the changing nature of injury, the contingency of trauma and of trauma remembered, the inherent infidelity of 'facts' to their facticity. It cannot take into account the changing of the world, of the social and political environment in which stories are told and retold. It cannot take into account the mobility of language and meaning. It cannot take into account the disruption or break in time – the multiple temporalities and ways in which trauma crashes through the thin skin of everyday life.

For Jenny Edkins, the difference between 'normal time' and 'trauma time' marks the survivor and disrupts narrative attempts at the co-optation and appropriation of both events and our reactions to them. Trauma time fundamentally disrupts temporal linearity and thus defies attempts to incorporate the traumatic event into the narrative corpus of our lives. In effect, the experience and recall of trauma acts as an intrusion into the linearity of everyday life or 'normal time'. In Edkins' words: 'This is a sort of parallel existence; the two worlds cannot be synchronized because of the different temporalities each invokes. Events from the period of the trauma are experienced in a sense simultaneously with those of a survivor's current existence. They have not been incorporated into a narrative.'[13] Furthermore, '[bearing] witness or giving testimony is problematic. In order to tell the story it has to be translated into narrative form.'[14] Not only does this undermine the immediacy of the (memory of) trauma, but it loses the characteristic of being fundamentally oppositional to any form of understanding.[15] Thus, the need to bear witness is juxtaposed with the simultaneous inability to ever do so. And it is also the case that, for many, trauma time *is* normal time.

## Silence

God keeps silent about his reasons for demanding Isaac of Abraham. Kierkegaard, who has not put his name to the text, instead invokes a pseudonym to speak for him, and he himself remains silent. As Derrida notes: 'one often thinks that responsibility consists of acting and signing in one's name. A responsible reflection on responsibility is interested in advance in whatever happens to the name in the event of pseudonymity, metonymy, homonymy, in the matter of what constitutes a real name. Sometimes one says or wishes it more effectively, more authentically, in the secret name by which one calls oneself, that one gives oneself or affects to give oneself, the name that is more naming and named in the pseudonym than in the official legality of the public patronym.'[16] Stojan Sokolović gave me another name. I speak from it only to him. With this other name, I speak Serbian.[17] I speak it poorly, but I speak, I listen, I try to understand. I abandon the language of reassurance that is the reason we call these our mother tongues and I speak to Serbs in Serbian, and I listen to Serbs speaking Serbian. Very often, though, I am forced to struggle with silence because I do not understand what is being said or asked of me. For Barbara Johnson, 'The original text is always already an impossible translation that renders translation impossible.'[18] Abraham is silent before God and his family – he does not seek to explain what he will do, his motives, or his reasons for having acquiesced to the demand to sacrifice Isaac. According to Derrida however, 'in some respects Abraham does speak. He says a lot. But even if he says everything, he need only keep silent on a single thing for one to conclude that he hasn't spoken. Such a silence takes over his whole discourse. So he speaks and doesn't speak. He responds without responding. He responds and doesn't respond.'[19] Kierkegaard postulates that Abraham cannot speak, because 'he speaks no human language. And even if he understood all the languages of the world, even if those he loved also understood them, he still could not speak – he speaks in a divine language, he speaks in tongues.'[20]

In this formulation, there may well be meaning in the event of sacrifice, but the meaning is beyond and apart from anything that can be said of it. The attempt to order the command, to express meaning, must always fail because it is impossible to know God, who, for Levinas, is always the absolutely Other. Human language cannot capture the meaning that God holds in secret, and so the only response is silence. Kierkegaard observes that, 'Abraham cannot speak, because he cannot say that which would explain everything (that is, so it is understandable): that it is an ordeal such that, please note, the ethical is the temptation. Anyone placed in such a position is an emigrant from the sphere of the universal.'[21] But Abraham does not speak, also, perhaps, because he cannot order what has been asked of him; perhaps he does not speak because what has been asked of him is unspeakable. Perhaps it is unable to be vested with universal meaning, or with meaning that is universally understandable. Perhaps to attempt to give it meaning is itself an exercise in obscenity, not because of the inscrutable divinity of God or the faithfulness of Abraham, but because of the terror that befalls Isaac in the response to God's command. What is at stake in the structure of the command that God gives: that Isaac die – and in the structure of the command given from Berlin: that the Jews die?

For Caputo's pseudonym, 'the encounter with the absolutely other . . . with one capable of issuing a categorical call, leaves one in a state of absolutely ineffable obedience, which is the structure of the pure or absolute violence that makes the Nazi analogy possible . . . when people are convinced they speak in the name of God, then it is time for the rest of us to head for the doors.'[22] Obligation, then, is not a call that emanates from 'on high' – irrefutable, and ineluctable. Obligation does not equal obedience. Rather, 'obligation means the obligation to reduce and alleviate suffering, not to produce it, not to augment it, not to spill blood in the name of the voices one hears. Sometimes prescriptions are to be followed by disobedience.'[23] And yet, it remains so that my response to the Other is always made possible by my exclusion of other Others – of those to whom I do not respond, for whatever reason, whether I intend it or not. My responsibility to Stojan Sokolović is made possible by my failure to respond to others – perhaps to those Others who are the victims of Stojan Sokolović – to those who are victims of Serbs, who are also, in other places, and at other times, themselves victims. How shall I answer Stojan Sokolović, who simply asks me to embody the same ethic that I charged him with having disavowed? My response to Stojan Sokolović is one that emanates from the murdered of Bosnia, without whom my gaze would not have rested as it did on Bosnia, and without whom I would have had no occasion to write about it nor, in turn, Stojan Sokolović occasion to charge me with indecency. Our interaction depends fundamentally on the dead. How shall I respond? Stojan Sokolović is implicated in genocide, regardless of whether or not he personally engaged in it. He is implicated even so because he remains – a Serb unwilling and unable to be something else, moving back and forth between two territories implicated in some measure of disaster, upon which disaster unfolded and continues to unfold.

In his testimony *The Sunflower*, the concentration camp prisoner Simon Wiesenthal is summoned to the deathbed of Karl, a young Nazi soldier. The soldier has asked his nurse to bring a Jew to his bedside – presumably any Jew would suffice – so that he might confess his crime of helping to drive Jewish families into a house in Dnepropetrovsk to be burned alive. As some tried to escape the flames by jumping out of the second story windows, the soldiers were waiting in the courtyard below with guns at the ready. Karl testifies: 'Behind the windows of the second floor, I saw a man with a small child in his arms. His clothes were alight. By his side stood a woman, doubtless the mother of the child. With his free hand the man covered the child's eyes . . . then he jumped into the street. Seconds later the mother followed. Then from the other windows fell burning bodies . . . We shot.'[24]

For several hours, Karl and Wiesenthal struggled together over the deathbed with these memories. Karl says: 'I know that what I have told you is terrible. In the long nights while I have been waiting for death, time and time again I have longed to talk about it to a Jew and beg forgiveness from him. Only I didn't know whether there were any Jews left . . . I know that what I am asking is almost too much for you, but without your answer I cannot die in peace.'[25]

Wiesenthal writes of this encounter: 'Two men who had never known each other had been brought together for a few hours by Fate. One asks the other for help. But the other was himself helpless and able to do nothing for him . . . At last I made up my mind and without a word I left the room.'[26]

In the deluge of commentary that has sprung up from the central question of this testimony[27] – the question of whether Wiesenthal should have granted forgiveness or not – one issue, that of Wiesenthal's silence, seems to reappear over and over again. For Matthew Fox, Wiesenthal's silence is all that he can give. Staying at the deathbed and allowing the soldier to confess his crime does not require, indeed, does not even warrant, some facile gesture of forgiveness that Wiesenthal is not empowered to give anyway. Wiesenthal's attentive silence is the most ethical option in the face of so hideous a crime.[28] For Hatley, 'Wiesenthal is helpless before the perpetrator's suffering at precisely the moment when he might have reasonably been tempted to cruelty, to cold revenge, or at the very least, to a lasting indifference.'[29] In other words, Wiesenthal's silence has both transcended and borne witness against violence. In sympathy and horror and with a violently pounding heart, Wiesenthal stays with the dying soldier seemingly against his own will. Forgiveness in that moment is as out of the question as it is urgently necessary. For '[f]orgiveness, no matter how transcendent remains infected with the burden of atrocity, with an irreparable harm.'[30] Only the victim of violence is empowered to forgive her tormentor. Wiesenthal cannot forgive in the place of the father, the mother, or the child burned alive at Dnepropetrovsk, although he may honour the memory of both their lives and deaths. He may speak of them, about them, but he may not speak for them – an ethical choice which Wiesenthal almost instinctively understands as he sits at the edge of Karl's deathbed. Is it significant here that Wiesenthal has not had the pleasure of stretching his body out across a real bed for several years at the time of this encounter? Is there to be understood some good fortune for Karl to die, medicated between crisp hospital sheets, as a result of his injuries – juxtaposed against the fortunes of Wiesenthal, who lives in one hour and not in the next, whose experience of crisp white sheets is a memory almost too distant to recall in the tortured state of the concentration camp prisoner?

The ethic of silence is part of our response to the victim who has already been crushed, and to the perpetrator who would deny the Other his voice. As Hatley argues:

> In ethical silence, the [witness] finds her or himself in crisis. One confronts the treatment of another human being that is so outrageous, so indefensible that one must intervene. But the very capability to intervene is taken away from one because the person one confronts has already been crushed. No recourse is possible that would undo the other's suffering. One finds oneself in an impossible situation – one ought to care for this other, one ought to be outraged, but the very care and outrage one feels are utterly useless. For this reason, one's energy is sapped, one's feelings are muted, one's consciousness is traumatized.[31]

But here we see that there are many kinds of silences – as many kinds of silences as there are tones of voice, or faces, kinds of suffering, deaths. We may identify, for example, the silence of friendship – the silence which is necessary for the preservation of friendship. For Derrida: 'Friendship does not keep silence, it is preserved by silence.'[32] Silence may also emanate out of respect for the dead. Jenny Edkins notes that there are also official silences, and that these, too, are not without effect. 'By stopping all "everyday" activity, by halting the flow of traffic, the flow of time itself is stopped. "Time stands still": and we are open to the "moment". This is the ethical moment, the moment of decision, the moment of the political, which is outside (and escapes) politics.'[33] We can identify the silence of Wiesenthal, which is the silence of what cannot be made up, of one who does not know what to say. This silence is the only way in which Wiesenthal can respond – and his silence *is* a response. Wiesenthal's silence not only serves as its own indictment against the Nazi genocide, but it is the only possible way he can respond ethically to acknowledge the family burned alive at

Dnepropetrovsk. Likewise, Karl's silence during his tenure with the SS is manifest in his failure to speak against the events in Dnepropetrovsk while there was still time to do so; in Dnepropetrovsk and everywhere that men in the SS murdered hideously and shamelessly. We may identify the silence of secrets, as responsibility for a promise (not to betray), as protection of oneself – the keeping of silence because one cannot explain oneself. There is silence in love. Indeed, sometimes love *demands* silence. In some cases and in some ways, the saying and the said are obscene. Silence also proceeds from the experience of trauma, as illustrated by Hannah Arendt:

> There are no parallels to the life of the concentration camps. Its horror can never be fully embraced by the imagination for the very reason that it stands outside of life and death. It can never be fully reported for the very reason that the survivor returns to the world of the living, which makes it impossible for him to believe fully in his own past experiences. It is as though he had a story to tell of another planet, for the status of the inmates in the world of the living, where nobody is supposed to know if they are alive or dead, is such that it is as though they had never been born.[34]

The trauma of witnessing renders mute as it intrudes into and disrupts completely the 'normal' course of one's life; it makes facile gestures difficult, it makes 'getting on with one's life' impossible. Edkins argues: 'Trauma is that which refuses to take its place in history as done and finished with. It demands an acknowledgement of a different temporality, where the past is produced by – or even takes place in – the present.'[35] Furthermore, 'the language we speak is part of the social order, and when the order falls apart around our ears, so does the language. What we *can* say no longer makes sense; what we *want* to say, we can't. There are no words for it.'[36] We are found, in other words, in silence.

The perpetrator's attempt to silence the victim is the attempt to deny his existence and the manner of his death. Yet, silence is also complicity in the commission of these acts. It is the silence between the ones who do the killing that is as much a denial of the deaths themselves – it is a denial of the responsibility of one's comrades, and thus a denial of one's own culpability.

## Defiance

In May 2003, Dragan Obrenović signed a confession at the ICTY detailing the measure of his responsibility for the commission of war crimes in Srebrenica in 1995.[37] In the content of the confession, he notes that he was asked by one of his superiors 'not to make a record of the activities involving the killing operation or speak on the radio about it.' Is it the case that the order to silence is really for one's protection from future prosecution? Is it really a conspiracy for future protection from future tribunals? Surely, in the moment when such a decision is made, prosecution is the furthest thing from one's mind. Is it not the case that the admonition to silence is rather a means of denying the complicity of oneself in the process of inhumanity? Is it not the case that silence insulates one from the confrontation with oneself, from the recognition of oneself as the agent of torture and death?

Obrenović goes on:

> Sometime in August 1995, General Krstić came to Zvornik and requested me to take him to the soldiers in the field who had been involved in the most fierce fighting. I decided to take him to the right flank of the 7th battalion where the men were manning the trenches. I stood with General Krstić next to a trench where one of the soldiers was listening to a transistor radio. A survivor from one of the executions was giving an account of what happened to him over the radio broadcast from Tuzla. We stood there for about two minutes listening to the survivor and then General Krstić ordered that the radio be switched off and said we should not listen to enemy radio. He asked me if I had issued orders that enemy radio should not be listened to and I said that I had not. On the way back I thought about the survivor's story on the radio and this led me to ask General Krstić why the killings took place. I had said that we knew the people killed were all simple people and asked for the reason why they had to be killed. I said that even if they were all chickens that were killed, there still had to be a reason. General Krstić asked me where I had been. I said that I went to the field at Snagovo as ordered. Krstić cut me short and said that we would speak no more about this.

Silence and denial protect one for a time from having to address one's actions, from having to address the suffering that one has caused, from having to address the damage one has done in the destruction of the Other. If the Serbs in the trenches only turn off the radio, the dead will disappear. Making the dead disappear is a feat unto itself. The mass burial of the mass of nameless bodies, entangled limbs, frozen musculature, emaciated forms, allows one to wipe the memory of their deaths from one's conversations and in turn, it is hoped, from one's thoughts. One does not leave the dead above ground not because the bodies will later bear witness for prosecutors (satellite technologies pinpoint graves that already bear witness enough), but because leaving the dead above ground allows the dead to bear constant witness against you, witness against you in that moment, in every moment that they remain in the realm of the visible. Once the bodies of the murdered are underground, once they are reduced to carbon and ash fused with the walls in the crematoria, the one who destroyed them can find repose for a time, can believe that they were never there, that there was no crime, but only a battle, that the dead were other than

116

innocent, that they, insofar as they existed, deserved not to have existed. Thus, the perpetrator insulates himself from the forms of the bodies outlined in the light of day and protects himself from the accusation that their absence must nevertheless always level.

It is a peculiar aspect of our cultural life that we speak *to* the living, but *about* the dead.[38] We don't ask questions of the dead, because the dead cannot answer in the way that we are used to divining answers. The murdered repose in a silence which is understood to be outside language, and even outside existence. And yet, it is a paradox that the very scientism that would deny us the logic of talking with the dead is the same phenomenon which produces technologies that allow the dead to speak for themselves, as it were. DNA technologies, the near perfection of the autopsy as an indicator of the cause, time, and manner of death, and advanced forensics, which can pinpoint places of execution, all facilitate in a certain manner the testimony that the dead cannot speak from the other side of existence. And in The Hague, at Arusha, at Nuremburg, one attempts to find justice for the dead as much as for the living and for the securitization of society. It is the dead in the indictment against Dragan Nikolić whose proper names are inscribed on the public record. It is the living who require him to answer for the dead, whose very absence – whose very inability to return – is the cause of the indictment. It is the very absence of Ismet Dedić and Galib Musić that bears witness against Nikolić, and for whom he is understood to be accountable. And yet, it is also this very absence associated with the deaths of these men which causes them to be spoken *of*, but not *to*, that announces the need for, and the simultaneous impossibility of, justice. For Derrida, 'from the moment they are spoken of instead of being spoken *to*, it is to say that they are no longer, or not yet, there: it is to register their absence',[39] whether real or implied, voluntary or imposed. It is to register the exile that is inherent in an absence – in an excommunication – which is the basic form of our spatially oriented existence. Ismet and Galib, Osman and Sead, are subsumed beneath the imperatives of testimony, which they could not return to give. For Blanchot, 'to be silent is still to speak. Silence is impossible.'[40] Even in death.

However, for Hannah Arendt, the camp inmate is also unintelligible in the 'normal' world of everyday existence precisely because there is no chance of the survivor's testimony making sense in the context of 'normal' life. In short, even if language permitted the expression of that which is unspeakable, it would be unbelievable. The world of the camp, then, is as much outside our world as it is a fundamental component of it; the world of the camp underwrites the scenario in which the crushed bodies of the mass-murdered in Other, unpronounceable places allows us the means to identify our own good fortune. It is precisely that divide which provides us an alibi with respect to our being 'elsewhere' as the bodies piled up. It provides us with the ability, indeed the necessity, to be silent because we cannot give testimony for what we did not suffer. And yet, that silence is also the substance of an aporia – it is an impassable blockade in the road of ethics – because the interior substance of our silence is *both* guiltlessness *and* complicity.

Lea Wernick Friedman argues that: 'To dwell on the silence that is linked to the killing process, that is the very mark of the killing process, is to dwell precisely on the unintegratable and traumatic fact, and hence to begin to hear a silence profoundly resisted and, therefore, profoundly silent, at the chaotic heart of history.'[41] Silence, then, is not the opposite of language, but here becomes its very condition. As Bernard Dauenhauser argues: 'Rather than being that which thwarts language, silence is that which opens the way for language's potency . . . for speech is born from silence and seeks its conclusion in silence.'[42] But here, we find another paradox, an in-between space, which is not devoid of, and in fact, may very well be characterized by the inherent violence of representation. As Jenny Edkins argues, when we think we have found the language to describe what happened – when we give it the name 'Holocaust', 'genocide', 'ethnic cleansing', it is as if we no longer have to confront it. We have filed it away in the historical record to be dusted off from time to time to look at it, admittedly, with a species of detached horror, which, as events pass temporally further away, further ensures our professed innocence. However, when we stand in silence, we are saying that there is nothing that can be said, thereby underwriting an equally serious danger. For Edkins, the paradox is that 'when we acknowledge the event as unimaginable and unsayable . . . we are excused from further inquiry.'[43] Further, the assignation of actors to their proper narrative place:

> is already to have translated [them] into a conceptual formulation. In order to speak *about* someone, one must translate that person into a defined quality or set of qualities. In doing philosophy, one ceases to be addressed by the victim but instead speaks *about* her or him. The very act of reasoning is continually in danger of betraying the situation of the victim, or transforming the particularity of his or her suffering into a category that can be given an explicit significance for all who reason. The victim enters into a *logos* in which he or she becomes one of many examples of the same type.[44]

Dragan Nikolić, Dragan Obrenović, Stojan Sokolović address me directly, they appeal to me, they ask me not to make sense of what has come to pass, not to order, but to recognize that I am not outside the events in which they were swallowed up and implicated. They ask me to recognize that I am equally swallowed up and equally implicated by virtue of my having watched at the keyhole so that these events could come to serve me in a professional future I could not have planned at the time. I ordered, I categorized, I filed my interviews, created patterns, recognized misfortunes. They ask me to accept that it is precisely my complicity in the ordering of events and of the reification of their meaning that provides the logic in which mass murder becomes a politically sensible move. For James Hatley: 'The very struggle to make sense of the world, to render it in a manner that allows it to be illuminated, to show forth in a logos, a pattern that is self-consistent and reasonable', provides a reasoned and reasonable place for the abject destruction of infinite numbers of others.[45]

## Perpetrators

The inherent dignity of the victim is the authority under which the command is made to remember the victim as being stripped of dignity in the extreme.[46] Similarly, the inherent humanity of the perpetrator betrays our desire to dehumanize him in the face of his dehumanizing actions. Our attempt to explain, understand, and memorialize the dehumanized victim can also be understood as an attempt to bear the suffering that lies at the core of dehumanization. In our identification of the victim as a victim of inhumanity, however, the victims' dignity can somehow only be restored through the stripping of the perpetrator, through the distancing as far as possible of the Self from the perpetrator. In so doing, we abandon the perpetrator. The perpetrator becomes Other. It is not me who injures, who betrays, who kills, who identifies those who will become victims. I have washed my hands. But I injure, betray and kill the perpetrator with impunity. Is this not the sentiment that lies at the core of corporal and capital punishment? Is this not what lies at the core of Levinas's statement with regard to the Palestinians that 'there are people who are wrong'?[47] Has Levinas not excluded the Palestinian from the circle of those to whom the Self is responsible through his identification of the Palestinians' violence? Is this not the manner in which we insulate ourselves from the crimes of the Other and, in so doing, identify the Other as the absolutely Other? Is this not the way in which we convince ourselves that we could not perpetrate the violence that is perpetrated by the perpetrator? The perpetrator must deny the command of the Other, and just as the perpetrator denies the face of the Other, so I deny the face of the perpetrator and thus become myself perpetrator in my turn. The perpetrator must proceed as though the Other has no right to make any claim, to speak, to query, to protest. As the perpetrator attempts to silence the victim, so the system of corporal punishment seeks to silence the perpetrator, or to determine beforehand what he will say. For Hatley, 'the address of the other haunts the perpetrator, no matter what he or she does to forget the other. In fact, the very activity of forgetting the other, an activity that the perpetrator then had to attempt to forget that he or she had forgotten, becomes itself an insistent witness to the contrary that the other could not be forgotten.'[48]

The excision of the perpetrator from the realm of those to whom I am responsible is made possible precisely through the identification of victims and of victimhood, ontological categories which require a nameable – and denounceable – perpetrator. In the main, the move toward responsibility is primarily a juridical, not an ethical, gesture.[49] The relation here is necessary. Just as the perpetrator and the victim authorize one another's existence through the symbiosis of their relationship, so the facticity of fact exists by virtue of its (in)ability to excise from itself all fiction, lie, and simulation. In other words, fact is fact precisely because it can identify fiction, and thus identify what it does not identify with. As Derrida notes, 'without the *possibility* of this fiction, without the spectral virtuality of this simulacrum and as a result of this lie or this fragmentation of the true, no truthful testimony would be possible. Consequently, the possibility of literary fiction haunts so-called truthful, responsible, serious, real testimony as its proper possibility.'[50] Thus, it is the very binary construction of fact versus fiction itself that causes claims of fact to be haunted by fiction and that causes victims and survivors alike to be haunted by the depth of their potential responsibility, by the responsibility of having survived because others could not. The attempt to destroy the Other reveals the technology through which the Self is made salient and unitary. If the Other is always in the Self, so, then, the fiction is also always in the truth. The trace of the Other always remains. The trace of the literary always remains in the factual, just as the trace of the factual is always found in the literary. But is literature not also testimony? Is poetry also not a means for the witness?

> Slowly, boring a tunnel, a guardian mole makes his way,
> With a small red lamp fastened to his forehead.
> He touches buried bodies, counts them, pushes on,
> He distinguishes human ashes by their luminous vapor,
> The ashes of each man by a different part of the spectrum.[51]

Czesław Miłosz, powerless perpetrator, watching the ghetto, witness plagued by responsibility:

> I am afraid, so afraid of the guardian mole.
> He has swollen eyelids, like a Patriarch
> Who has sat much in the light of candles
> Reading the great book of the species.
>
> What will I tell him, I, a Jew of the New Testament,
> Waiting two thousand years for the second coming of Jesus?
> My broken body will deliver me to his sight

120

And he will count me among the helpers of death:
The uncircumcised.[52]

Hatley argues that 'in spite of all the power I might exercise upon or against the face [of the Other], its vulnerability to suffering at the hands of my power utterly escapes my power.'[53] In other words, the ability of the Other to suffer at my hands is an a priori aspect of her condition that remains fundamentally independent of me and my choices. In this way, the vulnerability of the Other to my power simultaneously exceeds my power. Derrida expresses this through his identification of death as unique to the one who undergoes it. We dwell in the face of death, which is the death that awaits the Other – the Other's unique death, for which I am singularly responsible because it cannot be substituted. Death is universal insofar as it comes to all of us, but it is absolutely particular in the uniqueness of each of our deaths. Death involves communities of mourners, individual mourners, and sometimes it destroys even the mourners themselves. The eagerness with which we give death, assign death, belies that each death is unique. Even as I kill, the murdered one's death remains his own, and not mine.[54] Even in Sead Sinanović's death, which appears exactly like Osman Osmanović's, it remains his own, and no Other's.

Yet 'to be responsible before another is to answer to the appeal by which he approaches. It is to put oneself in his place, not to observe oneself from without, but to bear the burden of his existence and supply for its wants. I am responsible for the very faults of another, for his deeds and misdeeds.'[55] For Hatley, following Levinas, this is expressed through the notion that: 'One is born into the world already involved, already claimed, already addressed.'[56] For Levinas, one is not an already-formed subject that turns toward the Other; it is not the case that discreet entities face one another across a divide, conceptual or physical. For Levinas, the Other is already in the Same, such that subjectivity itself is called into critical question. Responsibility for and to the Other 'could never mean altruistic will, instinct of "natural benevolence", or love.'[57] In the face-to-face with the Other, even the persecuted is responsible to answer for the crime that the perpetrator perpetrates against him. In this way, Levinas's formulation of responsibility is not a responsibility for the victim who occupies the a priori status of victim that merely remains to be identified by those who are already constituted as capable of being responsible – i.e. the state, international institutions, The Hague. Levinas's conception does not allow for a simple grafting of the division between murdered and murderer as the basis for responsibility. As Jenny Edkins notes, 'what happens is not straightforward; there is not a perpetrator and a victim with no ambiguity.'[58] Here the waters are murky, responsibility plagues and takes hostage, the Self is an accusative (in French, *soi, se*; in Serbian *sebe*) without a corresponding nominative.[59] My responsibility is 'prior to dialogue, to the exchange of questions and answers, to the thematization of the said.'[60]

The absolute command of the command transcends reason because it does not give one time to distinguish between calls or to weigh their relative merits. As Hatley notes: 'In the face-to-face encounter, no time is given for me to ask whether the command of the other face is justified.'[61] If I attempt to distinguish between the innocent and the guilty, the command *in which I have already found myself* is radically undermined. 'Suddenly, some of the others command me more than the rest of the others.'[62] The absoluteness of the command is destroyed in the rational categorization of which commands matter over other commands.

For those of us who write from the comfort of our offices, the experience of conflict and violence is always inscribed on Other bodies and dwelling places, relying fundamentally on the insulation of the immersed academic body from the physical and political implications of the conflicts we explore. Our self-importance and the self-importance of our narratives reflects our commitment to our own professional advancement, and says far more about our own institutional cultures than it does about the Others who bear the weight of our attempts to produce meaning about their situations. And yet, 'to be called as Levinas is called, one must write the text again for oneself. No one can write it for anyone else, since the very urgency of the relationship precedes its thematization.'[63] My encounter with the Other is singular and unique insofar as I am uniquely commanded by that Other and insofar as no one can stand in my place. For Hatley: 'Before one is guilty, one is already uniquely and irreplaceably in a position of shame in regard to those about whom one is to write.'[64] One does not face the Other as a unitary subject. One's identity is formed within that facing:

> Certainly, one might have suspected that some hidden dimension of one's existence was yet to be uncovered, an ecstatic return of an absence into presence, but the analysis itself seemed to neglect that the very words one was using to formulate it were already haunted by the voice and voices of [those Others] involved in one's historical inheritance. The very voice established in this text, *the one who is now speaking*, was not constituted from the vantage point of a particular identity self-sufficient to itself but was already intertwined with and suffering under the address of the other and all the other others as well.[65]

I am thus responsible to Stojan Sokolović before he ever speaks, as a matter of course, prior to my ability to identify him, to ontologize him, to cast a replica of him for my colleagues and students, or for the replay of my narrative of the Bosnian war to weigh down a shelf already groaning under the weight of such narratives in my academic discipline. His face is always shrouded in ambiguity. This ambiguity does not hide any true nature, but rather highlights the inherently fractal space of both the Self and the Other. For Levinas: 'In the trauma of persecution it is to pass from the outrage undergone to the responsibility for the persecutor, and, in this sense from suffering to expiation for the other.'[66] For Bernasconi, the ambiguity of Levinas's missive on responsibility may mean that 'I am both persecuted and oppressor to the extent that the face which confronts me is both judge and accused.'[67] The faces that face are inherently two-faced, multiple-faced, they do not and cannot occupy one instantaneous zone of being.

Just as there cannot be a single, universal type of persecuted, there can not be a single, universal type of persecutor. We are persecuted and persecutor simultaneously, in different contexts and temporalities and degrees. The point here is that I am equally responsible for the persecutor, responsible for his crimes, and responsible to him as Other. I am responsible to speak to him, not of him, not about him, not for him, I am responsible not to silence him, but to regard him in that instant with silence, to stand in silence for the suffering he has caused and for the suffering caused still. I am obligated to silence before the perpetrator in the space that awaits justice. Silence accuses without formulating a narrative on the violence which struggles always to justify what is not justifiable – which is to say, itself.

NOTES

1   Maurice Blanchot, *The Writing of the Disaster*, p. 13.
2   International Criminal Tribunal for the Former Yugoslavia, The Prosecutor of the Tribunal Against Dragan Nikolić (Third Amended Indictment), Case No. IT-94-2-PT, 31 October 2003.
3   Caputo, *Against Ethics*, p. 152.
4   Hatley, *Suffering Witness*, p. 15.
5   Hans Morgenthau, 'Death in the Nuclear Age', *Commentary*, Vol. 32, No. 3, September 1961.
6   Hatley, *Suffering Witness*, p 14.
7   *Ibid.*, p. 42.
8   Agamben, *Remnants*, p. 35.
9   *Ibid.*, p. 34.
10  Bernard-Donals and Glejzer, 'Introduction: Representations of the Holocaust and the End of Memory', in Bernard-Donals and Glejzer, eds, *Witnessing the Disaster: Essays on Representation and the Holocaust* (Madison, WI: University of Wisconsin Press, 2003), p. 7.
11  Rade Drainac, 'When the Poet Without Lying Verses in His Heart Returns to His Native Country', in Charles Simić, ed., *The Horse Has Six Legs: An Anthology of Serbian Poetry* (St Paul: Graywolf Press, 1992), p. 40.
12  Jacques Derrida, *Demeure: Fiction and Testimony*, Elizabeth Rottenberg, trans. (Stanford, CA: Stanford University Press: 2000), p. 33
13  Edkins, *Trauma and the Memory of Politics*, p. 40.

14  *Ibid.*, p. 41.

15  *Ibid.*

16  Derrida, *The Gift of Death*, p. 58.

17  The division of Serbo-Croatian into 'Serbian', 'Croatian', and 'Bosnian' is an extremely political one. I might even venture to say that it is a largely instrumental division. I say here that I speak Serbian to Stojan Sokolović because the version of that language that I learned to speak was *ekavica* – the variant spoken mostly by Serbs in Serbia. Stojan Sokolović speaks *ijekavica*, which is spoken by Bosnian nationals (and most Croats) of all 'ethnicities'. I often have a hard time understanding *ijekavica* speakers because they use a different series of vowel sounds. When one struggles as I do in a language that is not mine, even minor differences raise obstacles.

18  Barbara Johnson quoted in Trinh T. Minh-ha, *Framer Framed*, p. 80.

19  Derrida, *The Gift of Death*, p. 59.

20  Kierkegaard in Hong and Hong, p. 114.

21  *Ibid.*, p. 115.

22  Caputo, *Against Ethics*, p. 145.

23  *Ibid.*

24  Simon Wiesenthal, *The Sunflower: On the Possibilities and Limits of Forgiveness* (Paris: Opera Mundi, 1969); With Symposium (1998), p. 42.

25  *Ibid.*, p. 54.

26  *Ibid.*, p. 55.

27  A 1998 reprint of *The Sunflower* included a Symposium in which guests were invited to respond to the question of whether Wiesenthal had behaved ethically in his choice not to forgive the German soldier.

28  Wiesenthal, *The Sunflower*, p. 143.

29  Hatley, *Suffering Witness*, p. 8.

30  *Ibid.*, p. 9.

31  *Ibid.*, p. 21.

32  Derrida, *Politics of Friendship*, p. 53.

33  Edkins, *Trauma and the Memory of Politics*, p. 84.

34  Arendt, 'The Origins of Totalitarianism', p. 125.

35  Edkins, *Trauma and the Memory of Politics*, p. 59.

36  *Ibid.*, p. 8.

37  All quotations appear in 'Statement of Facts as set out by Dragan Obrenović' (Tab A to 'Annex A' to the 'Joint Motion for Consideration of Plea Agreement Between Dragan Obrenović and the Office of the Prosecutor'), ICTY, May 2003.

38  See Bob Brecher, 'Our Obligation to the Dead', *Journal of Applied Philosophy*, Vol. 19, No. 2, 2002, pp. 109–119.

39  Derrida, *Politics of Friendship*, p. 172.

40  Blanchot, *The Writing of the Disaster*, p. 11.

41  Lea Wernick Fridman, *Words and Witness: Narrative and Aesthetic Strategies in the Representation of the Holocaust* (Albany, NY: State University of New York Press, 2000), p. 61.

42  *Ibid.*, p. 53.

43  Edkins, *Trauma and the Memory of Politics*, p. 176.

44  Hatley, *Suffering Witness*, p. 37.

45  *Ibid.*, p. 33.

46  *Ibid.*, p. 73.

47  Emmanuel Levinas, 'Ethics and Politics', in Sean Hand, ed., *The Levinas Reader* (Oxford: Blackwell Publishers, 1989), p. 294.

48  *Ibid.*, p. 92.
49  Agamben, *Remnants*, p. 22.
50  Derrida, *Demeure*, p. 72.
51  Czesław Miłosz, 'A Poor Christian Looks at the Ghetto', *Selected Poems* (Hopewell, NJ: The Ecco Press, 1973).
52  *Ibid.*
53  Hatley, *Suffering Witness*, p. 84.
54  Derrida, *The Gift of Death*, p. 44.
55  Levinas, *Otherwise Than Being*, p. xx
56  Hatley, *Suffering Witness*, p. 13.
57  Levinas, *Otherwise Than Being*, p. 112.
58  Edkins, *Trauma and the Memory of Politics*, p. 11.
59  See Levinas, *Otherwise Than Being*.
60  *Ibid.*, p. 111.
61  Hatley, *Suffering Witness*, p. 104.
62  *Ibid.*, p. 105.
63  Levinas, *Otherwise Than Being*, p. 106.
64  Hatley, *Suffering Witness*, p. 112.
65  *Ibid.*, p. 140–141.
66  Levinas, *Otherwise Than Being*, p. 111.
67  Robert Bernasconi, '"*Only the Persecuted . . .*": Language of the Oppressor, Language of the Oppressed', in Adriaan T. Peperzak (ed.), *Ethics as First Philosophy: The Significance of Emmanuel Levinas for Philosophy, Literature, and Religion* (New York: Routledge, 1995), p. 78.

# 7

# *Mourning*

It is always the other who saw with an eye that was too natural, too carnal, too external, which is to say, too literal.[1]

Judith Butler argues that our opacity to ourselves is precisely the condition upon which an ethic of responsibility can be formed. It is the inherent fragmentation of the subject, the inability of the self to provide a thorough accounting of who or what one is, the sense that we are only ever partially knowable to ourselves, and that even this partiality is shrouded in indeterminacy, that forms the condition in which the imperative to identify can be loosened. It is only when we find that the question *čija si ti?*[2] is impossible to answer, or fraught with so many possible answers that the question itself becomes meaningless, that we cease to demand of the Other the answer to our relentless question 'who are you'? The reciprocity of recognition is blown apart in this formulation, and we are forced to accept that we do not – cannot – know one another. The density and the depth of our souls are too much for recognition; recognition cannot contain or reckon on souls. This requires a new way of thinking about both ourselves and others. For Butler, a new sense of ethics emerges from 'the willingness to acknowledge the limits of acknowledgement itself, that when we claim to know and present ourselves, we will fail in some ways that are nevertheless essential to who we are, and that we cannot expect anything different from others.'[3] Here we find the fluidity of identity, the partiality of any and all accounting, the incongruity that necessarily emerges in the spaces between language and our existence in language and space. We are always operating in borrowed space, with borrowed languages from which we borrow terms, concepts, and ideas that precede our existence even as they necessarily frame our accounts and the lives that intersect them. We can only express what we are in borrowed terms, and this necessarily limits our capacity for expression – for explanation. It limits who we are, and who we can be. Yet, this is not to suggest that there might someday exist the perfect conditions in which we can express ourselves completely, in which we can become transparent. To operate outside of the bounds of the existent is, if existence is predicated on our ability to be recognized, to cease to be, and to cease to be expressive. We are obligated to relate, or else we cannot exist.

For Butler, the opacity of that which constitutes us informs the notion that the completeness of our exposure cannot be precisely narrated – it overflows in us – it is an excess that cannot be contained by expression or by any possibility of explanation. We exist in relation to Others, partially known and partially unknown, partially knowable and partially unknowable. Our accounts of ourselves are always already enmeshed with the accounts that Others might give. Thus, the mainstay of my existence is not autonomy, but dependence and interdependence in an inherently social frame. It is this very sociality that denies me my autonomy. 'In a sense, my account of myself is never fully mine, and is never fully for me . . . If I try to give an account of myself, if I try to make myself recognizable and understandable, then I might begin with a narrative account of my life, but this narrative will be disoriented by what is not mine, or what is not mine alone.'[4] In a world marked fundamentally by sociality, events never just happen to *me*; I am always a part of a community of shared experiences which are nevertheless experienced, marked, and remembered differently. As David Campbell notes with respect to the narratives of Srebrenica: 'For Bosnians, it was an instance of "ethnic cleansing" or "genocide"; for Serbs it was a "battle." For nobody was it simply a place where people "were killed", a figuration, bland though it seems, that nonetheless implies different entailments and responsibilities than saying, for example, "people died there."'[5] What is more, narratives are told, retold, and categorized accordingly into hierarchies of value from fantasies to stories, to accounts to testimonies, to knowledge, and so on. Regardless of the mechanisms through which we measure their acceptability, all narratives emerge in space and time, subject to and subsumed within the intensity of the pain or the defence of the ones who tell them. They are not told over and over again in the same way consistently – a legal statement of facts that seeks to minimize our exposure to uncertainty, incongruity, or paradox. They change as we change.

## Narrativity

Storytelling is about securitizing; it is about securitising narratives and enshrouding them in a protective layer of reproduction so that their salience, relevance, and accuracy cannot be questioned. The witness,

Derrida notes, is committed to telling the same story in the same ways each and every time. It is only in the ability to seamlessly corroborate what was previously claimed that 'facts' are developed and witness accounts deemed accurate and acceptable. Insofar as anyone survives to witness the account of Srebrenica as a genocide, he must be prepared to repeat in the same ways, and on command, the narrative account of what he suffered and saw. In the witnessing, and in the telling, he denies the vulnerability which he was forced to bear; he claims, against the grain of his intuitive sense, that it is precisely his survival and his telling of the ordeal that overcomes his assignation to death. He is no longer assigned to death – he has managed to defer it for another day, and he has also thereby helped to secure, however paradoxically, the narrative of Srebrenica as a genocide. This is the paradox of which Primo Levi speaks when he refers to the survivor as unable to witness. Those who witnessed could not return to narrate their fate. What befell them is an opacity that cannot be organized and narrated into a coherent teleology of events without the commission of a further violence against the individuals who were made to surrender their lives.

Yet, we mark off these instances of violence as genocides, holocausts, massacres – exceptions to the normative play of politics; the perpetrators, exceptional in the measure of their cruelty; the victims, exceptional in the abject, nameless destruction to which their identification as 'victims' assigns them. The victims of the Shoah, the victims of Tuol Sleng, the victims of Srebrenica and Guernica and Hiroshima become a nameless horde of wronged people – and their namelessness in our conceptual reckoning works to secure us from their deaths.

The desire to secure and to securitize – to insulate ourselves from the stain of the Other's vulnerability or from his crimes works to harden and immobilize our sense of who we are and, most importantly, how we differ from Others, and how Others differ from us – for example, through their criminality or their weakness. We recognize and recoil from the Other's vulnerability to injury, illness, disease, and disaster. And we purge the Other on the basis of his crimes, identifying him as violent and evil. This is not to say that violence, and even evil, are never appropriate ways to understand and explain events. What is at stake here, however, is not the inherent, immutable characteristics so often assigned to the Other, but rather the ways in which the Other is identified that serve to excise him from the community of those toward whom we feel any sense of ethical responsibility. This, in turn, works to enshrine our own subjectivities as normatively ethical.

Indeed, it is precisely the practices associated with 'condemnation, denunciation, and excoriation [that] work as quick ways to posit an onto-logical difference between judge and judged, and even to purge oneself of another so that condemnation becomes the way in which we establish the other as non-recognizable.'[6] And an Other that is non-recognizable is a dangerous Other; she is an Other who cannot be welcomed as she crosses the threshold of our borders, our homes, our classrooms, our lives. We work to repel or contain her in the name of justice – or ethics. Our sense of security is thus predicated on the denial of our vulnerability, even as we work to patch those same vulnerabilities. We work tirelessly to minimize our exposure to the Other, to deny the frailty which characterizes the surfaces of our bodies; the thin stretch of skin over our bones, the weakness of the ribcage over our hearts and lungs, our spindly necks and exposed abdomens. Yet to recognize the partial truths of shared weakness is to orient our thinking toward a new ethics, toward an ethics which does not inquire after or demand hardened, fixed identities, toward an ethics which regards as violent the imperative of identifying oneself as this or that, of suffering identity as a liability which is more liable – even subject to punishment of death – than the identities of others. This is an ethics, which, as Butler notes, does not ask the question 'who are you?' once and for all with the expectation of a complete, trans-existential answer. Rather, this is an ethics which asks 'who are you?' over and over again, in different ways and in different times and places, always aware and agreeable to the idea that the only possibility of making answer can never satisfy what the question requires.[7]

## The measure of things

Responsibility requires that we accept the exposure that follows from the framing of the question. It requires us to 'take the very unbearability of exposure as the sign, the reminder, of a common vulnerability, a common physicality, a common risk.'[8] We are not substitutable for one another, but neither do we occupy discrete subjective positions marked fundamentally by separation. We are, all of us, 'in our skins, given over, in each other's hands, at each other's mercy.'[9] The situation in which we find ourselves is not one of our choosing – we do not will it – yet our painful vulnerability to suffering and death is undeniable. The commonality among those of us who have nothing else in common is precisely that vulnerability – that exposure to the Other for which and for whom we are responsible to answer, but through the very strictures placed upon the possibility of answering, we cannot answer.

In this way, we are always more and less and other than what we think and do and are. My relationship with Stojan Sokolović was always about more and less and other than the text in which he now appears, however opaquely, however unjustly, however violently, however painfully. It was

always about more and less and other than fulfilling professional require-
ments, or even completing them with the tangential goal of having something to say that was worth all the time it took to say it. Indeed, I wrote
what I wrote because it pleased me to write it, even as it simultaneously
drew from me grief, frustration, neurosis, sleeplessness, and a measure of
depression. As I cannot account fully for myself and my multiplicities, so I
cannot fully account for what I wrote or, perhaps more importantly, what
I failed to write. Like Butler:

> I begin somewhere, marking a time, trying to begin a sequence, offering
> perhaps causal links or, at least, narrative structure. I narrate, and I bind
> myself as I narrate, give an account of myself, offer an account to an Other
> in the form of a story which might well work to summarize how and why I
> am. But my effort at self-summarization fails, and fails necessarily, when the
> 'I' who is introduced in the opening line, the 'I' who serves as a narrative
> voice, cannot give an account of how it became an 'I' who might narrate
> itself.[10]

Yet, this failure, far from precluding the possibility of responsibility, is actually integral to an understanding of responsibility, which takes as its goal
the loosening of the metaphysical ropes in which we have bound ourselves
and others – the cracking of the edges of ontology – the fragmentation (the
obliteration) of objectivity.

Indeed, the failure to adequately account for ourselves, our choices,
and our actions does not release us from obligation, but actually underwrites it. It is precisely because I cannot fix myself as a Self in time and
space that I must release the Other from the command to do the same,
that is, to show himself in a complete accounting. How can I ever ask Petar
Kujundžić, for example, to give a full and complete and verifiable account
of the reason why he chose to capture the priest in the photograph at
Gračanica? It will always have been about more and less and other than
what he, or we, can say about it. How might I ask Stojan Sokolović to
explain himself to me as an unproblematic subject who can remain unproblematically unitary? Stojan Sokolović has kind, steady hands that serve
coffee to strangers. But those hands have also sown landmines.

Observing that our sense of ourselves is always fragmented is quite
different, however, than saying that what we might say could be contested.
Our exposure to the Other is also fundamentally about contestation – it is
about the possibility – indeed, the necessity, of facing the Other's facing
and allowing oneself to be contested, challenged, temporarily silenced. I
am silenced by Stojan Sokolović. I undergo this facing, it comes upon me
ineluctably and I am caught, trapped always in the inability to verify or
justify my thoughts and actions, and beliefs. We are lodged in the gaze of

the Other, and we have no alibi which could clear us – we have no absolution that could release us – from responsibility.

It is for this reason that I have argued that we are bound to answer
for the crimes of the Other as though they were our own. We are obligated to answer for them not because we are personally responsible for their
commission in particular times and places and against particular Others,
but because there is no possibility of ever claiming that we are incapable
of committing them, and because we *do* commit them, or they are
committed in our names, in other times and places, against other Others.
Thus, all the work we undertake to denounce and punish the perpetrator
– from war to juridical proceedings, to incarceration, to execution, to fieldwork conclusions that reify and immobilize, to writing and publishing, and
to narrating events in ways that insulate us from the disease of the Other's
violence – only underwrites our own desperate attempt to evade that which
would implicate us in the commission of violence; namely, that violence
is the normative condition within which we operate, and that all of our
claims to the contrary are their own, further violence. Indeed, identifying
ourselves as implicated in the ways in which the very forms of our identities are underwritten by violence disallows us a retreat into justifications
or into obfuscation through the identification of the violence of the Other
as exceptional.

## Opacity

The exceptionalization of the Other passes first through the attempt to grasp
the Other – to arrange the Other into a taxonomy of characteristics, along
a teleology of recognition, along an alien route. The Other's exceptionality
is achieved only after we have satisfied ourselves that we can accurately
identify what it is about him that makes him *not us*. In the process of identification, we ourselves produce the supposed qualities of the Other: his
backwardness, his barbarity, his criminality. We locate the Other as a
knowable phenomenon with particular qualities that in turn explain his
situation of abjection. It is the moral or economic poverty of the Other, or
his addiction, or his ethnicity, or his primitive sense of politics and religion;
it is his inability to relate, to feel, to struggle, to resist. The Other slips away
and we have, before the Other is even lost, already calculated the reasons
why it happened, and why he – and we – could do nothing against it.
These are the questions which are precisely borne and play out within the
context of an applied futility. It is pointless to speak with them – they are
barbarians. It is pointless to provide financial aid – they cannot manage it
properly. It is pointless to make a ceasefire with them – they will betray it.
It is pointless to intervene – they only want to kill one another.

The Other is subsumed even in the face of the best intentions, and *particularly* when there is no intention to commit violence, to harm or injure or outrage. Indeed, the scholarship associated with fieldwork, for example, is perceived by its practitioners as a crucial source of data-gathering, which enhances our corpus of scholarly knowledge, not as a violent appropriation, representation, and manufacture of the form of the Other's body and the content of her life, and of her society. Field researchers, like tourists, arrive having already purchased the right to access the Other – the right to write the Other as adventure, danger, erotic, exotic pleasure, and risk; as primitive, pristine. Even Kujundžić, for whom the priest and the penitent are Other in different ways, differently, found something exceptional in the moment in which the photograph was taken; the slant of the sun on his hair, the black rope measured out in thirty-three repetitions wound round his hand, his patient, downturned face. Something about him was exceptionalized in that moment – an exceptionality that made the photograph seem worthwhile: the attempt to grasp what is essentially unexceptional, and thereby render exceptional.

The rigidity of taxonomies and other models and processes of identification is precisely what enables the relegation of Others into spheres that are fundamentally outside our sense of ethical obligation. Trundling up the side of a hill in a tour bus in Bosnia, one does not think that one's photographs will form a body of violence, one does not think that one's hastily written observations, or that one's carefully thought out interview questions, have already predetermined the terrain of engagement such that the Other's resistance can never be heard. Once the Muslim is identified by the Serb, he is not seen as anything other or additional to what has come to constitute the only politically recognizable possibility of 'himself'. Once the genocidaire is properly identified by documents, witnesses, or international observers, he is distilled into only that figure. All other points of relationality, all other possibilities, are subsumed beneath the identification: war criminal. This is the exceptionality that takes place in the categorization, in the claim to know who the Other is, and how he relates to me. Regardless of whatever else the priest in the photograph might be – a woman's son, a sister's brother, another man's friend, someone's lover or husband – he is only capable of being a priest in the photograph. Whatever else Dragan Nikolić might be, in front of the court, he is only an indicted war criminal. Whatever else Osman Osmanović and Sead Sinanović might be – professors or poets or police chiefs, fathers, brothers, husbands, sons, their deaths at Srebrenica immobilize them as victims representative of victimhood par excellence – paradigmatic examples of loss – the perfect, silent referents of a mummified system that organizes representation in such a way that the individuality of loss becomes meaningless in and for itself; the loss of one's own life, or of one whom one loves – the loss of one's voice – of one's ability to protest. This system of referents forms the onto-logical groundwork for the exceptionality of the Other, whether it is the Serb to me or the Muslim to the Serb. And there is a fundamental elision of responsibility in the face of the exceptional.

## Genocide

The exceptionality of the Other is achieved as a means of securing the Self from that for which it cannot take responsibility without destroying its sense of righteousness, namely, responsibility for violence and murder. The genocidaire is the absolutely Other – the committer of mass murder, of a measure of violence that can never be justified. We have seen the Levinasian Other personified in the figure of the widow, the orphan, the stranger, or in Caputo's formulation, the one who has been laid low, the victim of disaster. But the Levinasian Other faces us *before we can identify who he is.* We are faced with that which is anarchical, a traveller without a passport or an identity card, a figure with no discernable history; we do not know what he has been up to; we cannot pause and ask for a curriculum vitae or a brief narrative history of his deeds before we decide whether or not we are responsible to him. We are simply responsible. Hostages. This means that the one who faces me – the one who turns to me and to whom I am responsible in a Levinasian infinity – may not simply be the one who knelt down on the edge of a precipice to be shot to death, but may, in fact, be the one who pulled the trigger. The one who faces me may bear the weight of the crime – of the genocidaire – and this is a weight that I must shoulder as my own, because I do not get to choose to whom I will find myself responsible.

We should be afraid of this moment – we should be afraid, even terri-fied, that our ethical relation to the one who has been killed will be destroyed in the facing of the killer. But this does not free us from the *aporia* that is inherent in the facing: If we fail to respond to the genocidaire, then we become in our turn the committer of genocide. If we excise the genocidaire from the realm of those to whom we are responsible, then we have destroyed the possibility of the ethical, even as our facing the genocidaire imperils the ethical position itself by risking its obliteration. This, it seems to me, is the terrifying limit condition of difference. We risk the possibility that our colleagues will find us repellent – that we, too, will be excoriated from the realm of acceptable existence. In *Precarious Life*, Judith Butler begins with 'the question of the human ... We start here not because there is a human condition that is universally shared – this is surely not yet the case. The question that preoccupies me in the light of recent global violence is,

Who counts as human? Whose lives count as lives? And, finally, *What makes for a grievable life?*'[11] That some lives are grievable and others are not is the very subject of this fearful conversation about our measure of responsibility to the genocidaire. We rightly grieve, and identify those who grieve, over those whose lives have been torn from them in violence and genocide. We bear witness to them, we mourn them, we seek justice. But we are also bound by the inability to locate justice in any permanent, enduring way. Surely, resorting to ethical violence in which murder is avenged by murder only distances us that much further from other possibilities and conversations. Yet, we are left with the sense that court proceedings – that the law – cannot restore what has been taken. The law cannot restore the life, the soul, the future that is already lost, to the broken body. Dragan Nikolić's incarceration in a European prison for the rest of his life cannot possibly justify the murders of Galib Musić or Ismet Dedić. Dragan Obrenović's confession of responsibility at Potočari cannot undo what was done there, and he knows it. It cannot restore the lives of Osman Osmanović or Sead Sinanović, or any of the other several thousand dead at Srebrenica and everywhere across Bosnia and Hercegovina. Those murders can never be made right – what is broken and lost cannot be made whole again.

We survive in the myth that order is restored by proceedings that remove the perpetrator, both physically, and conceptually through the entire corpus of the law and of the theory that underwrites and legitimates law. We persist in the myth that mourning is temporary, that it will end as we push back into our regularly scheduled programming – another manifestation of exceptionality. Yet this also assumes the unproblematic existence of a fully knowable, fully accountable and narratable subject. It assumes that loss and grief, too, can be narrated, incorporated, and overcome. 'There is losing, as we know, but there is also the transformative effect of loss, and this latter cannot be charted or planned. One can try to choose it, but it may be that this experience of transformation deconstitutes choice at some level . . . I think one is hit by waves [of grief], and that one starts out the day with an aim, a project, a plan, and finds oneself foiled. One finds oneself fallen. One is exhausted but does not know why. Something is larger than one's own deliberate plan, one's own project, one's own knowing and choosing.'[12] If we are constituted relationally, and if I cannot secure a sense of myself, then how shall I secure a sense of what the one I loved who was lost meant to me? How can I say how she helped to constitute me? How can I say that the loss of her life is not the loss of my own to some extent and to some degree? 'If I lose you . . . then I not only mourn the loss, but I become inscrutable to myself. Who "am" I, without you? When we lose some of these ties by which we are constituted, we do not know who we are or what to do. On one level, I think I have lost "you" only to discover that "I" have gone missing as well. At another level, perhaps what I have lost "in" you, that for which I have no ready vocabulary, is a relationality that is composed neither exclusively of myself nor you, but is to be conceived as *the tie* by which those terms are differentiated and related.'[13] If the loss is the tie, then the priority is the relationship – in Levinas's terms, the relationship of the face-to-face which is prior to everything that could constitute it. In other words, we are constituted in the facing, one to another, and what we need to worry about in this is the death of the Other, for which we are always already responsible.

Perhaps the ethic of encountering the Other, then, is one that is necessarily steeped in mourning – in mourning for all that we are witness to and responsible for, and for those horrors that chip away at us, victim and perpetrator, and witness, all. We are inexorably tied to one another, and any attempt to excise and excoriate – to deny and destroy the Other – is implicated in the crime we are trying to evade in the first place.

## Justice

The singular objection to all of this is perhaps that, in our responsibility to the perpetrator, our sense of responsibility to the victim is diminished. Indeed, if Derrida is right, then my hands are only free for one because I withheld them from another. This implies, as Caputo argues, that we have to choose to whom we will be responsible and that this necessarily entails the elision of responsibility to the one who is not chosen. Thus, for Caputo, Levinas's conception is flawed because it marks an impossibility, that is, the impossibility of the form of the absolutely Other. For Caputo, the absolutely Other cannot exist, and thus, the Other is *not* a fundamental alterity; we *can* identify Others on the basis of their criminality or their victimhood; we *should* understand the Other as the widow, orphan, or stranger. 'When the Other is shooting at us, then we say, that is not the Other', Caputo reminds us.[14] For Caputo, Levinas's infinite alterity is 'the dream of virgin lands and arctic snows, of absolute nonviolence, of full presence utterly unmarked, unmediated, unmodified. It is the dream of absolute presence in the mode of absolute absence, the dream of a world without difference, without textuality, without phrases, without horizons, contexts, settings, frameworks, or any form of mediation.'[15] *Yet, here I am faced with Stojan Sokolović, who has laid landmines.*

The ineluctable entry of the Levinasian Third – the interruption that the Third effects – both tempers and heightens my responsibility to the Other. Indeed, the Third is the witness against Stojan Sokolović – the Third who accuses, who remembers, who narrates, and who appeals to me for justice. The Third *is* justice in his position as the Other of the Other. For Derrida, the entry of the Third also brings justice to the relationship of the face-to-face. The Third stands vigil, protecting against the possibility of my absolute affinity for the Other. The Third preserves the alterity of the Other, his uniqueness, which is in danger of being subsumed. Is there not the possibility of 'a violence in the pure and immediate ethics of the face to face?' asks Derrida. 'A violence potentially unleashed in the experience of the neighbor and of absolute unicity? The impossibility of discerning here between good and evil, love and hate, giving and taking, the desire to live and the death drive, the hospitable welcome and the egoistic or narcissistic closing up within oneself?'[16] How does one adjudicate? The Third stands vigil against the ever-present possibility that I experience the Other, and thus subsume him, in ecstasy. 'The [T]hird would thus protect against the vertigo of ethical violence itself. For ethics could be doubly exposed to such violence: exposed to undergo it but also to exercise it. Alternatively or simultaneously. It is true that the protecting or mediating third, in its juridico-political role, violates in its turn, at least potentially, the purity of the ethical desire devoted to the unique. Whence the terrible ineluctability of a double constraint.'[17] The Third thus protects against the violence of unicity in the facing of the Other, but also heralds violence for this very same reason: because the entry of the Third interrupts the impossibly perfect relation of the face-to-face. Thus the Third both announces justice and denies it. The Third reminds us, in short, that there is no possibility of non-violence.

The awareness that there is no possibility of non-violence – that the neighbour of the neighbour is not only another neighbour, but also the Other of the neighbour – means that the move toward justice is not a move toward innocence. If even the ethical relation to the Other is haunted by an ineradicable violence, then my capacity to make a non-violent decision is radically undermined. This does not mean that I cannot adjudicate – indeed, I do, and I must. What it means, however, is that the place from which I adjudicate is radically different from the system of referents that posits the synchronicity of binary relationships. This means that I cannot pass judgment on Stojan Sokolović on the cornerstone of my own presumed innocence; instead, any judgment of Stojan Sokolović that I undertake must recognize that he and I are guilty together – simultaneously guilty – though not interchangeably and not identically. My judgment cannot rest on his excision. Stojan Sokolović cannot be excised because there is no originary innocence – there is no sphere of non-violence – from which to excise him. And thus, there is nowhere for him to go that does not implicate us equally for his crimes.

### Refuge and exile

In his Talmudic lecture on the cities of refuge, Levinas takes up the theme of sanctuary for the manslayer. Appearing in Deuteronomy 4: 41–43 and 19: 1–10; in Numbers 35:1–34; and in Joshua 19:1–10, the cities of refuge are founded by Moses to provide a safe haven for those who accidentally commit murder, and who would otherwise be in peril of being murdered in revenge by the family members of the killed. Here, as Levinas notes, we find a question of competing rights – that is, the right of the involuntary murderer to retain his life over the right of the avenger to take it from him. The city of refuge offers a safe haven for the manslayer by prohibiting the avenger from taking revenge within the gates of the cities. Yet, Levinas notes, that same asylum is also an exile, and the hospitality of the city of refuge is also an incarceration. The city of refuge, then, both offers forgiveness and condemnation simultaneously.[18] For Derrida, this double-bind illustrates that 'the objective or involuntary murder does not have to be totally excused. Levinas insists on this double finality. Indeed, it is there to remind us that there is no real discontinuity between voluntary and involuntary murder. Sometimes invisible, always to be deciphered, this continuity forces us to infinitize our responsibility: we are also responsible for our lack of attention and for our carelessness, for what we do neither intentionally nor freely, indeed, for what we do unconsciously – since this is never without significance.'[19] The status, then, of the cities of refuge is thus highly ambiguous, and is such for this important reason. For Oona Eisenstadt, we are all in cities of refuge – simultaneously in sanctuary and exile. [20]

Levinas's missive on the cities of refuge provides a way of understanding human connectivity as one of vigilance. In this formulation, however, we are vigilant not against the Other, who we fear may kill or injure us. Rather, we exercise vigilance within the possibility that we might injure or kill the Other. The relationship here is not synchronous, but diachronous; it is not a relationship of binary opposites arrayed simultaneously along an axis of space and time. Rather, understanding responsibility, and thus justice, as leaking out and across time and space means that we can respond to what has already taken place; we can, and do, exercise vigilance in regard to those events which exceed the temporal space of our own lives or of our own ability to act. We read the names at Yom Shoah, we trace the gold-leaf letters in the museum at Victory Park, we walk slowly amid the ruins at Srebrenica, holding hands, surviving, some of us more responsible than others, but none wholly excusable. However much we may wish to defy it, we remain obligated to answer to one another, even if we can never adequately do so. The form of our address – the manner of our speaking

– always assumes that another is there, listening, waiting to respond, or to be responded to. We do not address ourselves, but Others. It is this thread that ties.

NOTES

1 Derrida, *Memoirs of the Blind*, p. 18.
2 *Whose are you?*
3 Judith Butler, *Giving An Account of Oneself: A Critique of Ethical Violence* (Assen, Netherlands: Koninklijke van Gorcum, 2003), p. 33.
4 *Ibid.*, p. 27.
5 Campbell, *National Deconstruction*, pp. 40–41.
6 Butler, *Giving An Account of Oneself*, p. 36.
7 *Ibid.*, p. 34.
8 *Ibid.*, p. 58.
9 *Ibid.*
10 *Ibid.*, p. 45.
11 Judith Butler, *Precarious Life: The Powers of Mourning and Violence* (London; New York: Verso, 2004), p. 20.
12 *Ibid.*, p. 21.
13 *Ibid.*, p. 22.
14 Caputo, *Against Ethics*, p. 123.
15 *Ibid.*, p. 82.
16 Jacques Derrida, *Adieu to Emmanuel Levinas*, p. 33.
17 *Ibid.*
18 Emmanuel Levinas, *Beyond the Verse: Talmudic Readings and Lectures*, trans. Gary D. Mole (Bloomington, IN: Indiana University Press, 1994), p. 39.
19 Derrida, *Adieu to Emmanuel Levinas*, p. 108.
20 Oona Eisenstadt, 'The Problem of the Promise: Derrida on Levinas on the Cities of Refuge', *Cross Currents*, Vol. 52, No. 4, pp. 474–482, 2001, p. 475.

## 8

# *Letter to Stojan Sokolović*

I have thought for a long time, and I'm always followed by this same thought – guilt. I find it very hard to say this truth. I am to blame for everything I did at that time. I am trying to erase all this and to be what I was not at that time. I am also to blame for what I did not do, for not trying to protect those prisoners ... I ask myself again and again, What could I have done that I didn't do? ... I am responsible for this. The guilt for this I feel remorse and for which I apologise to the victims and to their shadows.[1]

Dear Stojan,

When we met last, we drank two brown bottles of beer in Republic Square in Belgrade. We walked around the walled fortress at Kalemegdan, built on the headland at the juncture of the Dunav and Sava Rivers. We wandered up Knez Mihajlova, ducking in and out of the cafes and shops. The last war had just ended again. You said you knew that Kosovo was gone. We laughed over a postcard depicting the American Stealth bomber that Serbs had managed to shoot down. The text read: 'Sorry, we didn't know it was invisible'. After a few drinks, you said that you thought Serbia did not deserve to keep Kosovo after what had happened there. A lot of the Bosnian Serbs I know felt it was fitting that the Serbian Serbs were the last ones who had to answer for themselves. Somebody was getting rich while we were dying and killing in those hills, they said, but it was not us.

What does it mean to profit from another's loss? Does it not mean simultaneously more and less than, as Czesław Miłosz wrote, 'sending others to the more exposed positions, urging them loudly to fight on, [while we ourselves withdraw] in certainty of the cause lost'? Does it not mean simultaneously more and less than, 'having the choice of our own death and that of a friend, we chose his, coldly thinking: let it be done quickly'? Does it not mean both more and less than stealing bread, sowing land-mines, moving into the house of your neighbour after she has fled or been

139

executed or disappeared? Is it not more and less, even, than this letter, which is addressed to you, but which is still inevitably doing other work, too, because I am still answerable in some measure to those who provide me with a space to write and teach? And I am still, after all, inserting this letter into the fabric of claims about the way we are in the world – about the way the world is, even if the claim is to say that the world is not anything in particular at all, but rather a series of endless possibilities which can only be realized from time to time in fragmented, momentary ways?

What would it mean for me to say that I know you? To say that I know the way that your skin stretches across your cheeks and over your brow, and how it deepens in colour on the coast in the summer? What would it mean to say that I know the tenor of your voice, the luminosity of your eyes, the fringe of dark lashes that frame them, the curve of your fingers laced through one another on the tabletop as you fold your hands together in a manner that is uniquely yours? What can it mean, then, to say that those are the same hands with the same laced fingers that rested casually on your rifle in the high hills around Sarajevo? What can it mean, then, that these are the same eyes that sought, found, and followed the figure of the person through the cross hairs – perhaps carrying his own gun, or perhaps waiting in line for a loaf of bread, or a kilogram of flour? What could it mean to say that this is the same hand that mapped the trajectory before firing the mortar round into the side of a building that slid away like a slice of butter from the perspective of your distance, with just the far-away echo of the explosion and the memory of the women hanging their laundry out on the balconies to make it seem real at all? Some of the Serbian women in Sarajevo say that they hung out their laundry with blue, red, and white clothes pegs – the colours of Serbia – to avoid drawing your sniper fire.

Here, on the other side of the train compartment, you laugh and a moment of misunderstanding becomes the core of a priceless joke. You laugh and laugh – a moment of ecstasy or madness – of forgetting what will never pass. 'Here', you pointed out to me from the train – 'that is the house that I slept in.' And you murmured, 'that is the field I stayed in – that is where the front lines were.' And sure enough, a moment later, the train inches past the de-mining teams moving on narrow lanes marked by orange flags. 'Here', you whisper, 'it was like this.' And 'Here, it was like that.' Here, with your hands – with those very same hands – you point things out – you peel oranges, handing me section after section. Those oranges refresh me. The train slides out of Doboj and into the Federation. They pause to change the engine (which takes forever), because the Serbian engine cannot pull the train into the Federation, as the Federation engine cannot pull the train into Republika Srpska, even now, these years after . . .

140

## Letter to Stojan Sokolović

You measure our coffee – you carefully wash out the delicate cups. Here, with your hands, Stojane, you carry candles to graves, you wash the floor of the neighbour who is too old to do it herself, you count out my money again at the exchange so I don't make a mistake. You prepare lunch. Here, when we come now to Ilijaš, you take care to give no offence by asking a man to direct you 'in the name of Christ'.

Can I ever greet you, or you me, with perfect faith? Perfect faith – *potpuno povjerenje?* Is there not always that element of suspicion – that moment in the space before we know what we are going to ask of one another? Before you know why I came to speak to you, and what I want to know? Before I know who you might turn out to be?

Submitted to you: my thoughts, my words, these prayers and admonitions, the tenor of my admission, this appeal to you for mercy, this desire to stay in the prior place, where you are inaccessible and unknowable. It is precisely in the lag time between the statement and the response, precisely in the fraction of time that separates our speaking, that you escape beyond any possibility of representation – that you become the contestation that points to the destitution – and the arrogance – of my own claims all throughout this life. You become the fundamental defiance of the symmetry of my self and of the world in which I think I have found myself. You defy the categories of perpetrator and victim because these categories can never be complete – can never capture what is said of them. You resist the categories of Serb and Muslim because you move back and forth between figures of speech and words and ritualistic traditions without even being aware of which moments are Serb, and which moments are Muslim. You repel my attempt to formulate meaning. You defy my desire to fix you in time and space and relationships. We are in a place now where singular truth as a possibility is long gone. We speak, you and I, neither knowing who the other is, was, could be – under these circumstances or others. We sit across from one another on a borrowed balcony, a scratched milk carton serving as a makeshift table for the coffee cups. We are knee-to-knee in that small space, regarding each other with our different-coloured eyes and trying to communicate in a language that is not yours in a country that is not mine. There is a patch of dry summer grass below the railing. We try to make sense of ourselves and one another. We try to explain ourselves. But we don't – we can't – succeed.

Perhaps by the end of this, we will walk away from one another in confusion, disgust, misunderstanding, outrage, condemnation, excoriation. This is what it means to risk our potential commonality – perhaps we share nothing at all. Perhaps we are, as a philosopher I like claims, a community of those who have nothing in common. Yet, when we sit down together at the same table and contemplate one another over those two cups of thick Turkish coffee, we are assuming goodwill each on the part of the other – we have lowered our guard to allow for the possibility of friendship, which is not the same as commonality. You peel oranges for me. You tear off section after section.

It is precisely through the dissymmetry of friendship that I can speak in your favour without speaking in your place. I am responsible to you both for the things that I wrote, said, and did, but also for the things that you decided and did. I am responsible to answer to you, even for your own decisions, even for the decisions you took prior to my having found you. I am responsible to you both because of those decisions, and despite them. I am responsible to answer as though in your place, which is not the same thing at all as answering in place of you. Answering as though I am in your place means that I am responsible in equal measure for your actions – they are also mine, always potentially mine in this endless process of friendship and faith. I cannot, however, answer in place of you – I cannot answer for you, in other words, in order to protect you from having to answer for yourself. In this way are we responsible to and for one another without knowing what it is each of us has done or not done – before we know, in other words, what it is that we are answering for. This is the movement of perfect faith – *potpuno povjerenje* – wherein we are willing to answer for one another before we know what it is we are answering for, to whom, and what the consequences might be. This is the movement wherein we are willing to answer for one another before any formulation of other can be made.

This is not the imperative to answer for some particular instance of murder out of juridical guilt, but rather to answer to and for individuals out of friendship and faith – out of responsibility, which is required for Ismet Dedić and Galib Musić, but also to Dragan Nikolić, who killed them at Sušica. This is the imperative to answer to you, Stojan Sokolović, to answer to Sead Sinanović, to Osman Osmanović, buried at Srebrenica by units of the Zvornik Brigade that Dragan Obrenović sent for that purpose. This is the imperative to answer to Dragan Obrenović, who also found the guts to answer for himself – to stand exposed and undone – to say, 'yes I did this, and I did that, and the responsibility is mine'. This is the sinking down to the floor before the proper names of the dead, because the proper names bear witness to themselves, and they also bear witness to those whose proper names have been forgotten, whose bodies simply succumbed. But it is also the sinking down to the floor before the proper name of Dragan Obrenović, because he managed to stay on his feet when the orders to execute the prisoners arrived (would that he had not!).

'Here is the front line', you murmur in English as the train slides past. And I felt the tremor pass over your skin.

Ours is a friendship of fear and trembling, which contains a measure of responsibility that I do not want to bear. And yet, we know – don't we know – that it is precisely our denial of responsibility that paves the way for Omarska and Sušica, for Srebrenica – for these places which bear proper names but also for those nameless events which crush people whose names we never knew, but whom we did not love well enough because, as you yourself said: our lives went on.

But here, now, Stojane, my life does not go on as it would have gone had we never sat down together on that balcony in the summer rain. My life was changed there while you poured your viscous Turkish coffee into those little china cups. My soul was intersected – revealed as having been constituted in the first through its fundamental fragmentation. I didn't want to know what you would tell me. Even then, I saw that it would complicate things unbearably – that it would destroy my sense of equilibrium – the sense that I and all my colleagues had already concluded on how your war had been, how it should never have been, on how and who you were in it, on what should have been done about it. There is no city of refuge that could contain us all within its bounds, and no measure of remorse or forgiveness that can make these things right.

Stojane, do you remember when we walked through that village graveyard in Gučevo – in the ancestral hills of Romanija – humming with overgrown grasses beneath the still summer sun? And so many stones bore the proper name of Karišik – four brothers each, Veljko, Željko, Gojko, and Bojko, cut down in 1944 all at once – an entire generation extinguished on the spot – the work of a woman's whole adult life destroyed without a second thought. In the low hills around Sarajevo, in the low hills before they become high hills, the stark white sentinel stones of Muslim graves are stuffed in beside one another, left and right on east-facing slopes, each one bearing a proper name. All of the visitors to Bosnia, researchers and thanotourists, follow the splash marks of grenade explosions in the concrete while we lick the white honey halva from our summer-stained fingers. We pass beneath the white marble commemorative plaques that mark the spot where 'Serbian criminals' murdered shamelessly sixteen people, ten people, twelve, three, forty-three. We pass through the narrow alleys of the old shops on Baščaršija. We walk there with less than perfect faith because it is here in these narrow, smoke-choked cobbled alleys that we feel the skin of that other close in on us all around in the shapes of the brass vases and copper *džezve* and the distinctly Sarajevan inflection of words shouted back and forth across the shop fronts. You already always contain that within yourself.

But where is the one for the other? Where is the one who will stand in the place of the other man? Who will answer as though in his place, out of equal responsibility? What is the distance between you and me, that one crosses into the other's path unexpectedly, unannounced, with nothing in common? What is the distance between faith and perfect faith that it exists and can exist only between strangers? There is no need to have perfect faith among family and friends – one's faith is not faith, but expectation. It is only between you and me – neither family nor friends nor even colleagues – it is only in this space where we are not yet aware of our connections (if we have any at all) – that perfect faith becomes possible.

Here, I am standing before you. Here is the place where I am with you in totality and infinitude, without recourse or reconsideration, without a sunset clause that would allow my accountability to lapse. The loss of you – like the loss of those who lie beneath the soil in cities and villages across this lost federation – is also in some measure mine. Here, we find ourselves sharing in common the death of the other in the interconnectedness of loss itself, toward which each of us must eventually turn our faces. Here, it is the other, who, in the face of the absolutely Other – that is, death – becomes my brother, stands in my place not instead of me, but with me – before me, hand in hand, the one for the other, in my place. Stojane.

I know it was indecent for me to show up speaking English, mispronouncing names and villages, refusing the food and drink which is the very core of your hospitality, maintaining and marking my place on the other side of the world. To whom was I responsible for the content of my publications when they were populated by others? I answered to myself, which is to say, to no one. What do I owe to the soldier with the colourless eyes at the Karakaj crossing that he can ever exact from me? I owe only if I decide I do, which is no obligation at all. This is the prior condition within which the soldier at the Karakaj crossing crashes through the armour of my training and traumatizes me absolutely with the very manner of his presence. This is the manner in which you utterly destroyed my sense of what constitutes justice with your inescapable allegation, and trapped in the trauma of your gaze – of your demanding. At a workshop in San Diego in 2006, Annick Wibben, a mother and feminist, tells me that my silence will not protect me. So I still write. I still try, all the while asking you to understand that this text can ever only be part of all that I would say if I could. All the while, I am asking you to let me go for all that I cannot express, because I am constrained by so very many things, and there are so many things I have forgotten, and other things that I don't have words for.

This is the manner in which we sat facing one another across the scratched table on the balcony, while I thought of the smoke from burning tyres that hangs low over the Vrbas River on Petrovdan. (The Vrbas starts in the Federation, but I have never met a person who knows what sound it makes at the point of its origin.) There is no exchange, no equivalent – we are not two sides in the same space – I cannot project myself into your skin – you are fundamentally different from me. And here we brush up against one another almost accidentally, both because of and despite my intentionality to find you. I intended to find you, but you were not who I thought you would be – you were not who I had searched for. You ruined my research agenda. You were too much for my discipline. You were too much for me. You were too much for ethics.

Here, outside any possibility of non-violence, the question of loosening up, of letting you try again, is the only one that remains. Here, the recognition of the bind that this life and this hope have caught us in is the only thing that can allow for perfect faith. How could it be otherwise? It is only the unforgivable that can be forgiven. It is only in the unbinding that the possibility of perfect faith emerges. I am here, standing before you without having meant to, without having wanted to. But here I am.

Stojane, evo me . . .

NOTE

1    Dragan Obrenović, Statement at Sentencing (ICTY case number IT-02-8 60/2-S), 30 October 2003.

# BIBLIOGRAPHY

Agamben, Giorgio, *Homo Sacer: Sovereign Power and Bare Life* (Stanford, CA: Stanford University Press, 1998).

——, *Remnants of Auschwitz: The Witness and the Archive*, Daniel Heller-Roazen, trans. (New York: Zone Books, 2002).

Arendt, Hannah, *Eichmann in Jerusalem: A Report on the Banality of Evil* (New York: Penguin, 1964).

——, 'Organized Guilt and Universal Responsibility', in Peter Baehr, ed., *The Portable Hannah Arendt* (New York: Penguin, 2000).

——, 'The Origins of Totalitarianism', in Peter Baehr, ed., *The Portable Hannah Arendt* (New York: Penguin, 2000).

——, *Responsibility and Judgment* (New York: Schocken, 2003).

Ashley, Richard, 'The Achievements of Post-Structuralism', in Steve Smith, Ken Booth, and Marysia Zalewski, eds, *International Theory: Positivism and Beyond* (New York: Cambridge University Press, 1996).

Baudrillard, Jean, *Impossible Exchange* (London; New York: Verso, 2001).

——, *Simulacra and Simulation*, in Mark Poster, ed., *Selected Writings* (Stanford, CA: Stanford University Press, 2001).

——, *Simulacra and Simulation* (Ann Arbor, MI: University of Michigan Press, 1995).

Bernard-Donals and Glejzer, eds, *Witnessing the Disaster: Essays on Representation and the Holocaust* (Madison, WI: University of Wisconsin Press, 2003).

Bernasconi, Robert, '"Only the Persecuted . . .": Language of the Oppressor, Language of the Oppressed', in Adriaan T. Peperzak, ed., *Ethics as First Philosophy: The Significance of Emmanuel Levinas for Philosophy, Literature, and Religion* (New York: Routledge, 1995).

Blanchot, Maurice, *The Instant of My Death*, Elizabeth Rottenberg, trans. (Stanford, CA: Stanford University Press, 2000).

——, *The Writing of the Disaster*, Ann Smock, trans. (Lincoln, NE: University of Nebraska Press, 1995).

Bleiker, Roland, 'The Aesthetic Turn in International Political Theory', *Millennium: Journal of International Studies*, Vol. 30, No. 3, 2001.

Bourdieu, Pierre, *Homo Academicus*, Peter Collier, trans. (Cambridge: Polity Press/Blackwell, 1988).

Brecher, Bob, 'Our Obligation to the Dead', *Journal of Applied Philosophy*, Vol. 19, No. 2, 2002.

Buber, Martin, *I and Thou* (New York: Touchstone Books, 1996).

Burke, Anthony, 'Poetry Outside of Security', *Alternatives*, Vol. 25, 2000.

Butler, Judith, *Giving An Account of Oneself: A Critique of Ethical Violence* (Assen, Netherlands: Koninklijke van Gorcum, 2003).

——, *Precarious Life: The Powers of Mourning and Violence* (London; New York: Verso, 2004).

# Bibliography

Campbell, David, 'The Deterritorialization of Responsibility: Levinas, Derrida, and Ethics after the End of Philosophy', in David Campbell and Michael J. Shapiro, eds, *Moral Spaces: Rethinking Ethics and World Politics* (Minneapolis, MN: University of Minnesota Press: 1999).

——, *National Deconstruction: Violence, Identity, and Justice in Bosnia* (Minneapolis, MN: University of Minnesota Press, 1998).

——, 'Post-Cold War Conflict and the Failure of Democracy', in Shawna Christianson and Robert Dick, eds, *Order and Disorder: Domestic Sources of Regional Instability*, Occasional Paper #31, Centre for Defence and Security Studies, University of Manitoba, February 1995.

Caputo, John D., ed., *Against Ethics* (Indianapolis: University of Indiana Press, 1993).

——, *Deconstruction in a Nutshell: A Conversation with Jacques Derrida* (New York: Fordham University Press, 1997).

——, 'Goodwill and the Hermeneutics of Friendship: Gadamer and Derrida', *Philosophy and Social Criticism*, Vol. 28, No. 5, 2002.

——, 'Reason, History and a Little Madness: Towards an Ethics of the Kingdom', in Richard Kearney and Mark Dooley, eds, *Questioning Ethics: Contemporary Debates in Philosophy* (New York: Routledge, 1999).

Cheong, So-Min and Marc L. Miller, 'Power and Tourism: A Foucauldian Observation', *Annals of Tourism Research*, Vol. 27, No. 2, 2000.

Clegg, Johnny, *Jericho* (Capitol Records: 1990).

Connelly, William E., *Identity/Difference: Democratic Negotiations of Political Paradox* (Minneapolis, MN: University of Minnesota Press, 1991).

——, 'Suffering, Justice, and the Politics of Becoming', in *Moral Spaces: Rethinking Ethics and World Politics* (Minneapolis, MN: University of Minnesota Press: 1999).

Collins, Patricia Hill, *Black Feminist Thought: Knowledge, Consciousness, and the Politics of Empowerment*, 2nd edn (New York: Routledge, 2000).

Dauphinée, Elizabeth, 'International Intervention, Discourses of Representation, and the Production of Subordinated Sovereignties', in Kyle Grayson and Cristina Masters, eds, *Theory in Practice: Critical Reflections on Global Policy* (Toronto: Centre for International and Security Studies, 2003).

——, 'Rambouillet: A Critical Reassessment', in Florian Bieber and Zhidas Daskalovski, eds, *Understanding the War in Kosovo* (London: Frank Cass, 2003).

Department of National Defence, Security and Defence Forum Annual Report, 1998–1999 (Ottawa, Canada: Department of National Defence, 1999).

Derrida, Jacques, *Adieu to Emmanuel Levinas*, Pascale-Anne Brault and Michael Naas, trans. (Stanford, CA: Stanford University Press, 1999).

——, *Aporias*, Thomas Dutoit, trans. (Stanford, CA: Stanford University Press, 1993).

——, *Demeure: Fiction and Testimony*, Elizabeth Rottenberg, trans. (Stanford, CA: Stanford University Press: 2000).

——, 'Force of Law: "The Mystical Foundations of Authority,"' in Drucilla Cornell, Michael Rosenfeld, David Gray Carlson, eds, *Deconstruction and the Possibility of Justice* (New York: Routledge, 1992).

——, *The Gift of Death*, David Wills, trans. (Chicago: University of Chicago Press, 1995).

——, 'Hospitality, Justice and Responsibility', in Richard Kearney and Mark Dooley, eds, *Questioning Ethics: Contemporary Debates in Philosophy* (London: Routledge, 1999).

——, *Memoirs of the Blind: The Self-Portrait and Other Ruins*, Pascale-Anne Brault and Michael Naas, trans. (Chicago, University of Chicago Press, 1993).

——, *Politics of Friendship*, George Collins, trans. (London: Verso, 1997).

——, *The Work of Mourning* (Chicago: University of Chicago Press, 2001).

Dimon, Anne, 'Visiting Another Place, Another Time', *Toronto Star*, 10 April 2004, J14.

Doebele, Justin, 'Club Dead', *Forbes*, December 15, 1997.

Dominguez, Virginia R., 'For A Politics of Love and Rescue', *Cultural Anthropology*, Vol. 15, No. 3, 2000.

Dostoevsky, Fyodor, *The Brothers Karamazov*, Andrew R. MacAndrew, trans. (New York: Bantam Books, 1970).

Drainac, Rade, 'When the Poet Without Lying Verses in His Heart Returns to His Native Country', in Charles Simić, ed., *The Horse Has Six Legs: An Anthology of Serbian Poetry* (St Paul MN: Graywolf Press, 1992).

Edkins, Jenny, *Trauma and the Memory of Politics* (Cambridge: Cambridge University Press, 2003).

Eisenstadt, Oona, 'The Problem of the Promise: Derrida on Levinas on the Cities of Refuge', *Cross Currents*, Vol. 52, No. 4, 2001.

Ewart, Vian, 'Images of India', *Toronto Star*, 3 April 2004, J1.

Foucault, Michel, *The Birth of the Clinic: an archaeology of medical perception* (London: Routledge, 1989).

Fridman, Lea Wernick, *Words and Witness: Narrative and Aesthetic Strategies in the Representation of the Holocaust* (Albany, NY: State University of New York Press, 2000).

Geertz, Clifford, *Works and Lives: The Anthropologist as Author* (Stanford, CA: Stanford University Press, 1988).

Girard, Rene, 'Literature and Christianity: A Personal View', *Philosophy and Literature*, Vol. 23, No. 1, 1999.

Hammer, Espen, 'Adorno and Extreme Evil', *Philosophy and Social Criticism*, Vol. 26, No. 4, 2000.

Haraway, Donna, *Simians Cyborgs and Women* (New York: Routledge: 1991).

Hatley, James, 'Beyond Outrage: The Delirium of Responsibility in Levinas's Scene of Persecution', in Eric Nelson, Antje Kapust and Kent Still, eds, *Addressing Levinas* (Evanston, IL: Northwestern University Press, 2004).

——, *Suffering Witness: The Quandary of Responsibility After the Irreparable* (Albany, NY: State University of New York Press, 2000).

Herwig, Holger, 'What Price Victory?' *University of Calgary Gazette*, 1 May 2000.

Hibbitts, Bernard, 'War Correspondence', *Jurist* (Pittsburgh: University of Pittsburgh, 1999).

Hilberg, Raul, 'I Was Not There', in Berel Lang, ed., *Writing and the Holocaust* (New York: Holmes & Meier, 1988).

'Historic Bridge Reopens in Bosnia', CBC Online, 23 July 2004.

Hutnyk, John, *The Rumour of Calcutta: Tourism, Charity, and the Poverty of Representation* (London; New Jersey: Zed Books, 1996).

Hyde, Jeannette, 'Ban the Extremists Says LP', *The Observer*, 17 November 2002.

International Campaign to Ban Landmines, *Landmine Monitor Report*, Human Rights Watch, 2000.

International Criminal Tribunal for the Former Yugoslavia, Judgement in the Case of the Prosecutor V. Stanislav Galić, ICTY Press Release, The Hague, 5 December 2003.

——, The Prosecutor V. Stanislav Galić: Separate and Partially Dissenting Opinion of Judge Nieto-Navia, para. 109.

——, The Prosecutor V. Dragan Nikolić (Third Amended Indictment), Case No. IT-94-2-PT, 31 October 2003.

——, Dragan Obrenović, Statement at Sentencing, 30 October 2003.

——, 'Statement of Facts as set out by Dragan Obrenović' (Tab A to 'Annex A' to the 'Joint Motion for Consideration of a Plea Agreement Between Dragan Obrenović and the Office of the Prosecutor'), May 2003.

Irigiray, Luce, 'The Fecundity of the Caress', in Richard A. Cohen, ed., *Face to Face With Levinas* (Albany, NY: State University of New York Press, 1986).

Jantzen, Grace, *Becoming Divine: Towards a Feminist Philosophy of Religion* (Manchester, UK: Manchester University Press, 1998).

Keenan, Thomas, *Fables of Responsibility: Aberrations and Predicaments in Ethics and Politics* (Stanford, CA: Stanford University Press, 1997).

Kierkegaard, Søren, 'Fear and Trembling', in Hong and Hong, eds/trans., *Fear and Trembling/Repetition* (Princeton, NJ: Princeton University Press, 1983).

——, 'Fear and Trembling', in Robert Bretall, ed., *A Kierkegaard Anthology* (Princeton, NJ: Princeton University Press, 1936).

Kujundžić, Petar, *Globe and Mail*, 29 June 1998 Photograph and captioning: 'A MAN PRAYS DURING LITURGY IN GRAČANICA. A man prays next to a Serbian Orthodox priest during a liturgy marking the 609th anniversary of the battle of Kosovo against the Ottoman Empire, outside the 14th century Serbian Orthodox monastery Gračanica, some 10 km from Priština, the capital of Serbia's troubled province of Kosovo June 28. US envoy Richard Holbrooke warned on Saturday that Europe was only a few steps away from a general war in Kosovo but said there was still time to pull back from the brink. PEK/ME YUGOSLAVIA KOSOVO GRAČANICA. Photo by PETAR KUJUNDŽIĆ. © REUTERS 1998. 28/06/1998 [x001500020010920du6s001e2, X00150]'

Lang, Berel, *Writing and the Moral Self* (New York; London: Routledge, 1991).

Levi, Primo, *The Drowned and the Saved* (London: Abacus, 1989).

Levinas, Emmanuel, *Beyond the Verse: Talmudic Readings and Lectures*, trans. Gary D. Mole (Bloomington, IN: Indiana University Press, 1994).

——, 'Ethics and Politics', in *The Levinas Reader*, Sean Hand, ed. (Oxford, UK and Cambridge, MA: Blackwell Publishers, 1989).

# Bibliography

——, 'Ethics as First Philosophy', in *The Levinas Reader*, Sean Hand, ed. (Oxford, UK and Cambridge, MA: Blackwell Publishers, 1989).

——, *Of God Who Comes to Mind*, Bettina Bergo, trans. (Stanford, CA: Stanford University Press: 1998).

——, *Otherwise Than Being Or Beyond Essence* (Pittsburgh: Duquesne University Press, 1998).

——, 'The Trace of the Other', Alphonso Lingis, trans., in Mark Taylor, ed., *Deconstruction in Context* (Chicago: University of Chicago Press, 1986).

Lingis, Alphonso, *The Community of Those Who Have Nothing in Common* (Bloomington, IN: Indiana University Press, 1994).

——, *Foreign Bodies* (New York: Routledge, 1994),

——, 'Introduction' in Emmanuel Levinas, *Otherwise Than Being Or Beyond Essence* (Pittsburgh: Duquesne University Press, 1998).

——, *Trust* (Minneapolis: University of Minnesota Press, 2004).

Lisle, Debbie, 'Consuming Danger: Reimagining the War/Tourism Divide', *Alternatives*, Vol. 25, No. 1, Jan–Mar 2000, pp. 91–116.

Little, Kenneth, 'On Safari: The Visual Politics of a Tourist Representation', in David Howes, ed., *The Varieties of Sensory Experience: A Sourcebook in the Anthropology of the Senses* (Toronto: University of Toronto Press, 1991).

Lloyd, Anthony, *My War Gone By, I Miss It So* (New York: Atlantic Monthly Press: 1999).

Miłosz, Czesław, 'A Poor Christian Looks at the Ghetto', *Selected Poems* (Hopewell, NJ: The Ecco Press, 1973).

——, 'Child of Europe', *Selected Poems* (Hopewell, NJ: The Ecco Press, 1973).

Molloy, Patricia, 'Face-to-Face with the Dead Man: Ethical Responsibility, State-Sanctioned Killing, and Empathetic Impossibility', in David Campbell and Michael J. Shapiro, eds, *Moral Spaces: Rethinking Ethics and World Politics* (Minneapolis, MN: University of Minnesota Press: 1999).

'More Explosions in Yugoslavia; Civilian Casualties Reported', CNN, 5 April 1999.

Morgenthau, Hans, 'Death in the Nuclear Age', *Commentary*, Vol. 32, No. 3, September 1961.

Murdoch, Iris, *Metaphysics as a Guide to Morals* (London: Chatto & Windus, Ltd, 1992).

N'Dour, Youssou, public comments at Harbourfront, Toronto, 6 July 2004.

Nietzsche, Friedrich, *Thus Spoke Zarathustra*, R. J. Hollingdale, trans. (London: Penguin Books, 1969).

Obrenović, Dragan, Internatioanl Criminal Tribunal for the Former Yugoslavia, Prosecutor v. Dragan Obrenovic: Sentencing Judgement, 10 December 2003. www.un.org/icty/obrenovic/trielc/judgement/index.htm

O'Donoghue, David, 'Holocaust Tourism', *Sunday Business Post*, 13 January 2002.

Pelton, Robert Young, *The World's Most Dangerous Places*, 5th edn (New York: Harper Collins, 2003).

Rehn, Elisabeth and Ellen Johnson Sirleaf, 'Women, War, and Peace: The Independent Experts' Assessment on the Impact of Armed Conflict on Women and Women's Role in Peace-building', United Nations Development Fund for Women (UNIFEM), October 2002.

Robertson, Geoffrey, *Crimes Against Humanity: The Struggle for Global Justice* (London: Penguin-Allen-Lane, 1999).

Rose, Gillian, 'Practising Photography: an Archive, a Study, Some Photographs and a Researcher', *Journal of Historical Geography*, Vol. 26, No. 4, 2000.

Ross, Fiona C., *Bearing Witness: Women and the Truth and Reconciliation Commission in South Africa* (London: Pluto Press, 2003).

Segan, Sascha, 'Iraq: The Next Adventure Travel Destination?' *Frommer's News and Highlights*, 23 April 2003.

Shapiro, Michael J., 'The Ethics of Encounter: Unreading, Unmapping the Imperium', in Michael J. Shapiro and David Campbell, eds, *Moral Spaces: Rethinking Ethics and World Politics* (Minneapolis: University of Minnesota Press, 1999).

Simmons, William Paul, 'The Third: Levinas' Theoretical Move From An-archical Ethics to the Realm of Justice and Politics, *Philosophy and Social Criticism*, Vol. 25, No. 6, 1999.

Sontag, Susan, *On Photography* (New York: Farrar, Strauss, and Giroux, 1977).

——, *Regarding the Pain of Others* (New York: Farrar, Straus, and Giroux, 2003).

Strain, Ellen, *Public Places, Private Journeys: Ethnography, Entertainment, and the Tourist Gaze* (New Brunswick, NJ: Rutgers University Press, 2003).

Thompson, Allan, 'Canadian Troops Smuggled Bosnian Refugees, Memos Say', *Toronto Star*, 28 November 1999, A2.

Torpey, John, *The Invention of the Passport: Surveillance, Citizenship and the State* (Cambridge; New York: Cambridge University Press, 2000).

Trinh T. Minh-ha, *Framer Framed* (New York: Routledge, 1992).

Urry, John, *The Tourist Gaze: Leisure and Travel in Contemporary Societies* (London: Sage, 1990).

Vučetić, Srdjan, 'Identity is a Joking Matter: Intergroup Humour in Bosnia', *Spaces of Identity*, Vol. 3, No. 2, July 2004.

Walzer, Michael, *Just and Unjust Wars* (New York: Basic Books, 2000).

Ward, Graham, 'On Time and Salvation: The Eschatology of Emmanuel Levinas', in Sean Hand ed., *Facing the Other: The Ethics of Emmanuel Levinas* (New York: Curson Press, 1996).

Waters, Roger and Pink Floyd, 'Your Possible Pasts', *The Final Cut* (Phantom Records, 1983).

Weber, Cynthia, 'Performative States', *Études Internationales*, XXIX, 1, 1998.

Wiesenthal, Simon, *The Sunflower: On the Possibilities and Limits of Forgiveness* (Paris: Opera Mundi, 1969); with Symposium (1998).

Williams, Stephen, *Tourism Geography* (London; New York: Routledge, 1998).

# INDEX

Note: 'n.' after a page number indicates the number of a note on that page.

# Index

# Index

Filipović, Zoran 37
forgiveness 14, 113–14, 145
Foucault, Michel 41
fragmentation: of objectivity 130
    of narrative events 70
    of the self 89, 92
Friedman, Lea Wernick 118
friendship 114, 142, 143

Galić, Stanislav 81, 117
gaze *see* tourist gaze
Geertz, Clifford 53
genocidaire 132, 133–4
genocide: of Bosnians 96, 112
    and naming 118, 127, 128
    as a televised event 74
Girard, Rene 90
glas: in French and Serbian 92
*Glas Srpski* 92
Glejzer, Richard 109–10
*Globe and Mail* 62–3, 69, 78
'good' and 'evil': and Arendt 87
    identification of 94
    in law 84, 85, 86
Gračanica 58, 60, 60–1, 63, 67, 68, 69,
    130
grief 9, 10, 15
    Butler on 134–5
Guantanamo Bay 88
Gučevo 143
Guernica 128
guilt 1, 2, 14, 15, 93
    Dragan Obrenović's statement at
        sentencing 139

Hague, The *see* International Criminal
    Tribunal for the Former Yugoslavia
    (ICTY), The Hague
Haraway, Donna 16n.17
Hatley, James: on the command 107,
    122
    on forgiveness 113–14
    on formulation into *logos* 118, 119
    on irrecoverable loss 108, 109
    on responsibility to the Other 1, 33–4,
        93, 119–20, 121, 122
Herwig, Holger 48–9, 65, 66, 67, 68,
    76
Hilberg, Raul 13
Hiroshima 108, 128
history: issues of ethnicity and
    nationalism 28
    as politics 29–30
    and naming of events 118

Holocaust: as cinematographic 73, 74
    and naming 92, 95, 118, 128
    as a singular event 95
    *see also* Shoah
Hutnyk, John 39–40, 41
hyperreal 75

identification: and naming 89
    of the Other 128–9, 131–3
identity: and fluidity 126–7
    and politics 28
impressions 5, 8, 9, 10, 15n.4
India 46–7
individual: discourse of 96, 102
innocence 2, 14, 15, 30-31, 95
International Criminal Tribunal for the
    Former Yugoslavia (ICTY), The
    Hague 81–2, 84–5, 86, 106, 115–16,
    117, 121
international law 81, 107
Israel: and responsibility 26, 27, 94

Jantzen, Grace 17n.26
Jasenovac 92
Jews: murder of 113, 114
    excision from European body politic
        94
    and meaning of Auschwitz 72
    Nazis' annihilation of 27, 73
    and role of Israeli state in the protection
        of 94, 95
journalists 50–2
justice 15, 24, 25, 101, 134
    call for 100–1, 136
    Derrida on law and 82–4, 101, 136
    relationship with law 85, 88
'just war' 26

Kalemegdan 37, 139
Karakaj border crossing 6, 7–8, 9, 93,
    144
Karišik brothers 143
Keenan, Thomas 102
Kierkegaard, Søren 24, 28, 108
    on Abraham and Isaac 99, 111,
        111–12
    and de-universalizing ethics 5, 99–100,
        101–2
    on faith 84, 100, 102
killing 2, 93
    in indictment of Dragan Nikolić 106,
        107
    silence linked to process of 118
    *see also* mass murder; murder

154

# Index

## Index

# Index

EU authorised representative for GPSR:
Easy Access System Europe, Mustamäe tee 50,
10621 Tallinn, Estonia
gpsr.requests@easproject.com

www.ingramcontent.com/pod-product-compliance
Lightning Source LLC
Chambersburg PA
CBHW061743270326
41928CB00011B/2352